# The Cat Did What?

*Chicken Soup for the Soul: The Cat Did* **What***?*
*101 Amazing Stories of Magical Moments, Miracles and… Mischief*
Amy Newmark. Foreword by Miranda Lambert
Published by Chicken Soup for the Soul Publishing, LLC www.chickensoup.com



The publisher gratefully acknowledges the many publishers and individuals who granted Chicken Soup for the Soul permission to reprint the cited material.

Front cover photo courtesy of iStockPhoto.com/Andrey Kuzmin (© Andrey_Kuzmin).
Interior photo courtesy of iStockPhoto.com/Dixie_ (© Dixie_).
Back cover headshot of Miranda Lambert courtesy of Randee St. Nicholas.
Childhood photo provided by Miranda Lambert.

*Cover and Interior Design & Layout by Brian Taylor, Pneuma Books, LLC*

Distributed to the booktrade by Simon & Schuster. SAN: 200-2442

**Publisher's Cataloging-in-Publication Data**
*(Prepared by The Donohue Group)*

Chicken soup for the soul : the cat did what? : 101 amazing stories of magical moments, miracles and... mischief / [compiled by] Amy Newmark ; foreword by Miranda Lambert.

pages ; cm

ISBN: 978-1-61159-936-7

1. Cats--Behavior--Literary collections. 2. Cats--Behavior--Anecdotes. 3. Cat owners--Literary collections. 4. Cat owners--Anecdotes. 5. Human-animal relationships--Literary collections. 6. Human-animal relationships--Anecdotes. 7. Anecdotes. I. Newmark, Amy. II. Lambert, Miranda, 1983- III. Title: Cat did what? : 101 amazing stories of magical moments, miracles and... mischief

SF446.5 .C45 2014
636.8/02 2014940365

PRINTED IN THE UNITED STATES OF AMERICA
on acid∞free paper

24 23 22 21 20 19 18 17 16 15 03 04 05 06 07 08 09 10 11

# The Cat Did What?

## 101 Amazing Stories of Magical Moments, Miracles and… Mischief

Amy Newmark
Foreword by Miranda Lambert

Chicken Soup for the Soul Publishing, LLC
Cos Cob, CT

Chicken Soup for the Soul®

www.chickensoup.com

# Contents

❸
## ~Who Rescued Who?~



❹
## ~That Little Rascal~



❺
## ~Four-Legged Therapists~

8

## ~Meant to Be~



9

## ~There's No Place Like Home~

**10**

## ~Bad Cat!~

# Foreword

As a lifelong lover of pets and a lifelong lover of the Chicken Soup for the Soul book series, I was honored when they asked me to contribute the foreword to *Chicken Soup for the Soul: The Cat Did* ***What****?* The truth is that I can't remember far enough back when either of these wasn't a part of my life. So I started thinking about memories of all of the cats I have loved throughout my life. All rescue pets of course, which I assume most cats are. They either wandered up to their owner's house or else they were the result of the never-ending sign: Free Kittens.

So begins my story of "The Cat Did **What**?" I've always heard "some people are dog people, some are cat people." I guess I'm blessed to be both. When I was six years old, my family hit on some financial hard times and we ended up losing our home. My parents were devastated. By that time, a new baby brother, Luke, had joined me, two cats, Mollie and Daisy, and our dog, Cooter Brown. The entire Lambert family was homeless. After looking into shelters, considering moving in with relatives, and living in a campground, we finally lucked into moving into my uncle's home. The only problem is that he is allergic to cats. What made a sad day even sadder was saying goodbye to Mollie and Daisy as they went to their new home.

After a year or so, we got back on our feet and moved into our own house again, which turned out to be the house I sing about in "The House That Built Me," my biggest hit song to date. With little or no money for Christmas gifts, Mom fell prey to the sign I referred to earlier—Free Kittens. Prancer entered my life at nine years old.

In typical cat fashion, it took her weeks to get over the car ride and stop pouting. Eventually we became "friends." Prancer wasn't anything like Mollie or Daisy. She didn't like to play, she didn't like to go outside to the sandbox, she didn't like to sleep with me. She was aloof. She found the best warm spot on the couch, constantly found ways to serve her own needs, and pampered herself in every way. But in spite of our strange relationship, we learned to tolerate, then tolerate and finally like each other. My little girl playtime turned to crushes, then school dances, and finally to proms and boyfriends. From the very first visit by a boy to my house, Prancer started to turn on the charm. She purred, she cuddled, she batted her eyelashes and swished her tail. She curled up in the lap… of my boyfriend! Every single guy that came over for the next three years would ask the same question: "What is your problem with this cat. She is adorable!" She soon garnered a new nickname in our house…. Her first name was Kitty and her last name started with a B and ended in tch! She was unstoppable with the flirting. That's what she did.

Soon, an opportunity came for me to audition for a new TV show called *Nashville Star*. It was my first chance to get in front of a national audience with my music (my other lifelong passion). I auditioned and made it! My family and I were thrilled, even though it would mean a move to Nashville and would be my first time away from home. We said yes! I started packing and the contracts arrived, four thick copies in all. Mom spread them out on the bar and we started signing (what we feared might be my life away!). Dad stayed up all night reading every word and left them stacked up and ready to put into the folders for mailing. The next morning we woke up to an awful sight. Kitty B had jumped on our counter, and managed to throw up on every copy. My signatures were ruined. How do you call the producers and say what happened? It's worse than "the dog ate it" excuse, but that's what the cat really did.

We managed to clean them, make copies, re-sign and get them mailed. Off I went to Nashville and into the big new world. Mom took care of my cat, changed the litter and tried to keep her out of trouble. Nine long Tuesday nights passed with me making the cut week after week. Eventually I came in third on the TV show and signed a recording contract with Sony Nashville. I came back for a homecoming concert feeling ten feet tall, with a suitcase full of new clothes, a little bank account, a big record deal, a new sense of self, but it still felt good to step back into my childhood room and sleep in my own bed. Then came the big day, the parade, the concert, the fire trucks… I was to be the Grand Marshall! What to wear? I started going through the suitcase on the floor. During the night KB had jumped into my suitcase and peed on ALL of my new clothes. Not one item was spared! She had been litter trained her entire life. We couldn't believe it, but that's what the cat did.

Adding insult to injury, Mom said, "Before you leave for the parade, you need to change your cat litter." Was anyone in my house aware that I came home feeling like a rock star? Off to the pantry I went to do the deed. Kitty B followed along (though she now had no need for the box). I decided then and there it was time for a face-to-face talk with her. I sat down in the pantry and let her have it. I told her about all the times I had fed her and changed her litter and stood by while she flirted with my boyfriends. I told her that I had loved her all her life and it was time she loved me back. Right then and there, on the pantry floor, she curled up in my lap, purred, batted her eyelashes and swished her tail. She told me in the only way that she could that she loved me, that she had missed me and that she was sad that I was going away. I couldn't believe that she was actually trying to connect with me, but that's what the cat did.

I hope reading the pages to follow in *Chicken Soup for the Soul: The Cat Did* ***What***? finds you laughing and crying. I hope that you learn a little about love and the strange ways that animals (and humans) show it. Mostly I hope that you remember the place in your life where you found patience and understanding in spite of getting so mad you could scream. I hope someday when you are faced with a situation that calls for a long needed talk, you are able to sit down and finally see the situation thorough someone else's eyes. Ten years after first meeting Prancer on Christmas morning, I came to realize that animals teach you things about patience and responsibility as well as lessons about life and affection shown in their own unique ways. I learned that they, like humans, have their own methods of communicating love, loneliness, frustration and independence, because that's what the cat did.

Don't forget… love a shelter pet.

~Miranda Lambert
May 15, 2014

# Introduction

We are so pleased to bring you our latest collection of stories about cats, and this time with a special guest, Miranda Lambert, writing the foreword. In addition to being one of the most popular and well-liked entertainers on the planet, Miranda has been an incredibly dedicated and effective spokesperson for animal welfare and for the benefits of working with and adopting rescue animals. She is a big supporter of the American Humane Association and we are happy to report that the royalties from this book will go the Association to further its good work.

Chicken Soup for the Soul makes every effort to support the work of shelters and to promote adoption of cats and dogs. We use rescue cats and dogs as models on the packaging for our pet food, and we have been contributing to shelters for years. With this book, through the generous participation of Miranda Lambert, we undertake our biggest effort yet to financially support the welfare of animals.

You will read many stories in this book about the love and devotion between cats and their human families. You'll read about cats that demonstrate surprising intuition about the needs of their humans, cats that change people's lives, and cats that teach people important life lessons. You'll read about the wonderful volunteers and professionals who have found new meaning and joy in their lives by adopting, fostering, and working with pet rescue organizations and shelters. You'll also read dozens of really funny stories about the mischievous things that our little rascals do. It seems like every cat owner can't help but smile, even when relating his or her cat's most dastardly deeds!

Most importantly, the stories in the book make the point over and over again—shelter cats and abandoned cats are the best! They add so much value to your lives, and you have saved them from a grim future. So enjoy these stories from your fellow cat people, make some new stories of your own with your cats, and remember to adopt those abandoned cats… and don't forget the black ones and the older ones. They really need you too.

~Amy Newmark

# The Cat Did What?

## Who Me?

# The Collar

*A foolish consistency is the hobgoblin of little minds.*
*~Ralph Waldo Emerson*

"He won't keep his collar on," I complained as I attempted to re-secure the protective gear around Nero's neck. I knew that being neutered would be traumatic for the young kitten, but apparently being forced to wear an E-collar was worse. That was the third morning in a row I had found the crisp fabric flung onto the living room floor.

"Well, he needs to," my husband responded. "Otherwise, he'll lick his sutures and bust them open."

"You hear that, Nero?" I warned. The silky black cat squirmed in discomfort as I fastened the ties of the collar. When I finally finished, he immediately started clawing at the apparatus secured around his neck. He couldn't wait to remove the hindrance. But he was stuck, at least for the time being.

This pattern repeated each morning for the following week as Nero's sutures continued to heal. Somehow, during each night, he managed to squeeze his head through the hole or loosen the ties of the collar to set himself free. Sometimes he gave up halfway through his endeavor and left the collar hanging around his waist like a skirt. To him, even that feminine look was preferable to having the nuisance tied around his neck. His perseverance was remarkable, though nonetheless annoying.

Finally, when according to the aftercare sheet provided by the veterinarian Nero no longer needed to wear the collar, I removed it ceremoniously. "You're free! You're free!" I announced. I cast the collar aside with gusto to emphasize his newfound freedom.

When I woke up the next morning, I expected to find Nero reveling in his independence. Instead, I saw him walking around the living room with the collar around his neck! I don't know how he got it back on, or why he even wanted it after enduring a week of torture, but there it was in all of its Elizabethan glory. Despite all of Nero's resistance, I think he secretly liked looking like a clown.

~Nicole Starbuck

# Mandir the Magician

*A cat is more intelligent than people believe,*
*and can be taught any crime.*
*~Mark Twain*

"What are we going to do with the kids?" I asked my husband. "I've asked them repeatedly to keep the door closed so that the cats don't get out, but I might as well be talking to a wall."

When we designed our new home, we had a large cattery built exclusively for our five indoor cats. The room consisted of a picture window, several catwalks, platforms, hanging toys and their litter boxes. It also included human seats in case we wished to visit all of them at once.

Not only was this unique room designed to keep our feline family from prowling the house at night, but it served as a safe place to keep them out of harm's way while certain home projects were being completed.

We had only been in the house for a few days and were still unpacking our boxes when the cats discovered that we had a basement. There were too many unfinished places that could cause harm to our four-legged friends, so I'd pleaded with the children to keep the cats in the cattery until it was safe for them to roam.

As I worked in the Great Room, unpacking a box of dishes, I spied Mandir trotting merrily on her way to the basement stairs. "Kids…

can you come down here, please," I spoke loudly, so that all three of them would hear me.

When the children gathered in front of me I showed them the open cattery and asked which one of them had been in there last. The responsible party grudgingly came forward, but insisted that the door was fastened tight when he left.

"Listen," I said, "the cats aren't magicians. They cannot open the door any time they want to and come on out, so please—make sure it's shut!"

Less than half an hour later, while I was setting up items in the sunroom, Mandir once again appeared strolling toward the basement stairs. Once again I gathered the kids and of course, the responsible party came forward but denied leaving the door ajar.

This happened several times throughout the day and each time either the children swore they hadn't been in the cattery or swore that they had shut the door.

That night, as we sat together eating dinner, Mandir passed us on her way to the basement stairs.

"What the heck?" said my husband. "Did one of you kids leave the door open again?" Good, I thought. He can finally deal with this. The children shook their heads no.

My husband got up from the table, lovingly picked up Mandir and placed her back in the cattery with the other cats. He had barely been seated again when Mandir appeared.

The children roared with laughter. "I know I shut that door tight," said my husband. The kids were now laughing hysterically, because it was his turn to be accused of leaving the door open. "There must be a flaw with the door," he exclaimed. "It's the only answer."

"Has anyone else noticed that Mandir always comes out first?" I asked. Eventually the rest of the cats would escape, but Mandir always led the way.

My husband excused himself from the table and asked the kids to follow him. "Help me get the cats into the bedroom, all except Mandir. Leave her in the cattery."

The kids giggled as they worked placing all the cats in the room except Mandir. Then, they closed the bedroom door. After they placed Mandir in the cattery, each one of them tested the door to make sure that it had closed properly. None of them could get it to budge, including my husband. "There's nothing wrong with the door," he announced.

As we took our seats and started eating our dessert, sure enough, here came Mandir. By this time we were laughing so hard we had tears in our eyes. My husband picked her up and placed her back in the cattery. After he shut the door and made sure it was closed all the way, he motioned us over.

He put a finger to his lips, motioning us to be quiet. Pretty soon, we heard the sounds of frantic pawing on metal as we watched the doorknob twist to and fro. Then like magic—it opened and Mandir proudly appeared.

The next day we took turns sitting patiently in the cattery, anticipating the moment when Mandir would open the door, but she never tried it when someone was watching.

After several more escapes, my husband pulled out his toolbox and put an outside lock on the door. The children sat around giggling.

"I guess I owe you kids an apology," I laughed. "Cats can be magicians after all and they can come out any time they like as long as Mandir is with them."

"Mandir the magician," said my husband and put the final screw in place. "Let's see if she can open a locked door," he chuckled.

Only a few minutes after the bolt was in place Mandir tried to open the door. As the kids roared with laughter we observed the knob turning to and fro, but Mandir the magician had met her match!

~Jill Burns

# The Audition

*You call to a dog and a dog will break its neck to get to you.*
*Dogs just want to please. Call to a cat and its attitude is, What's in it for me?*
*~Lewis Grizzard*

My cat Bette is a talented, black and white, New York City cat who I named after Bette Davis because of her large, green eyes. Like a true actress, Bette likes to be center stage. In fact, one of her routines is such a hit with my friends that I make her perform it whenever there's an audience.

Bette likes to stand on her head on top of the refrigerator.

First, she sits upright on top of the stage (i.e., the refrigerator). When I sing out "Bettteeee" in a high, piping voice, she curls down, rubs her face into the top of the fridge, lets all four paws go limp and stands on her head. I have to move quickly to catch her before she slides head first off the refrigerator to the floor.

One day my friend Ken declared that Bette's unusual talent was remarkable enough for David Letterman's show. "She's perfect for Stupid Pet Tricks," he told me. All my friends agreed, so I began staying up past my bedtime to catch *Late Night with David Letterman*, which was on NBC back then.

Each night as I watched, Bette would sit on my lap. We saw a sporting dog who could shoot basketballs with his nose and an intellectual dog so clever he could select *War and Peace* from a bookcase. Pretty silly stuff, I thought.

"Bette," I said, "you're a shoo-in!" She tucked her paws neatly under her chest and purred.

Ken contacted David Letterman's casting director and Bette's audition was set for a Tuesday evening at NBC Studios. We held several rehearsals with Bette and she performed perfectly every time.

Arriving at Rockefeller Center, we were asked to wait in a hallway with the other *Late Night* "wannabes." Ken chatted with the other hopefuls in the waiting area, then whispered, "No other cats." I felt encouraged.

Soon, a couple shuffled in with a large, squat, pasty English Bulldog, who snuffled at Bette's carrier. She let out a loud hiss. The couple proceeded to dress the dog in a ridiculous cowboy costume, complete with a bandanna, toy holster, miniature cowboy hat and funny-looking boots. Bette immediately went to sleep.

Our turn came and we were ushered into the audition room. A young woman named Barbara checked off Bette's name on her clipboard. An upright piano was substituted for my refrigerator. I took Bette out of her box, carried her to the piano and placed her on top. She sat placidly looking around for a few moments, not the least bit nervous.

"Quite the professional," Barbara commented, making a notation on her pad. "Now, let's see her do her trick."

I walked over and stood beneath Bette as I had done so many times before. In my special high, piping voice I sang, "Bettteeee!" She looked down at me blandly. "Bettteeee!" I sang again. She looked over at Ken, then at Barbara, then quite calmly jumped to the floor. I caught her and placed her back on top of the piano. "Bettteeee!" I cried, "Bettteeee!"

She ignored me and tried to jump down again.

For ten minutes, Ken and I stood screeching "Bettteeee!" and Bette kept trying to climb down. Barbara finally said, "Let her explore." So we let her explore.

Bette walked around sniffing at the corners of the room, calm and unperturbed as ever. I picked her up and she purred.

"She seems happy now," said Ken. "Let's try again."

I set her up on the piano again and we called out "Bettteee!" in singsong unison. Even Barbara joined in. Bette gave us one bemused look, jumped down and ran over and began scratching at the door.

Barbara was sympathetic. "That's our problem with cats," she said. "They'll do it at home every time, but in the studio, they refuse. I had hoped Bette would be different."

She made a final notation on her pad as I put Bette back in her carrier. On our way out, the English Bulldog came clumping in, hardly able to walk in his cowboy boots. His eyes bulged, so it looked like the bandanna was choking him. "Stupid looking dog," muttered Ken.

As soon as we got home, I put Bette on the refrigerator and sang, "Bettteeee!"

She gurgled coyly and performed her routine flawlessly. After I caught her, she looked up at me with an unmistakable smirk.

"She did it on purpose," snorted Ken. I couldn't argue with him.

Some weeks later my phone rang late at night and an excited voice commanded me to "Put on *Letterman*!"

I switched the channel and there he was, the English Bulldog making a complete fool of himself. With a mini-guitar between his fat paws, he snorted along to a country western song.

David Letterman grinned.

The studio audience guffawed.

Even I laughed.

Suddenly, Bette leapt from out of nowhere onto the table next to the television set and sat staring at me. In contrast to the ridiculous dog, she looked proud and eloquent. As I admired her, a question formed in my mind.

"Bette, why don't cats do stupid pet tricks?"

I thought I saw the answer in her green eyes.

No self-respecting cat, and certainly not Bette, would sacrifice dignity for fame and fortune, not even for David Letterman!

~Morna Murphy Martell

# It Takes a Licking

*Sleeping together is a euphemism for people,*
*but tantamount to marriage with cats.*
*~Marge Percy*

My wife Julie hates cats. I use the word "hate" purposefully because she does not simply dislike, she most undoubtedly hates them. I believe what happened early in our relationship contributed to this animosity.

Julie was never fond of cats even though she grew up on a farm where there were cats, but these, she tells me, were outside cats—mousers. These cats would crowd around as she was milking the cows. Some cats would drop down from the rafters and scare her. Others would crowd around her feet hoping to trip her so she would spill some precious cream. At times, some would be bold enough to actually jump into the pail of milk, thus ruining the contents. On those occasions, Julie would then suffer the scorn of her parents who relied on the sale of the milk to make ends meet. So it is with these eyes—cats are mischievous, devilish, downright despicable and the cause of the many ills of the world—that she perceived all cats.

We both lived in the city when we met and were dating for over eight months when we were asked to Julie's sister's acreage to help put up a playground for her kids. I think it was a test to see if I was marriage material. If I could be around the potential in-laws for a day and be coerced into slave labour, then book the church, send out the invitations, and hire a preacher, the wedding was on.

We started at 9:00 a.m. The work was exhausting, as we were building a wooden jungle gym complete with rope ladders, a swinging bridge, a fort, a slide, a couple of swings, and roped monkey bars. By 8:00 p.m. most of the work was finished except for a few minor details that could be completed in an hour or two. But we were too tired to continue and decided we would complete the job the next day. So, with apprehension, Julie agreed to stay the night.

I say apprehension because her sister had a cat—a molly. This was a house cat—a beautiful marbled tabby with spectacular green eyes. It's funny how females tend to engage in competition and quickly establish their territory.

This cat loved me. She hissed at Julie.

As we sat around the supper table, this cat rubbed herself against me, sat on my lap, and purred, all the while glaring at Julie. Julie simply looked at me with disdain as I overtly showed my affection for this pristine feline.

That night Julie and I slept on a pullout couch in the middle of the living room. As I said, we were physically exhausted from the day's work, so I quickly fell into a deep sleep. And then it happened.

Around 4:00 a.m., when what one dreams and what is real become confused, my subconscious was slowly being tickled in a sensation of wakefulness. In a groggy, sleep-gravelled voice, I murmured my approval. My giddiness woke up Julie, and her clear, succinct, stark voice surprisingly woke me up to sudden awareness.

"In what world do you think I would be licking your armpit?"

I looked over to my right and there was the cat licking my armpit like a child licking ice cream. Apparently, she liked the combination of sweat and Old Spice.

"I thought you were being kinky," I said. "You know, all the fresh country air and..."

"Think again, buddy!"

My dear wife enjoys telling and retelling this story to people every time I suggest we get a cat, or when she wishes to explain to people how weird I am, or how she still married me even after this event, which is a testimony to the strength of her character.

To date, we have been married for twenty-five years. In this time, we have never owned a cat nor do I think will we ever have one. And just for the record, after all these years, my wife has never licked my armpit.

~Manley Fisher

# Feline Persuasion

*Some people say that cats are sneaky, evil, and cruel. True, and they have many other fine qualities as well.*
*~Missy Dizick*

Who else but you,
the originator of the runway stride,
could saunter down the slope
of a porch railing
with such nonchalance?
As I stumble through my morning,
tripping in flip-flops, rounding corners
with my sorely purpled hips,
grabbing at an avalanche
of ice-encrusted vegetables
when I open the freezer,
I envy your unpracticed grace,
the way you leap from ledges,
flaunting your sure-footed landings
like a born gymnast.

The moment my back is turned,
you prove yourself
the quintessential opportunist.
Every narrow gap is to you
an invitation. You Harry Houdini,

steal between bars, stalking shadows,
gliding through fences
seemingly without ever lifting a paw.
You discover opportunity ajar
and barge on in.
All barriers to worlds beyond
lift and roll back easily, exclusively for you,
as if they were remote-controlled
garage doors that you wander through
like royalty, mildly pleased
but unimpressed.

All through the slumbering winter hours
you hog the central heating grates
as if you pay a personal utilities bill
while the rest of us
flick ice chips off our shoulders.

When your mistress is away,
I am the one who feeds you,
wields the litter-sifting scoop,
opens the front door for you
three hundred times a day
with a towel on my arm,
chases the tornado of your antics,
and Swiffers the floors behind you.
I do this—I hope you are aware—
not out of a plebian desire
to appease you,
but because the rent is cheap.

Someone who has not lived with you
might mistake you for
a pleasant, ordinary house cat,
like your sweet-tempered affiliate,

who purrs like an idling engine,
content to gaze out the window
without any further ambition.
Her notable source of excitement in life
is a length of yarn
wiggled at her nose. As for you,
your handsome, dark gray stripes
and clean white socks belie
the mischief-plotting rogue you are,
who, in former lives, I've been told,
ran straight up the walls,
tearing at artwork, and tested the claws
of ragged-eared street cats
in the alleys of Prague.

Even now, you climb curtains
and summit the fridge,
your appetite for the forbidden
still insatiable.
The jut of your pointy white chin
pleads guilty defiance,
whatever your latest crime.
Yet there is no training, taming,
or punishing you.
My best weapon of defense
is the fine-mist sprayer I use
to water houseplants; the spritz
only fleetingly annoys you.

Food in any form left unattended
is endangered: a cup of juice,
a jar of peanut butter
carelessly left open
in the post-lunch hustle, even

a painstakingly wrapped care package
filled with homemade cookies, ready
to be mailed. I return to find
a colorful spill, a trail
of kitty-litter footprints
on the countertop,
layers of plastic chewed through,
crumbs of chocolate chips.
My rage explodes like a firework finale.
Cat! You slinking conniver.

Your favorite game is sniffing out
the very times and places
in which you are most unwelcome.
My bedroom has been fortressed against you
as the last bastion
of fur-free solitude, uninterrupted
by drama and destruction—
where I don't have to listen to you
laboriously coughing up hairballs
by way of "Good Morning"
or witness the hiss and scrabble
of the fights you pick
with your naïve intellectual inferior
out of sheer boredom, and where
there are no little mounds of rejection
for me to scrape off the floor.

When you stand outside my door
and start up your mewling, unlovely lament,
I have no sympathy for you.
By now I have learned
it is merely feline whining,
not to be confused with

the sob-song of loneliness.
You could have commandeered
any other room you desire.
Your intention is not to kindle a bond
but to coolly appraise my surroundings
once you have gained access
to this final frontier.

Never have I seen a flicker of fear
in your keen, green eyes.
I've seen you dodge and dart,
but only in pursuit of some creature
less fortunate than you,
or to evade discipline.
I might otherwise have been inspired
by your boldness, but as it is,
it merely infuriates me.

And yet, in moments of weakness,
I feel a strange, clawing fondness for you—
for the effortless charm
with which you sometimes
hop onto the couch with me
and deign to let me pet you.

How quickly I forget,
when the snuggle comes easy,
that you are still the poster boy
for narcissism, aloof and oblivious
to any emptiness except
the growl of your own stomach.
Your selective hearing
betrays your limited agenda:
you come bounding
down three flights of stairs

at the sound of a can lid
being opened in the kitchen,
whether or not the spoon is for you.

You flirt with anything that moves.
How convenient,
the way you lose interest,
thoughtlessly shedding
my hands, my fur-nested lap
quickly growing cold
as you step off the curb
of my thigh, distracted
by a millipede on holiday
from dinge of musty basement.
I suppose by now
it should not come as a surprise
when you leave me
like rumpled sheets on a hotel bed—
even for a dust mote
floating in a shaft of sun.

~Emily Ruth Hazel

# Indoor Hunter

*The cat is domestic only as far as suits its own ends.*
*~Saki*

We had to settle for a cat when our landlord wouldn't allow dogs. One thing led to another and we eventually ended up with three. One of them, the American tabby we named Snickers, was a natural hunter, confused by the unnatural environment in which we made her live—indoors.

Snickers had a few favourite "prey," and one of them was drinking straws. As you would walk through the house carrying a drink adorned with a straw, a pair of calculating eyes would be trained on the plastic tube. If you didn't keep your eyes on your drink, if you dared leave the room, the sound of your glass toppling over as she stole the straw would have you running back in.

Eventually Snickers perfected her skill. No sooner would you get comfy on the couch when the "ferocious" feline would stalk your drink. Delicately tilting her head to one side, she would grasp the straw with her teeth and gingerly pull it out of the glass without knocking the whole thing over.

With her prize in her mouth, she would proudly skulk away, a possessive deep-throated "kill" growl vibrating through your still-standing glass. The grand finale was her attempt at posing her hefty tabby body like the Great Sphinx of Giza, with the straw cradled between her paws.

But it wasn't the straws that were the real problem with our hunter.

Unfortunately, Snickers had decided that my husband's underwear constituted worthy prey as well, and we never knew when a pair of socks or knickers would be on display in our foyer or in the middle of the living room floor for the few guests we managed to invite over.

The mystery was, how did Snickers get "the drawers" out of the drawers? One day, we caught her in the act and watched the process in awe. She climbed up the side of the dresser, using each drawer's edge as a step, until she reached the underwear drawer at the top. With her back legs as leverage on the drawer below, she wedged her front claws into the drawer and pulled.

Then, dangling by her front legs, she hoisted herself into the drawer. After rooting around she emerged with her so-called "kill" clamped in her mouth and jumped down.

Even though we were right in front of her, she didn't care. Our presence was no threat. Down the stairs she stealthily crept, the underwear in her mouth muffling her trademark deep-throated "kill" growl. As she neared the living room the growling became more intense, and there she dropped her kill and lay on it.

We never figured out what made Snickers pick socks over underwear. What made it a sock day? What made it a knickers day? And it didn't matter whether we were home or not—her fetish had no scheduled time. Seeing as our house was small, we could hear when a drawer was being opened and knew what would come next.

Snickers is no longer with us, but her memory lives on through the claw marks on my husband's dresser drawers. And although I can finally stock straws in my house and use them without incident, I still sometimes hesitate, and reflect. And then I get a little nostalgic for the good old days when glasses got knocked over and I tripped on underwear in the front hall.

~Lisa McManus Lange

# At the Mall

*Like a graceful vase, a cat even when motionless seems to flow.*
*~George F. Will*

With great ceremony my husband reached into his coat and pulled out my perfect birthday gift, a tiny grey Persian kitten. We had been married a few short months but already I was experiencing the "nesting" urge. Children were still a few years off and I needed something to cuddle and spoil. Dogs were not allowed in our apartment so a kitten seemed the answer to my maternal impulse.

Gilligan (named after my husband's favorite TV show) was a delightful addition to our life. We were careful to raise him with just the right mix of affection and discipline, insisting on the best food available and a regular play schedule. The lucky kitty was even allowed to sleep with us every night, usually winning the battle for my pillow. He was promoted from pet to family member when he began joining us on all our excursions, even though he continued to treat us with disdain. We loved him anyway.

My great pride in Gilligan was that he had learned to walk on a leash. Yes, it was certainly quite an accomplishment and had taken a great deal of diligence and persistence, requiring just the right amount of creativity and bribery—but it had paid off.

My favorite outing was taking him for walks in the mall. For some reason my husband never seemed to be available for this venture. It was before animals were banned in many public places, and pet owners were known to frequent the shopping center with their precious darlings on a regular basis.

As we sauntered casually through the mall, people would stare at Gilligan, making ooh and ahh sounds as we went by. I got quite used to the attention and was proud of my obedient and talented kitty.

One particular day I decided to dress him up for our usual stroll through the mall. The latest purchase was brought out and a comical struggle ensued as we proceeded to put on his new green, knitted, turtleneck sweater.

Now I know that a Persian cat has no need of a knitted turtleneck sweater but I had no one else to dress up. We arrived at the mall and began our stroll through the maze of people and stores. Again, everyone looked at Gilligan in amazement, whispering to each other behind their hands. I simply walked on, staring straight ahead but thoroughly enjoying the looks on their faces.

As long as I didn't feel any drag on the leash, or a sudden jerk, I just kept going. When he went around a pole on the opposite side, it took a few moments of unwinding and we would be on our way again.

This day seemed like any other day. Children smiled, adults commented to each other and groups of people stopped to stare, but it suddenly dawned on me that shoppers seemed to be getting more than the usual enjoyment out of our performance. Smiles were more like snickers and chuckles had elements of hysterics. There had been no drag on the leash, but I turned my head to do a quick check anyway.

To my horror, there at the end of the leash was the cat, laying flat on his back with all fours reaching to the sky. He looked relaxed and quite comfortable with the new traveling arrangements. I realized this entire time I had been slowly dragging my twenty-pound cat around on the mall's slippery floor, on his back, in a green sweater! Drat that cat.

With lightning speed, I picked up Gilligan and tucked him under my arm—making a beeline for the exit. That was also the end of the leash walking. I figured next time we might find my picture in the evening paper under the heading—"Believe It or Not."

I'm sure there is some kind of moral to this story but I can't think of a single one. All I know is that at many dinner tables that night the conversation probably started with, "You won't believe the woman I saw today at the mall."

~Heather Rae Rodin

# A Tiger Sleeps

*God made the cat in order that humankind might have the pleasure of caressing the tiger.*
*~Fernand Mery*

A tiger sleeps inside our cat
where he sits, purring, washing paws;
jelly-bean pads so soft and flat
concealing predatory claws.

He hunts our antique catcher's mitt,
he hunts the pillows, hunts the sheets;
and when he was a naughty kit
he'd hunt unwary toes and feet.

He prowls about in feral form,
attacks toys with a savage joy
but always comes back, sweet and warm,
and is once more my loving boy.

A tiger sleeps inside our cat.
In feline dreams he'll roar and leap
—he's really on a fluffy mat:
tiny, cute and fast asleep.

~Cathy Bryant

# Gray Cat, Corner Pocket

*To play billiards well was a sign of an ill-spent youth.*
*~Herbert Spencer*

Our cat Spot was unique from the beginning. He was born in a kayak in our garage, which must account for his innate sense of adventure and interest in all things wild. Named for the tiny black spot on his ear, he was as soft and gray as the wild rabbits he liked to "hunt" through the windowpane, chattering with anticipation and drooling all over the woodwork as he went through his daily routine of jungle cat on the move. Birds were his other favorite obsession, but Spot was an indoor cat, so luckily for the local wildlife, his hunting escapades were limited to his imagination.

Spot was constantly finding creative places to hide, like a shoebox, where his excess poundage would drape gracefully over the edge in a feline version of a muffin top. He loved the cavernous dark mystery of the linen closet or hiding behind the shower curtain to pounce on an unwitting victim. But his favorite game of all was chasing pool balls across the billiards table in our family room. He would silently stalk the pool table, slung low like a panther on the prowl, skulking in the shadow of a red plaid couch before leaping onto the table mid-game to take down his prey. It was the source of constant amusement in our house, and with five kids, the pool table was always alive with action for Spot. Games of Eight Ball were constantly interrupted with cries of, "Spot, noooo!" or "Hey, no fair, Spot got that one in!"

One spring day, Spot upped the ante with the pool table hunt when we were all at school. Random balls had been left on the table, and Spot found such a bounty of prey irresistible. Ball after ball was chased down across the green felt lawn until each one escaped into its dark hideaway. With his bloodlust up, Spot chased his final victim, a solid green number six, into its corner lair. He could feel the tantalizing scrape of his claws on the smooth surface of the ball as it rolled around in the pocket, just beyond his reach. Taking a cue from his predatory ancestors and his mantra of no pool ball left behind, he dove head first into the hole to finish off his victim.

My sister, Pam, had just come in the door from the school bus when she heard a wail coming from the family room. She flew into the room and found the source of the mournful cry by the pool table. Spot's head was wedged firmly in the corner pocket. She called my mother and together they tried to gently dislodge Spot from his trap. They tried turning him, slowly pulling him straight back, then gently pushing his head to one side to see if they could find the right angle to slide him out. No luck. They called our neighbor, Paul, a teenage boy who was good with animals. He came running across the street to help and they tried easing Spot backwards, slathering butter on his neck, then adding vegetable oil to grease the track, with no better results. Spot's head was wedged in the corner pocket of the table.

Along with the three of them, Spot was starting to panic, so my mother called the police department and started the conversation with, "You're not going to believe this, but…" Our town was so small that phone calls could be made in town using only five digits, so the officer who took the call knew our family. After he stopped laughing, he said help would be on the way. Minutes later, the local police and fire truck rolled up our driveway and the firemen took over the rescue mission. Between making jokes about Spot's dedication to the sport of billiards and comments like "Isn't this what their whiskers are for?" they worked on trying to free him.

Spot wouldn't budge, and after fifteen minutes he was becoming exhausted and dizzy. Four men gently turned the pool table on its side so Spot wouldn't lose consciousness, and then an executive decision was made. "Are you sure you want to do this, Mrs. Graham? Okay, look away," said the chief to my mom. "This isn't going to be pretty." As one of the volunteer firemen came into the room with a saw, my mom said, "Do what you have to do."

The firemen converged on the table, one holding Spot's writhing body while the other positioned the saw. "What a shame," said the guy before firing it up.

The saw sprang to life with a hideous screech, matched by a howl from Spot. My sister cried, Paul shuddered and my mom closed her eyes and cringed. Two minutes later, the firefighter cried, "Okay!" and turned around. In his arms was Spot, still in one piece, looking sheepish and exhausted. His head looked ridiculously small, covered in vegetable oil and flecks of sawdust, while the rest of his fur puffed out like giant dust bunny. Behind him, a big square was missing from the corner of the pool table. "The guys are never gonna believe this one," the chief said with a laugh as my mom reached out to hug him. Spot lived through a move to a new home with our family and another fourteen years of adventures, but none quite as dramatic as his pool table escapade. The pool table survived a transformation into a ping pong table, which was much safer for everyone.

~Susan Graham Winslow

# Trick or Feat

*Where there is no imagination there is no horror.*
*~Arthur Conan Doyle, Sr.*

Sebastian, my tuxedo cat, dashed through the living room, with me in hot pursuit. He went into capture-and-conquer mode every time I used the feather duster. His fascination for it grew beyond merely taking it from me. Finding its newest hiding place had become one of his favorite pastimes.

I caught up with him by the sofa and grabbed the duster. "You can't have this." I sat on the sofa and dropped the tempting cleaning tool next to me.

He hopped up and swatted at the feathers.

"No." I shoved the duster under my sweatshirt. "I don't have time for this."

In addition to my regular housecleaning chores, this was Halloween. I had to finish dusting, sweeping, and mopping before I could set out the pumpkins, scarecrows, and candy.

Sebastian flipped his tail expectantly.

I laughed and stroked his black and white forehead. "You understand every word, don't you, boy?"

I carried the duster, still hidden within my clothing, from room to room, searching for a nook or canny my clever cat hadn't yet discovered.

"Aha. He'll never think to look in here." I glanced back into the living room. Sebastian sniffed and pawed at the sofa, where he had last seen his catch of the day. I tossed a couple of toys in his direction, hoping to distract him. It worked.

"Now," I said to myself, "time to finish my chores. Trick-or-treaters will be here before dusk."

After the last costumed child begged his treat, I locked the front door and turned off the porch light.

Sebastian toyed with his favorite catnip mouse as I watched TV. The feather duster was tucked safely in its latest hiding place.

Later that night, I sat in bed with my book, hoping to finish at least one chapter. The first paragraph blurred on the page. "I'll have to wait until tomorrow to find out who done it." Sebastian curled up next to me as I set the novel on the nightstand and scooted between cozy sheets. I turned off the lamp and was fast asleep in minutes.

A creak, thump, and scrape woke me in the middle of the night. The LED numbers on my clock radio read 1:45.

I had lived alone for many years, so normal household sounds rarely disturbed me. But those strange noises made my blood run cold. Had some goblin invaded my home?

I climbed out of bed and, following the sounds, tiptoed into the kitchen.

TV cop shows taught me not to turn on a light when investigating a noise. If it was a burglar, I wanted to see him before he saw me.

My eyes strained in the darkness. I could barely make out the half-opened pantry door.

Another creak, thump, and scrape came from the pantry. I crept forward and opened the door all the way.

Movement on the top shelf caught my attention. I could barely make out a small, strange creature with a crouched torso. Two silvery-green eyes glowed from the Medusa-like head rolling back and forth in a wavy motion. A muffled growl sent shivers down my spine. I couldn't move.

The creature lunged at me. I screamed when the monster landed on my shoulders, its claws digging into my flesh. Something hard hit my cheek. Then the creature emitted a familiar purr before leaping to the floor.

I turned on the light.

"Sebastian?" The nightmarish beast was my cat, his size enhanced by the feather duster protruding from his mouth. He dropped his prey and meowed his conquest.

I looked at the pantry. How did he open the door? The top shelf was eight feet high. He couldn't have climbed up there without knocking everything off the four shelves beneath it. Did he really jump from the floor to the top? And how did he know the feather duster was up there?

I turned to my acrobat cat. He stretched up a paw as though expecting a high-five. With his amazing top-shelf flight, I considered giving him one, or at least a good boy treat.

I scooped up Sebastian. "Back to bed, little guy."

He jumped out of my arms and grabbed the feather duster in his mouth, padding toward the bedroom.

"Uh, no. I'm not sleeping with a feather duster," I said to his retreating backside. The ceiling fan caught my eye. Hmmm, ten foot ceilings. If I taped the duster to the top of the blade? I laughed at myself. You're getting desperate, girl.

Two o'clock in the morning was no time to match wits with a tricky cat. I took Sebastian's booty from him and put it in the refrigerator. As I headed back to bed, he sat staring at the refrigerator door. I shook my head. Wouldn't surprise me in the least if he found a way to open it.

~Janet Ramsdell Rockey

# The Cat Did What?

## Learning to Love the Cat

# Those Other Cats

*Any conditioned cat-hater can be won over by any cat who chooses to make the effort.*
*~Paul Corey,* Do Cats Think?

The ring was on my finger and my name was changed before I learned my husband hated cats—not that he'd ever had one. He just knew he didn't like them.

"Cats are sneaky, and they don't come when they're called," he said.

Since we were newly married, without pets, I shrugged away his attitude as irrelevant. Years later, we bought a home on five acres and soon learned motorists used our road to drop off unwanted pets. We'd acquired two dogs and a white rabbit before the skinny kitten huddled under our porch. The kids found it. I brought it inside. After it gulped down a can of tuna, I took a long look at the tiny thing. With barely enough fur to cover it, it was still shivering when my husband appeared.

"Take it to the pound," he said.

"Nope. As far as I'm concerned, it can stay. If you want it to go to the pound, you'll have to take it there," I said, and handed him the kitten.

He started the car, kitten on the front seat, and drove away. After a couple of hours, he returned. He brought a padded circular pet bed, a bag of litter, a bag of kitten food, a dozen cans of kitten formula and a cardboard cat carrier into the kitchen. I lowered my chin and stared at him over the rim of my eyeglasses.

He shrugged and grinned sheepishly. I said nothing and kept staring at him. He gave out a big sigh.

"Her name's Baby. I had to tell the vet something. He asked me what the cat's name was."

"The vet?" I asked. "The pound has a vet?"

Another big sigh huffed out of him.

"No, by the time I got to the end of the driveway, she'd curled up against my leg and the dang thing kept purring, so I rubbed her head. By the time I got to the pound's parking lot, she'd laid her head on my thigh and was asleep."

I wanted to laugh but knew not to. "So you decided to take it to the vet first?"

"Not an it, a she. That's what the vet said. He said I should bring her back before she's a year so he can spay her, unless I want more kittens." He walked over to our wall calendar, flipped pages and circled March, five months away.

Our four-year-old opened the cat carrier and reached inside. My husband lunged, grabbed the kitten, hugged her against him.

"She's easy to hurt, honey. You can hold her but you can't squeeze her," he said as he cuddled the kitten against his chest.

"So, all it took to change your opinion of cats is one who fell asleep in the car?" I asked.

He tilted his head, studied the ceiling, then leaned close to me, staring into my eyes.

"The difference, you see," he said, hesitating between words, "is she's not one of those cats. She's my cat."

~Alvena Stanfield

# An Accidental Cat Lover

*I used to love dogs until I discovered cats.*
*~Nafisa Joseph*

There was a time when I hated the sight of a cat. I was that person who went to a party and spent the night with the family cat in my lap, smiling through gritted teeth. Dogs and small children avoid people who clearly detest them. But cats are drawn to them. They'd spot me as I came through the door, and then spend the rest of the night shedding on my outfit as I did my best "nice kitty" routine.

All that changed when my husband and I moved to the country and encountered a mouse problem. We asked a neighbor for advice and he recommended we get what he called barn cats. He said females were the best mousers, that they worked better in pairs and his mother-in-law had a litter that was about ready to leave their mama. He'd chase us down a couple of kittens.

It was a lesser-of-two-evils decision for me. If I had to choose between cats and mice, cats won out—but not by much. So we put in an order for two female barn cats who'd earn their keep as mousers. Our daughters, Haley and Molly, were two and four at the time and for the next few nights I put them to sleep with bedtime stories about their new kittens. I laid it on thick, telling them how their baby kitties would sleep in their laps rolled into a ball, how soft they'd be, how they'd purr, and how, if you put a little cat food on your finger, they'd lick it with their little rough tongues. They liked the little rough tongues part and begged to hear it again and again.

After a few days, we received a call from the neighbor to say that our kittens were ready to be picked up. I strapped both girls in the back seat of the car and told them they'd each have a soft, warm ball of fur to hold on the way home. They begged for more so I told them that as a kitten slept, they could put their hands up to its mouth and feel sweet, little puffs of breath. They wanted the little rough tongues part again and we talked kitten, all the way to the neighbor's mother-in-law's house.

What we were given, however, was not a ball of soft fur to nestle into each girl's lap but a box—taped tightly shut—with instructions not to untape it until we got home and had them exactly where we wanted them to live. I settled the box between the girl's car seats and started home. They seemed to forget all about the balls of fur and little rough tongues for the time being and were content to give the box a poke every once in a while and hear a mad scrambling inside. Each time they'd emit peals of laughter. Not my idea of a pet, but they were happy.

When we got the box home, I took it into the living room, placed it on the floor with a girl on either side and worked the tape off. Haley and Molly held their breath, eyes wide as I tilted the box over, opened the lid and watched two streaks of fur—one gray, one black—bolt under the couch where they crouched together with absolutely no intention of coming out—ever.

I put out a bowl of food and a bowl of water, hoping to coax the kittens out of hiding. No such luck. Anyone who's spent any time around preschoolers knows that telling my girls to "Stay perfectly still and the kittens might come out" was a waste of breath. Each time one kitten would so much as move a muscle to creep toward the food, the girls would squeal, sending them further under the couch.

This went on for a couple of hours until my husband came home, opened the door and the gray and black streaks made a dash for freedom. For weeks after that, there were daily cat sightings and empty cat food bowls each morning. Other than that, we hardly knew we had cats. The mouse population seemed to decrease though, so they were fulfilling their job description. Stimpy and Massy (we let the girls name them) grew the tiniest bit more friendly. Now they waited for the girls to actually take a step toward them before them bolted for the nearest hiding place.

Chapter two of our cat story began when my sister, Denise, was visiting and informed us that the cats were getting so nice and round not because they were full of mice but rather full of kittens. Oops! We weren't housing two proficient mousers but two unwed mothers. That's when a funny thing happened. We decided that, since they were in a family way, the cats should be allowed to move into the house.

They seemed to agree and became amazingly tame in a short period of time. My first pleasant surprise came when I went to the library looking for a book on house-training cats. I'd trained a dog or two in my day and wasn't looking forward to it. What a delightful surprise to discover that all that's involved in teaching a cat to use a litter box is to buy the box. They do the rest. Cool! There were a couple of house plant incidents and Molly had to be convinced that just because the kitty litter looked a little like the sand in her sandbox didn't mean it was good for building castles. By the time our litters were born—a day apart—Stimpy and Massy were pampered house pets.

Haley and Molly are seventeen and fifteen now. Stimpy and Massy are no longer with us but we are proud companions to Kipling, Harper, Belle, and Opie. We've since learned to have all our pets spayed at a young age and—in that clairvoyant way that cats have—all our current felines have found their way to our front door on their own, then made it clear they were here to stay.

Who knew cats would enrich our lives the way they have? My girls and their two little brothers hardly know what it's like to fall to sleep without a cat or two curled beside them. And my husband has been known to sneak into a sleeping child's room to swipe a cat so he won't have to watch TV alone. As a work-at-home writer, I relish their companionship in my otherwise empty house all day. We've come to appreciate the unique personality and characteristics of each one. Besides it's awfully fun to host a party and watch some poor sap pretend to be thrilled that one of our cats has chosen him as its new best friend while covertly trying to shoo it away.

~Mimi Greenwood Knight

# Guilty

*Even if you have just destroyed a Ming Vase, purr.*
*Usually all will be forgiven.*
*~Lenny Rubenstein*

Were we so oblivious that we'd sat on the upstairs couch each night watching movies together, but never noticed the couch's upholstery had been shredded to pieces? "Don't you hear him or see him scratching?" I asked my sons, since they had their office and bedrooms upstairs within sight of the couch.

Little Man strutted his stuff throughout the rest of the house and was famous for scratching the furniture. When he got caught in the act he would be gently reprimanded by his owners: my sons. However as any cat owner knows, you need to catch them in the act. If Little Man had been scratching, whoever was inside should have heard it. The open, airy design of the house allowed noises to drift through the rooms and that included cat scratching.

As a deterrent, protection was placed on the couch, however the abuse continued. This called for desperate measures, but no matter how hard we tried, Little Man's criminal behavior eluded us.

Each day our family left the house to walk the dog. Little Man would be curled up downstairs when we'd leave and still curled up in the same place when we returned, so he must have been committing the act some other time, but when?

As the crime continued, the detectives went to work. First the weapons were examined as they searched for clues in Little Man's claws. In the morning, the pads of his feet were clean and empty, but later in the afternoon bits and pieces of foam appeared between his claws. Eventually we narrowed down the time frame when his criminal activity must have been occurring.

Weeks went by as my sons tried to catch our criminal in the act, but without any luck. One afternoon, after our dog walk, I'd remained outside to do some gardening. When I came in I heard uncontrollable laughter coming from upstairs. "What's so funny?" I asked.

"Come up and see for yourself," they answered.

My sons had their video camera out. As I watched the footage they had recorded, I found myself staring at their shredded couch. First I heard a bang. Then within minutes the camera showed Little Man sneaking quickly up the stairs. His blue eyes darted here and there making sure no one else was in the room. When his face came in view of the camera his expression showed a cat on a mission as he walked nonchalantly over to the couch, balanced on his hind legs and stretched his arms as high as he could on the couch arm.

With no conscience whatsoever, he proceeded to annihilate the couch, vigorously clawing and scratching with all of his might. Bits and pieces of foam flew from the couch as his claws scratched feverishly. Then, when he had finished, he strolled innocently over to the stairs and peered down, to make sure that we hadn't come in from the walk unexpectedly. With an expression of pure ecstasy, he gazed lovingly at the couch one last time and then proudly headed back downstairs to assume his sleeping position.

The mystery of the couch had been solved, but Little Man—in his twelve years—never got caught in the act. Today the couch remains upstairs as a monument to his guilt, but the video of him committing his crime is priceless—especially now that he's passed on. His cunningness, his expressions, and his passion for getting away with his crime will always bring a smile to our faces.

~Jill Burns

# Not Our Cat

*Women and cats will do as they please, and men and dogs should relax and get used to the idea.*
*~Robert A. Heinlein*

I am allergic to cats—violently allergic. Naturally, I found myself living with two of them.

My allergies used to be so intense that even as someone opened the door to their home I could tell if they owned a cat. The moment the knob turned, my eyes began to water and the sneezing would start. Once, when I spent the night at a friend's house I had such a severe allergic reaction to his two cats that I stopped breathing for a few seconds.

That's why I wasn't amused when Joey decided she was moving in.

Joey officially lived next door, but even as a kitten she'd race up to anyone who walked by her house to see who they were and what they wanted. Her "owners" included a three-year-old boy who viewed the cat as a cute furry toy. Not surprisingly Joey spent as much time out of the house as she could.

Joey was endearing enough that when she raced up to my car, I'd risk giving her a quick rub before bursting into a sneezing fit. My wife, Darron, always did the same (minus the sneezing).

Then, one afternoon, Joey followed Darron into the house. And from that moment on, any time the front door opened Joey raced inside.

She was small, sweet and so determined to charm us that I'd

swallow megadoses of allergy pills just so I could breathe during her visits. Suddenly I found myself with the best pet I never had. Joey would sit on my shoulders as I worked until she'd get bored and jump onto my desk until she'd get bored with that and casually stroll across my computer keyboard.

Then my allergies worsened—she'd rubbed against so many parts of the house that it felt like I was allergic to everything. We knew we couldn't have her in the house anymore but Joey didn't agree. Joey had discovered every possible entrance to the house—including a small third-story bedroom window she reached via a convoluted ladder consisting of a fence, a nearby tree and our roof. Once we discovered how she was getting in, we kept all the windows shut—and that's when Joey started holding cat symphonies, complete with window scratching, each morning at 3 a.m. until we'd surrender and let her in.

That was about the time we noticed Joey—who our friends had taken to calling by the name we'd given her—"Not Our Cat"—was getting bigger. We knew Joey was a she—but it never occurred to us she hadn't been spayed. Eventually the tiny black tabby looked like she'd swallowed a football. And the bigger she became the more determined she was to get—and stay—inside our house.

When we came back from a weekend vacation we discovered Joey was huge and furious. She looked so impatient that I suspect if we hadn't reappeared, she would have broken the door down to let herself in.

The next morning at 5 a.m. "Not Our Cat" let loose with a howl and gave birth to "not our kittens" in the middle of our bedroom floor. I immediately dubbed the first one that landed on the bedroom floor "Excalibur" because my 5 a.m. logic was that birth reminded me of the sword being pulled from the stone.

Darron, who grew up on a farm and knew far too much about animals, quickly set out a box for Joey, which she leapt into as the next kitten began to pop out. A few minutes later there were five impossibly tiny kittens cuddled up to their mom on a soft towel in a cardboard box in the corner of our bedroom.

As I looked at these little balls of fluff I knew it was time to buy every allergy pill in the city.

On the second day, two things happened. The first was that one of the kittens—a howler—began looking sick. She didn't make it through the night. The next thing was that Darron took all the kittens out of the box to insert a fresh towel.

"Look at this," she said, holding up the beauty of the litter—a sweet-faced calico. Darron counted the limbs and each time came up with the wrong number—three. Instead of a leg there was something dangling from her rear right hindquarter.

We raced the calico puffball to a vet who told us that the leg had been accidentally severed just below the knee by the umbilical cord. The cut was clean but this was definitely a three-footed cat. Then the vet told us that if we'd nurse this three-legged cat to health she would find a good home for it.

Darron and I quickly fell into a routine of cleansing the stump with iodine and painting it with medication four times a day—while also handling each of the other kittens to make sure Joey didn't think there was something wrong with her three-legged daughter (who we eventually named Scooter).

Aside from being the cutest of the lot, Scooter was everyone's first choice to adopt until they discovered her disability. But when she lost her leg she gained her mother's attitude. Scooter not only fought us as we tried to apply her medication—developing a way to withdraw her stump into her body so we couldn't reach it—she was also the first kitten to move onto solid food and the first to climb out of the box.

Once when my parents came to visit with their two Shih Tzus, we shut the cats in a room with a glass door. All the cats, including Mom, hid under the bed while five-week-old Scooter raced to the door, puffed herself up and hissed at the dogs through the window.

Then one morning I picked up Scooter and her stump was covered with blood. I wrapped her in a towel and raced her to the vet. The vet assured me Scooter was fine but when I got her back to the house I called Darron to announce that even if I had to leave the house, Scooter was staying.

When we took Scooter for her first checkup the vet admitted that we were the "good home" she'd suspected Scooter would end up in.

We found people for two of the other kittens, but since Scooter would never be allowed outside (for obvious reasons) we decided to keep Excalibur as her playmate.

I'm not sure how it happened but at about the time the other two kittens moved out, my allergies went with them.

~Mark Leiren-Young

# Paperwork

*It is impossible to keep a straight face in the presence of one or more kittens.*
*~Cynthia E. Varnado*

All we needed at the pet store was a bag of cat food and a box of litter. "I can get it—you two just go to the other stores, and I'll meet you in a few minutes," I advised my wife and daughter. But they wouldn't listen.

Together we entered the store with me taking a cart to collect our cats' needed items and the girls going to check out the newest additions to the adoption center at the back of the store. "We are not getting another cat!" I proclaimed. "We already have five and that is plenty!"

"We're just going to look, dear," my wife insisted, rolling her eyes. She quickened her pace to keep up with my little girl.

"No more cats!" I yelled after them. "I mean it!" Of course, the only people that heard me were an old man and his wife walking their Airedale, and a mother and her young son checking out the caged rats and guinea pigs. The senior citizen laughed and said, "Good luck, mister."

Quickly I picked out our items and threw into the cart a set of play mice from the clearance bin as an extra treat for our feline quintet at home. I hurried to the kitten display. "Okay, time to go. We need to pay now," I announced.

"Look, Dad," my daughter squealed pointing to a tiny, rambunctious orange tabby. "Can we get him?"

"I said no more cats! We're done. Let's leave."

"But he's so cute," my wife added. "Look how playful he is." I should have been stronger, but I looked. The kitten was jumping on top of his cage-mates and spinning around trying to catch his tail. He stopped and looked me in the eye, laughing.

"Can we get him?" I heard from behind me. Another little girl looked up at her father, tears forming in her eyes. Be strong, I warned him telepathically, but the message was not received.

"Let's go find your mother," he whimpered. "Let's see what she thinks about the cute little kitty."

"What a wimp!" I seethed under my breath.

My wife jumped into action. "Hurry!" she whispered. "Before they get back. Let's ask to hold him. He's so cute!" Obediently, I followed her to the little waiting room where the squirming ball of orange fur was handed to us. He hopped on our laps, rubbed against our chests and purred loudly. He looked me in the eye as if to say, "Listen to your wife, buddy. Take me home!"

As we filled out the necessary paperwork, the man returned with his daughter and wife. The girl took one look at us holding our new cat and burst into tears. Her father hung his head and mumbled, "Maybe we could get the little gray one?" I turned around and completed the forms, afraid to look him—or worse, his daughter—in the eye.

We took Buster home, and soon he was a part of the family. He jumped on the table and swatted the breakfast vitamins to the floor. He hopped on the counters and on the back of the sofa. He chased his new brothers and sisters around the house with the same intensity he exhibited at the store.

One Saturday morning—laundry day—I was moving the freshly washed towels into the dryer. The phone rang, and I went to answer it. When I returned, I closed the dryer door and pressed the "on" button. A loud banging came from within. I quickly opened the door, and a befuddled orange kitten stared up at me, shook his head and hopped out. He scratched at the machine in an attempt to bury it. Eight lives left, I thought.

Buster spent the next few months happily exploring the house, tormenting the other cats and jumping into our laps for some human attention when he was tired. He bumped our heads with his own, purred and generally made himself at home.

The ornery cat loved rummaging through the trashcans for paper to eat. We purchased garbage cans with lids. He pulled tissues from their boxes. We turned the boxes upside down. He unrolled the toilet paper. We flipped the roll so that it rolled under instead of over. Still, in the middle of the night, we could hear him pulling the toilet paper across the bathroom.

Late one evening, my daughter came running into the living room. She shouted, "Buster looks sick! He's not moving!"

We rushed to his side. He was lethargic, panting laboriously. His abdominal muscles clenched and heaved, yet nothing passed but tiny bubbles of mucus. With the vet's office closed for the evening, we decided to take him to the nearby emergency animal clinic.

He looked me in the eye and purred as I handed him off to the intake assistant. "We'll do a few tests and call you back as soon as we can," she said as she held him to her chest and left for the back room.

I sat in the lobby and noticed a former student and his mother nervously waiting for the assistant's report on their Cocker Spaniel. "A patio lamp fell on Chico's head," Benny whispered. His mother reached over and squeezed his hand.

Thirty minutes later, I was called to one examination room and Benny and his mother were escorted into an adjoining room. As I waited for news on Buster's condition, I sadly learned of Chico's through the uncontrolled sobbing of mother and son.

The veterinarian soon entered my room with my listless kitten. "We don't know what's wrong with him," she said. "We could open him up and do some tests. That would run you about $3,000. Or we can euthanize him so he is not in any more pain."

With a lump in my throat, I called my wife. We decided to bring him home, and if he died, he would be surrounded by those who loved him. The vet said she understood and handed me eight vials of painkiller—enough to suppress a St. Bernard. "In case he is uncomfortable tonight," she offered.

It was 2 a.m. when I finally brought him home. We woke up our daughter so she could say goodbye. Together we held him through the early morning and cried.

The next day, we took Buster to the vet. He informed us that the kitten's intestines were obstructed. "Probably something he ate from the trash," he said. He administered some medication and allowed Buster to rest in his office. That afternoon, we received a call telling us to come pick up our cat. He ran toward us purring and rubbed against our legs.

Deep in the night, we were awakened by the toilet paper being pulled from the roll. I took the roll off and hid it in the cupboard. "Bad boy!" I said petting his head. He purred.

"We don't need any more cats!" I hollered to my wife. But she didn't listen. A few months later she brought home a little black kitten—she said Buster needed a friend.

~Tim Ramsey

# The Christmas Cat

*The perfect Christmas tree? All Christmas trees are perfect!*
*~Charles N. Barnard*

I sat on the couch admiring our Christmas tree. My wife and I had searched several tree lots before finding the perfect blue spruce. It was about six-and-a-half-feet tall, full and plump. The tree smelled of fresh pine.

Though the tree smelled great and looked beautiful, it was a royal pain to set it up. My wife and I struggled to get the stubborn tree into its metal holder and to make it stand upright. Once it was standing, we pulled out our plastic crates full of ornaments and twinkle lights. We went to work making certain to place each ornament in its proper place on the tree. We hummed along to Christmas songs by Bing Crosby, Burl Ives and many others. We even laughed as we heard about Grandma getting run over by a reindeer.

We were young and very much in love. It was our second year of marriage and we had not yet started our family. All we had was each other and a black and white cat name Friday. This would be Friday's second Christmas with us. We had discovered the previous year that Friday really loved Christmastime. She loved batting Christmas bulbs off the bottom of the tree. She loved tugging on the stockings that hung from our mantle and she enjoyed sniffing and nibbling on pine needles. Cats are very indifferent creatures and Friday was no exception. But when it came to Christmastime, our cat was a downright festive feline!

Because of her propensity to bat at Christmas bulbs, my wife and I made sure to keep the more valuable ornaments higher on the tree as we decorated it. After we finished trimming the tree and decorating the mantle, my wife called the cat down to inspect our work. Both of us figured that Friday would be thrilled to see the condo all decked out for the holidays.

After an extensive search, we discovered the cat was upstairs napping. We decided we could show Friday the tree later and also decided that a nap was a good idea. My wife and I napped for an hour and then got up to work on Christmas cards. Once again we searched for the cat and this time we could not find Friday anywhere. I looked in each room upstairs and my wife searched diligently downstairs. Friday, the cat that loved Christmas, was nowhere to be found.

My wife became frantic as more time passed and there was still no sign of Friday. I grabbed my boots, deciding that maybe the cat had escaped and gone outdoors. Then I heard my wife laughing and saw her pointing at our newly decorated blue spruce. Our cat Friday was sitting in the center of our beautifully decorated Christmas tree. Somehow she had managed to climb into the tree and not knock off a single ornament or mess up the lights.

She peeked out at us and seemed to say, "What's the big deal? I'm just in the center of the tree enjoying another holiday season!" We laughed, and my wife grabbed a camera. She said she wanted to remember the moment forever. I thought to myself, I won't require a photograph to remember this!

That's the way it is with pets. They become a part of the family and they give you a lifetime of memories. Like all memories, some are happy and some are sad.

Several years later, my wife and I were decorating another Christmas tree. This time our daughter was around to help us. Unfortunately, this was the first Christmas without Friday. She had died a few months prior to the holiday season. We were now seasoned veterans at putting a tree safely into the stand and we had many more ornaments to cover our tree.

Once the tree was decorated, my daughter shouted, "Dad, get the stockings and candles for the mantle."

I went to the garage and opened a box full of extra Christmas decorations. At the bottom of the box sat a tiny red-and-white striped stocking that had once been filled with catnip for Friday, the cat that loved Christmas. I paused for a moment and took a deep breath. I showed my wife the tiny stocking and she cried. We both missed our cat.

A moment or two later, we laughed simultaneously as we recalled the year that Friday camped out in the center of our Christmas tree. My wife showed our daughter the picture she had taken of Friday sitting inside the beautiful blue spruce. Our daughter giggled at the photo. She told us that we were lucky to have a cat that loved Christmas so much.

Our daughter was right. We were lucky to have a cat that loved Christmas so much. We were also lucky to have a cat that gave us many great memories!

~David R. Warren

# Tommy Bangs Shampoo

*With the qualities of cleanliness, affection, patience, dignity, and courage that cats have, how many of us, I ask you, would be capable of becoming cats?*
*~Fernand Mery*

I didn't want Tommy Bangs. When my husband and I decided to adopt a cat from the local animal shelter, my choice was a gold and white Himalayan. But Larry liked an ordinary, shorthaired, white and gray tabby that was already curled in his arms.

My darling, regal Himalayan spat and swatted at Larry's arm. Larry's cat yawned and butted his chin.

I rolled my eyes. I already knew the outcome of this showdown. Sure enough, the tabby went home with us. I named him after a naughty boy in *Little Men*, Tommy Bangs, and left the males to bond. It didn't take long for my husband and Tommy Bangs to establish a routine. In the mornings and evenings after Larry returned from work, he'd trudge to the bathroom, the little gray and white cat trotting after him.

I didn't have to get up so early, so I'd drift back to sleep.

One morning, Larry shook me awake. "Kar, you have to see this."

I propped open an eyelid. "Now? Is it an emergency?"

Larry grinned and pulled off the covers. "It'll only take a minute."

Trailing a blanket, I trudged after him. I threw up my hands to shield my eyes from the brightness of the bathroom light. Tommy Bangs sat on the sink, admiring his profile in the mirror.

I glared, first at the cat, then at my husband. At 5:38 in the morning, I need a cup of tea before I can think, talk or function. Smiling isn't even a possibility.

"The cat? You dragged me out of bed to stare at the cat?"

Larry patted the creature's head. "He's so smart. He washes himself."

Before I said something that I would surely regret, I staggered back to the bedroom. "Unless he's juggling balls and singing, I really don't want to know!"

A couple of mornings later, I nudged Larry out for early morning necessities. Tommy Bangs was in the tub. We ignored each other while I finished my business and washed my hands. In the mirror, I glanced behind me.

Tommy Bangs caught several drops of water in his left paw. Instead of licking them off as I expected, he slapped the water on his face and scrubbed away. I rubbed my eyes and stared. He repeated the process with the right paw, the right side of his face. He methodically shampooed his chin, the top of his head, and even his ears the same way. He'd pause for a drink, then continue.

People take showers. Raccoons wash their food. Elephants cool down with streams of water. With the exception of tigers, cats are not supposed to like water. Not only did Tommy Bangs like water, but he shampooed his whole head.

Was he imitating my husband? Next, would he be requesting a washcloth and soap on a rope? I wouldn't be surprised. I went straight to the source.

"Larry, you didn't tell me that Tommy Bangs was your shower buddy." I tapped my big husband's arm. He shrugged on a blue shirt, a small grin on his face.

"I tried to, honey, but you aren't exactly at your best early in the morning." He kissed my cheek and fumbled with his cufflinks. "Hey, boy," he said, calling to the little gray and white cat who jumped on the bed. Tommy Bangs purred and washed the rest of his body in normal cat mode.

I stroked the top of the cat's wet head. "You can't get any cleaner than a shower."

"Yeah. But I'm sure he's thirsty. His tea should be cool by now. He prefers green tea with honey." Larry snapped on black suspenders.

Normally, I would compliment Larry on his dapper appearance, but my mind froze. My hand tightened on the cup of tea I'd been sipping.

Cat tea?

See what you miss when you sleep?

Weirdness.

~Karla Brown

# Good Vibrations

*I simply can't resist a cat, particularly a purring one. They are the cleanest, cunningest, and most intelligent things I know, outside of the girl you love, of course.*
*~Mark Twain*

Sometimes it feels like there are two major groups of people in this world: those who adore cats and those who hate them. My husband, Harry, however, exists somewhere in the middle. He enjoys snippets of their existence, such as playing with kittens or petting them when he wants. But when it comes to the constant shedding, sharpening claws on furniture or yowling to make their wishes known, well… he has had to learn tolerance. After all, when he fell in love with me it was clear that animals would always be a major part of my life.

One summer morning, I'd gone out to the barn to feed my horses. A low, guttural, eerie wail stood my neck hairs at attention. I found a large, orange and white tomcat lying on the dirt floor. A quick examination revealed two large abscesses that had swelled one back leg to twice its size. He also had a fever and was quite weak.

As I picked him up, the cat purred and head-butted his appreciation.

I set him up in our bathroom, cleaned and opened the abscesses to allow drainage and put a poultice on his leg. He purred quietly throughout the procedure and again each time I treated him, three times daily. In two weeks, he was healthy and ready to be introduced to our animal family.

For several months I tried to find him a good home, but everyone seemed to want him as a barn cat and he was far too interested in home life for that.

So, Orion became the newest member of our family.

Harry and I were closing in on thirty-eight years of being together when he was diagnosed, over Christmas, with Stage II colorectal cancer. Two weeks later, he was in surgery.

After ten days in the hospital, I brought him home and helped him get slowly out of the car and up the stairs. He sank into his recliner, lifting his feet and legs with the handle. Grimacing, he tried to find a comfortable position.

Orion was not allowed on that chair; Harry didn't appreciate the hairs he left behind. But once Harry was settled, Orion scrutinized him carefully, considering the situation. Then he made his move. Gingerly, he jumped onto the footrest. With careful consideration, one toe at a time, he inched up further, still surveying. And then, with a ballerina's grace, he slid onto Harry's lap, edging as close to the incision as he could without actually touching that painful area.

Finally, he'd found the exact spot he wanted and lay down. Within seconds, the whole room filled with a purr symphony—without a doubt, the loudest purr I'd ever heard. He didn't move or stop purring for a full hour. When he eventually left, he did so in the same careful manner.

Some scientists suggest that a cat's purr vibrates at a healing frequency. Orion certainly seemed to use it therapeutically for himself and then stepped up to help Harry. And although Orion and Harry eventually returned to their normal relationship, tolerating each other's presence in the house, for that one hour, the synchronicity and symbiosis between these two roommates defined pure harmony.

~Diane C. Nicholson

# The Nine Lives of Smokey

*Patience and perseverance have a magical effect before which difficulties disappear and obstacles vanish.*
*~John Quincy Adams*

I decided it was time for my young son to have his first pet. So for his third birthday, I brought home an eight-week-old kitten who was a fluff ball of long gray hair. My son immediately decided we should name him Smokey, the color of his fuzzy coat.

Two notable things happened by the time Smokey reached six months of age. First, he settled into a pattern of sleeping on my pillow right next to my head every night. Second, his gray kitten fluff fell out and his coat became sleek and jet black, no gray to be seen. The name Smokey no longer seemed fitting, but that's who he was, so the name stayed.

If Smokey could have talked, he would have told you he lived a perfect life for the next two years. That is until my new husband entered our lives. Mark was not a cat person. A cat sleeping between us on the pillow was not acceptable to him. Smokey eventually lost the battle and began to sleep elsewhere in the house.

When Smokey was five years old, we moved to a new city and rented a nice little house with a big back yard for our two children and two cats. We moved in on a Sunday and managed to unpack just enough to sleep there for the night. Monday morning, my husband left to start his new job. I quickly loaded my two kids into the car and set out to run errands, the first of which was to get the electricity turned on in the house. After about two and a half hours, the kids had reached their limit and we headed back to our new home.

As I turned into the quaint neighborhood, barricades blocked the street, the entire cul-de-sac filled with fire trucks and police cars. To my horror a column of black smoke was billowing from the house we had just rented. I jumped out of the car and raced toward the house, only to be stopped short by a police office.

"That's my house!" I exclaimed. "What happened?"

"It appears that there was an electrical problem in the kitchen, ma'am. The fire is almost out, but there is still a lot of smoke. You need to stay back."

"My cats. I had two cats in there. Do you know where they are? Are they okay?" Tears rolled down my face.

"Let me find a firefighter for you. Stay where you are."

I stood there in shock until a somewhat grimy firefighter exited the residence and followed the officer over to where I stood. "We found your cats huddled in a bedroom as far from the fire as they could get, they were unconscious but breathing. We transported them to the nearest vet. Here's the address. We aren't going to be able to let you in for a while, until we know it's safe. Why don't you go check on your pets?"

At the veterinarian office, a very kindly older doctor informed us that only one cat, the black one, had survived. They weren't equipped to handle such a severe case, so they had transported Smokey to a nearby veterinary school hospital, where he could receive the care he needed.

The enormous institutional building that was the vet hospital was a very different atmosphere from the small friendly clinic. We waited for what seemed like hours for a vet tech to come talk to us.

"Your cat is in very serious condition. He hasn't regained consciousness and his lungs have been damaged by smoke. If he survives the next twenty-four hours, we will see where we are then."

We trudged back to our car, the hope sucked out of us.

The following morning, I received a call from the hospital. "Smokey is awake but he doesn't respond. We believe he is brain dead. In addition, his back legs are permanently paralyzed. There is really nothing more we can do for him, except to put him out of his misery. You will need to come in and sign the paperwork so we can euthanize him."

Too overwhelmed by everything I had been through the past couple of days, I just couldn't face telling them to kill my beloved Smokey. My husband volunteered to go for me, taking along a large shoebox to bring back his body so we could give him a decent burial.

When Mark walked back into the house, shoebox in hand, I hid my face in my hands and dissolved into tears.

"Look at me," Mark said. "He's not dead."

"What?" I muttered raising my head.

"I told them I needed to say goodbye to him. When I walked in the room, he saw me and tried to pull himself up the side of the plastic cage to get to me. He can't be brain dead because he knew me! So I brought him home."

I reached my hand in the box to touch the head of my little buddy. He was burning up with fever and looked beseechingly at me with pain-filled eyes.

"Did they send some medicine for him?"

"No, they said he was going to die. But I just had to give him a chance."

Determination took over. I had a goal and I was not just going to sit there and watch my cat die. I had seen a small country vet's office less than a mile from where we were temporarily staying. We loaded Smokey back in the car.

"Well, I can't give you any guarantees, but we sure will try to get him better," the vet said. He sent us home with liquid amoxicillin and an eyedropper with instructions to get some of the antibiotic and fluids into Smokey's mouth every couple of hours.

My belief in cats having nine lives was affirmed in the next few days. We watched Smokey gain strength every day as he began to take in milk and his fever subsided. By the end of the week, he was able to lick canned cat food off our fingers.

Much to my surprise, my husband made getting our cat well his first priority. Smokey regained his cherished place on my bed pillow, and Mark spent hours every day rubbing his hind legs to help them regain strength. By the end of two weeks, Smokey began dragging himself from the bed to his litter box using his front paws. My cat was definitely not brain dead.

In the weeks and months that followed, Smokey's hind legs once again started functioning. He could run and play in the house and back yard, like any normal cat. The only visible sign of his trauma was a tremor that he would have for the remainder of his life.

Smokey, the cat who survived the smoke, taught all of us a lesson in perseverance and overcoming life's obstacles.

~Jill Haymaker

# Love Me, I'm Siamese

*Cats invented self-esteem.*
*~Erma Bombeck*

My fiancé and I agreed on most things, but not when it came to pets. I grew up with dogs, but he was a cat person. Reluctantly, I admitted that a cat was the practical choice for an apartment, especially with both of us working.

I had little experience with cats of any type when I surprised my husband-to-be with a Siamese kitten. He was thrilled and named her "Puss"—not very creative but she was his cat so what could I say?

Friends warned me too late that Siamese cats are in a class by themselves and not a good choice for a first-time cat owner. If you have never experienced one, maybe you saw the movie *Lady and the Tramp*. Remember when the Siamese cats sang, "We are Siamese if you please. We are Siamese if you don't please"? They meant it.

I knew cats tended to be aloof, but I'd seen other cats purr contentedly when petted. Puss swatted my hand away. When she wanted attention, however, she refused to take "no" for an answer. Often while my husband read the newspaper at the kitchen table, she jumped up and swatted the paper from the other side. At first, my husband just lowered the paper, smiled, said, "Hello, Puss" and gave her head a quick stroke before he went back to reading. Puss kept swatting until he put the paper down and devoted all his attention to her. She soon had him trained to stop reading on first swat. Who said husbands can't be trained?

More than once I found her a few feet above the floor, clinging to the sheer curtains on the living room windows, her belly flat against a curtain and her legs splayed. Was that her way of enjoying the breeze or had she pounced in attack mode as the curtains swayed? Maybe she wanted to get to the window ledge? We never knew because neither my husband nor I ever saw her jump onto the curtain, but numerous little holes from her claws in the curtains proved she did it often.

Kitchen drawers began opening by themselves. The "ghost" was Puss, who sneaked into the lower cabinets and pushed against the drawers above. Who can predict what a cat considers entertainment?

Her strangest habit of all was napping in the bathtub. Even during winter, when I thought she would prefer a warmer spot, she often chose the tub for her afternoon siesta.

One day I decided to pamper myself with a leisurely soak in the tub instead of showering. Home alone, I closed the bathroom door only partway. While luxuriating in the warm water I saw the bathroom door move. Puss sauntered in parallel to the tub and paused opposite my feet. We exchanged glances and I assumed she was miffed because I usurped her territory.

Suddenly she jumped. I jolted, anticipating the fury of Hades when Puss landed in my bath. When her body arched in the air over the side of the tub and she saw the water below, every muscle tensed in horror. She reversed herself mid-flight before even one paw touched the liquid terror below. After landing safe and dry on the floor, she ignored me as she slowly strutted out of the room, head raised haughtily and tail pointed straight up.

I never saw Puss nap in the tub again. As for me, I now close the bathroom door every time I take a bath, and I still don't attempt to understand cats.

~Janet Hartman

Chapter 3

# The Cat Did What?

## Who Rescued Who?

# Look What the Cat Dragged Home

*We all have big changes in our lives that are more or less a second chance.*
*~Harrison Ford*

I had been settled in my new home for only a few days when a loud voice brought me to my living room window. Concealed by lace curtains, I peered out at my new neighbor, my only neighbor. He stood in his driveway talking to himself, a cleaning rag clutched in one hand. When he gave the hood of his car a vicious swipe, my heart jumped. Even though I couldn't make out his words, his tone was clear. And even from across the road I could see paw prints on his car. Paw prints from my cat.

"See what you did, Duncan?" I murmured. Duncan jumped up on the back of the sofa, nestled comfortably beside me, and peeked out the window. A scratch behind his ears started him purring. Duncan was a shelter cat. When I moved from the city to a small house in a rural New England town to give myself a fresh start, I decided to give one to an adult cat as well. We would both be able to breathe out here.

I still remember the day I found Duncan. Out of a long row of cages at the animal shelter, as I passed by, he had stuck out his black and white paw and touched my arm. Being an older cat, he had been up for adoption for a long time. It hurt my heart to see him in that tiny space. "Let me see this one," I said, smiling at the attendant. Duncan snuggled in my arms. He was warm and sweet and he gave me head bumps and little cold nose kisses. He sure knew how to work me. Maybe he could tell how lonely I was. My fiancé and I had split up six months earlier and there had been no one since. I wasn't ready. It was impossible to put Duncan back in that cage now that we'd met, so he went home with me.

At the new house I felt confident it was safe to let him out. He had been cooped up for so long I couldn't bear to keep him inside. The property was situated at the end of a long dead-end street with only two houses nestled next to six acres of woods. Duncan roamed around the fragrant pine forest in obvious delight, sunning himself anywhere he pleased—stretched out on warm rocks, sprawled on the wooden deck, or sometimes all nice and tidy, arms folded under him, on a car hood. He never killed anything or brought anything home. I often found him snoozing on my neighbor's back porch. Thinking he just didn't know where he lived yet, I'd go fetch him, only to find him back over there the next day.

Although I hadn't officially met my new neighbor, a clerk at the market told me that he was a police officer, a detective by the name of Ken. It felt good to have a man like that nearby. And this particular man was sure easy to look at. The clerk also informed me with a wink that Ken had been asking about me, which made me panic a little. I didn't know what to do with that information.

That day when Ken stopped muttering and wiping at his car and finally drove off to work, I breathed a little sigh of relief and turned to face my day. Still in light summer pajamas, with a fresh cup of coffee, I wandered into my new den and turned on the computer. As it booted up, a woodpecker worked on the large maple tree that shaded the house. Working from home as a legal transcriptionist was heaven and my day went by quickly. When the afternoon breeze turned soft, Duncan and I enjoyed a little nap in the hammock.

There was a good view from my office window and around sunset I could see Ken's car as it made its way down our shared dirt road. He parked and exited, hesitated a moment, looked down at the ground, then over at my house. He banged a fist gently on his car roof as though he had made up his mind about something, slammed the car door, and started to walk across the lawn.

Well, here comes the conflict, I thought. I quickly combed my hands through my hair, patted down a spot in back that always sticks up, planted a smile on my face and opened the door as Ken was about to knock. He quickly jammed that fist in his pocket and offered the other in a handshake. "Hi, I'm Ken Stone." He jerked his thumb behind him. "I live over there. I wanted to come over and talk to you. I have a little problem."

"Oh?" I tried to look innocent and immediately wondered if a cop could tell I wasn't. His voice was pretty friendly for a guy who had a problem.

Ken rubbed his chin with the back of his fingers. "All right, here's the thing," he said. "I have two huge steaks I've been wanting to put on the grill, but I hate to eat alone."

That was not what I had been expecting. Duncan chose that moment to come to the door and wind around my legs.

"Hey, little fella, how are you?" Ken said.

"You like cats?"

"Always had a cat growing up. I'd have one now but my job keeps me out of the house too much. It wouldn't be fair."

"He's a shelter cat. I just got him a few weeks ago."

Ken crouched down to pet Duncan and the cat responded like they were old friends. "Those are the best kind."

I couldn't play dumb any longer. "Look, I know he left paw prints on your car, I'm sorry about that."

Ken gave me a dismissive wave. "No problem."

"I saw you this morning and you didn't look too happy."

"You were spying on me?" When he stood back up I realized how tall he was. He broke into a grin that brought out two perfect dimples. For a moment I almost forgot what we were talking about. Oh, yes, the paw prints. "No, not spying. I heard a voice and I looked out."

Ken turned his body slightly and tapped his ear. Nearly hidden under his dark hair was an earpiece. "I was talking to my partner." He shook his head and raised his eyes heavenward. "Our case is not going well. We lost a key witness this morning."

"But you were cleaning your car and—"

Ken cut me off. "Just bird droppings. Your cat is fine. In fact, bring him over for dinner. You will come, won't you?"

I felt a grin forming on my face. It had been a long time since I had been in the company of a nice man. Duncan was sitting between the two of us staring up at me.

You did this, didn't you? I thought.

"Sure, we'll be over," I told Ken.

Duncan and I had saved each other.

~Jody Lebel

# A Couple of Strays

*Our perfect companions never have fewer than four feet.*
*~Colette*

"Don't you dare feed that cat!" my mother would admonish us. "You feed a cat and it belongs to you forever."

Mom could always find a stray's rightful owner. "Instinct," she'd call it. We thought she worked for the FBI.

My mother liked dogs. "They're not so hoity-toity and full of themselves," she'd say. "They appreciate you and give something back."

And so it was that during our childhood we had dogs: a Poodle, two Greyhounds, and a Beagle.

Eventually we kids went off to college, married and started lives and homes of our own. For the next eight years my parents were free. They rekindled their courtship and traveled. No dogs and no kids. And then suddenly my father died.

My brother, his wife, and young son moved in to keep Mom company and look after her. She was grateful for their company, and although she wasn't alone, she said she felt lonely.

On one of my frequent visits home, I went to the back yard to find my mother. She was busy collecting mangoes from the tree when a cat came by her feet.

"Shoo," I said protectively. "Strays still coming around here?"

"Sort of," she said matter-of-factly. She brought the mangoes inside and returned with a small dish of salmon. The cat was still meowing and pacing beside the sliding glass door.

I watched Mom place the dish on the patio floor. The cat gulped down the twelve-dollar-a-pound fish and then brushed against Mom's leg.

"Mom, you're feeding a cat? You're a bona fide cat hater!" I protested.

"She comes around." She shrugged. "I think she's a she, I don't know."

"Does she have a name?" I asked.

"I don't know. I call her Cat."

Later that day, I found my mother and Cat nestled together asleep on the couch, my mother's hand buried deep in Cat's fur. I just shook my head and laughed.

"She's all right," my mother said simply. "We're a couple of strays that found each other." For four more years these "strays" lived together, each one giving and getting love in her own quiet way.

Then unexpectedly my mother died.

For another two years, my brother dutifully looked after Cat while Mom's house was on the market. Finally we found a buyer.

On the night before closing my brother and I went out for dinner. We shared memories of our childhood and laughed and cried about Mom's transformation from cat hater to cat lover. Then we agonized about what to do with Cat, since my brother's wife had allergies and couldn't bring her into their new home. We drove home to spend the last evening together in our house.

As we pulled into the driveway we saw Cat lying as she frequently did at the foot of the pathway. We walked by her, expecting her to get up, but she remained motionless. We bent down to pet her, but she was still. Cat had no visible injuries. She hadn't been ill. She was lying there peacefully, although her body was already cold.

I remembered my mother's admonition: "You feed a cat and it belongs to you forever." How lovely, I thought. How simple. Love, devotion, loyalty, and companionship all for a little dish of food.

We buried Cat that night in our back yard—no longer a stray, she was home where she would belong forever.

~Tsgoyna Tanzman

# My Healing Shadow

*The cat, it is well to remember, remains the friend of man because it pleases him to do so and not because he must.*
*~Carl Van Vechten*

After visiting with my parents one Sunday afternoon, my husband and I stood in their driveway saying our good-byes when we were interrupted by a high-pitched noise. It sounded like a wounded animal.

We soon realized the sound was coming from under the hood of my father's Buick. My mother and I stood back while my father lifted the hood. We could hear the cries getting louder but we had to look closely to see what it was. Hiding underneath the engine was a tiny gray striped kitten that had apparently found a warm place to hide on that crisp fall morning. This beautiful creature stopped crying the minute he saw us. I reached down under some engine parts, from where he was peeking out, picked him up and brought him inside. I had surmised that he was either feral or someone had abandoned him in my parents' neighborhood. He couldn't have been more than four weeks old.

My husband and I had just moved into our first home and I had been planning on getting a pet, so I decided to take the kitten home. I had always heard that rescued animals made the best pets because they knew that you saved them. On the way home I decided to name the kitten Shadow in hopes that he would be as close a companion as his name suggested. However, he hid under the seat of the car all the way home. "Come on out, Shadow. Do you like that name?" I talked to him and tried to get him out from under the seat, but I had to wait until I got home to pull him out.

For the first couple of days, he was very shy, hiding wherever he could in the most remote places, and scaring us into thinking we had lost him for good. We would find him on top of the kitchen cabinets, under the basement stairs or behind the couch. Days turned into months and months turned into years and he just never seemed to warm up to us, which made us think he may have been feral. He never wanted to be touched or held and he seemed to have an agenda of his own. If he was in one part of the house and we walked near him, he would run at breakneck speed into another room and hide. Over the years I tried everything I could to get him to change, but nothing I did worked. I continued talking to him in a gentle voice. "Shadow, I saved you from the streets, sweetie. You're supposed to be a loving pet." So much for my "rescued cat" theory. We came to terms with the fact that we had an "invisible cat."

In his twelfth year with us I had to have spinal surgery that would ultimately leave me bedridden for the better part of three years. Before my surgery, Shadow would never have come into our bedroom when we were in there. But when I had to stop working and spend all my time at home, he started to mellow a bit. He wouldn't sleep in bed with us but he slept in a laundry basket that I had placed on our dresser. I would call to him from my bed, "Come and lie in bed with Mommy," I would say, laughing at the thought. It had become a joke for us to call to him and expect him to come to us, even though we had seen some small changes in him.

Spending so much time alone and in bed had become like a prison for me. Every once in a while Shadow would come by the side of the bed and look up at me as if to say, "I know." All these prior years of me thinking he wasn't able to bond with a human had changed since my health had become compromised. He seemed to know I was in pain. And instead of spending his time under a table or behind a closet door, he now spent all his time by my side.

One night, after taking a new pain medication, I awoke from a sound sleep. My chest felt like it was going to explode and my heart was beating more rapidly than anything I had ever experienced. I was sure it was a reaction to the new pills and thought I might be having a heart attack. I couldn't speak because of the crushing pain in my chest. The sound of my beating heart seemed to fill the room. The accelerated pounding was all I could hear.

I lay there not able to move when I heard Shadow jump out of his laundry basket and onto our bed. He came closer to me than he ever had before and I could see a look in his big green eyes that let me know I was going to be okay. He came to save me. Ever so gently, he climbed onto my chest and placed both his front paws down over my shoulders. He was on a mission—I could tell. The look in his eyes had such an intensity—a warmth. Within minutes my chest pain subsided and my heart rate returned to normal. He spent the rest of the night in bed with me, cuddled under one of my arms. And from then on he slept in bed with me every night until he passed away, eight years later at the age of twenty.

During his final eight years we were able to draw closer together than I could have ever imagined possible. His name, Shadow, suited him well. In the beginning, I tried to give him more of myself than he apparently wanted. And in those last eight years of his life he gave me more than I was able to give back to him. He had been waiting for the right time, when it really counted. In the middle of that one frightening night, he showed me how much he had appreciated me for having saved him in his hour of need—and when I needed to be saved, he was there for me.

~Marijo Herndon

# Joey's Entourage

*Cats are endless opportunities for revelation.*
*~Leslie Kapp*

"Mack, stop it!" I yelled across the yard. My dog had treed yet another critter and was dancing at the base of the tall maple, his tongue lolling and his eyes bright with excitement. When he didn't stop barking and refused to abandon his chase, I sighed and walked towards him.

Grabbing his collar, I looked up to see a baby black squirrel clinging to a branch, its tiny body shivering in fear.

I clucked to it soothingly and dragged my dog away. To my surprise, the little fellow ran down the tree and followed us.

"Shoo!" I told it, trying to keep my dog from tearing my arm out of its socket in his rabid excitement to chase the poor thing again. "Go on, now. Go find your mother," I urged.

I finally managed to chase the squirrel away and get Mack into the house. A half hour later, thinking the coast was clear, I let him back out into the yard. He immediately charged over to the same spot, repeating the same capture.

"Go away," I ordered the fluffy-tailed rodent as he hopped behind us. He finally disappeared onto the neighbor's property.

I forgot about the incident until I heard another dog barking and my neighbor bellowing. I went outside to investigate and she waved me over. Sure enough, she was clutching her own dog as her kids tried to chase the squirrel off their property so it wouldn't be hurt.

I ran over to help, shocked when the tiny creature scampered right over to me. It crawled up my leg and torso to nestle against my neck, emitting frightened grunts as it tried to hide in my hair.

I didn't know whether to scream or tear it off my head. Visions of it ripping my face off and giving me rabies ran through my mind, but the squirrel calmed immediately against the warmth of my body and started to nuzzle for food.

I sighed. Evidently it was orphaned and decided I was its substitute mommy. I was accustomed to rescuing wild baby birds and nursing them until they could be returned to the wild. In fact, I'd pried several out of the jaws of my cats, much to their annoyance, and kept a cage handy just for such an occasion. I'd never rescued a squirrel, however.

I asked my neighbor for an old towel and gently pried the creature from my head. I brought it into the house, bathed it, dried it, and then dropped it into the cage lined with paper. I quickly showered myself in case there was any insect transfer.

I stepped out of the bathroom to find all three of my cats observing our new tenant. Two were licking their lips while a third was draped over the top of the cage, one paw clawing through the bars. I chased them all away and opened my laptop to figure out what to feed the little guy.

He took to the formula I found on the Internet very well, and was eagerly lapping it from a syringe an hour later when my family returned from work. My husband sighed in amused resignation when he saw him. We immediately named him Joey after he crawled into my son's hoodie kangaroo pocket to settle down for a nap.

Over the next two weeks, we tried to handle him as seldom as possible, not wanting him to become too accustomed to humans. He'd need to be released into the wild eventually, but he was still so small. I wanted to give him a fighting chance. I slowly introduced him to the food he would find in his own environment and he adapted well.

The cats, however, seemed to think I was fattening a luscious feast especially for them. They watched patiently, observing him through the bars of his confine. They would stare for hours at a time, almost unblinking, constantly glancing my way as if to ask, "Can we devour him yet? Is he ready?"

Joey took their attention in stride. He ran around his cage, batted at random paws that slipped through the bars. He sniffed at noses flattened against the latch that I took pains to shut with a tie wrap in case my felines managed to figure out how to open the hook. He even stood on his hind feet to swat at the underbelly of whichever cat happened to be splayed across the top of his enclosure.

After three weeks, my research told me Joey was ready to be free again. I couldn't guarantee his survival of course, but I could guarantee that if he stayed with us much longer he would become too tame to let loose.

I ensured the cats and dog were locked in the house. Carrying Joey, I walked deep into the woods behind our house. I gently placed him on the ground and watched him scurry off to climb up the nearest tree.

"Good luck, little fellow," I told him softly as I watched him disappear into the thick foliage.

I managed to walk about two hundred yards when I heard a rustling behind me. Sure enough, Joey was following me. He ran up my body to my shoulder. I attempted several more releases, but it was no use. He followed me every time. When I got back home, my husband chuckled as I placed the squirrel back in his cage.

Two days later, I tried again. This time I was successful. Joey did not follow me home. I could only hope he'd be okay.

Later that afternoon, as I sat on my patio, I saw my three cats coming toward the house. They were behaving oddly, taking several steps, stopping, then looking behind them. As they advanced closer, I saw a familiar black ball of fur following them. It was Joey. They were leading him home!

I was astounded. They could have easily killed him, yet they flanked around him like sentry, protecting him from harm. Together, the four of them climbed the stairs and sat at my feet waiting to be let in while I stared slack-jawed and speechless.

Tempted as I was to keep that persistently returning rodent, I knew it was in his best interests to be wild and self-reliant. Some squirrels can be domesticated, but I felt Joey would be happier in his natural habitat.

The next day, my husband drove him several miles away from our home and released him. We never saw him again. I placed the cage on the back porch to wash and disinfect it for a future inhabitant. Later that afternoon, I stepped out to see all three cats circling it and sniffing, as if trying to catch a scent of Joey's trail. They seemed confused, almost sad, when they couldn't find one.

Those cats have since done what most cats do—hunted and killed small prey—sometimes "gifting" me with the remains. Each time, I shudder and dispose of their trophies, and each time I remember how, completely out of character, they protected and guided a little black orphaned squirrel to the safety of what they believed was his home.

~Marya Morin

# A Captive Moment

*I have noticed that what cats most appreciate in a human being is not the ability to produce food, which they take for granted—but his or her entertainment value.*
*~Geoffrey Household*

Wildlife at Leap of Faith Farm was plentiful. From our window we watched deer grazing in our pastures in the green of summer and bedding down on the sheltering hillside as snow fell around them when the winter winds began to blow. Coyotes howled under the full harvest moon and haunted the winter nights. Birds flocked to the feeders that decorated our back porch eaves. Raccoons raided those feeders when food supplies dwindled and so did opossums. Those hardy creatures with their pencil sharp noses, black beady eyes and reptilian tails had changed little from prehistoric times. We had to admire their tenacity, but we preferred to do this from afar, not face to face. They reluctantly waddled away when we discouraged them from the birdseed feast with straw brooms and loud voices. They were not easily persuaded to find other eating spots.

Fall meant that we had to rethink our feeding pattern for the family of cats that had moved into our barn during the summer. Feeding in the old chicken coop worked well during warm weather, but now that winter threatened with each falling leaf, we decided to feed the cats upstairs in the loft near sheltering hay bales, cozy blanket-filled boxes, and strategically placed heat lights. The cats thought this was a grand idea, and readily tripped up the loft stairs behind us.

As our feeding routine became more familiar, our relationship with our new cat family grew. There was orange and white Peaches, tiny charcoal gray Jessie, black and white Chess, marmalade orange Larena, and her soft yellow son Justin. They all became used to our approach with kitty food each day and even tolerated an occasional chin rub or light brush of fingertips down their backs. Larena and Justin even trotted to meet us as we climbed the loft stairs with our kitty goodies. We were happy to see our cats snuggled in after a good meal when the night temperatures began to dip near freezing. What we were not happy about were the other creatures that decided this bed and breakfast was just what they were looking for. Occasionally a raccoon decided to try the tasty cat food on the barn's second floor. But more frequently, when we climbed the stairs, in addition to our furry pets, we also saw the grinning face of an opossum.

At first, while the cats watched the show from their warm beds, we were successful with driving the opossum down the stairs and out into the night with a short burst of yells and stamping feet. But as fall's crispness became winter's harshness, the ritual was repeated more frequently and with increasing difficulty. The opossum were intent on securing a good and easily obtained meal, and we were determined that they must learn the restaurant was closed. Opossums sometimes carry a disease that can be devastating to horses. Besides protecting our cats' food supply, we also wanted to eliminate the exposure of our guys to these cunning intruders.

And so we began an almost nightly opossum roundup. If we saw the escaping tip of a tail or the yellow glow of eyes in the deep recesses of the hay bales, we instituted a drive-and-capture technique that was almost always successful and surprisingly easy. With pole and broom, we prodded the little creatures from their haystack tunnels. While one of us would keep the opossum moving forward, the other held a trash can at the ready. Behind the opossum, the swish of a broom; ahead, a dark tunnel to hide in. The cats sat by wide-eyed as they watched the match unfold each night. Perhaps they were placing bets on whether the humans or the opossums would be victorious. And opossum by opossum they were loaded into a can and spirited away down the road or to the boat landing by the river and released to lead their lives away from us.

We must have captured at least twenty opossums over that winter. Most were amazingly easy to corral into our trash container, but some were a challenge for the two of us. One night I alone did chores. I fed the cats their evening meal, brought the horses into their stalls, and then went back upstairs to say good night to the cats. As I reached the top steps and turned to look down the barn aisle, I saw an opossum finishing his evening meal. I grabbed my broom and began urging him toward the stairs, but he doubled back and ducked into a hay bale tunnel. "Not so fast, opossum," I said. But when I dislodged him from his hiding place, he scurried between other bales. Our hide and seek game went on for some time and the cats advanced from their beds to the edges of the surrounding bales for a better view.

Exasperated, I thought perhaps I should just give up and wait until my husband could join in trying to capture this wily beast. "One more time," I promised. Then, whimsically, I called out to my furry audience. "Come on cats. Help me catch this opossum." I pried him from between the bales again and with broom in hand, began herding him down the aisle. Ahead of us was a stack of hay bales and the opossum headed straight for them. Just beyond, a trashcan sat waiting. I feared he would just skirt the stack and go into hiding again, but then ahead I saw movement in the shadows. Larena had reached the base of the stack and began climbing up one side. Justin approached from the other side. For a moment time stopped, with the cats on each side and the opossum on the top bale, mouth wide open and hissing, and me behind with the broom. The trashcan loomed ahead. Then, with a strong sweep, the opossum fell forward into the can.

My cats had come to my aid. These friends I looked out for each day had decided to return the favor. "Goodnight cats and thank you!" I called and I carried the trashcan out into the night for delivery of the opossum to his new home far away.

~Cheryl Suzanne Heide

# Daycare

*A good neighbor will babysit. A great neighbor will babysit twins.*
*~Author Unknown*

"Look, Mama. There's a white cat." Mary pointed out a white shape against the dark green of the pinion pines in our front yard. An elegant white cat surveyed us with piercing green eyes.

"I wonder who she belongs to," I murmured. Mary went over to the tree and stood on tiptoe, her tiny bare feet quivering with effort to reach our guest.

As if she knew the child was gentle and kind, the cat tilted her head to let Mary scratch behind her ear. "Oh, Mama," she breathed. "I'm going to call her Snowflake."

Our tiny home was already bursting with two adults, three children, two dogs, two cats, and two fish. I glanced at the For Sale sign posted next to our driveway. On top of keeping everything neat and tidy for the unexpected calls from potential buyers, the idea of taking in another cat overwhelmed me.

"Please, Mama!" Beth jumped up and down beside her older sister, straining to reach the kitty, who knew to stay out of reach of the smaller girl.

"Who do you think she belongs to, Mom?" At nine, Jim took his job as older brother seriously.

"I don't know. She's too beautiful to be a stray or feral. She's not very old, but she's certainly not a kitten. Let's ask around the neighborhood."

"Then can we keep her?"

"We'll see."

Deep in my heart I suspected that someone from the city had abandoned the cat. An hour later, we trudged back up our driveway. "Mom, no one lost a white cat," Jim said.

"Kids, we can't bring another cat into the house."

"But we can feed her. Right?"

"Yes."

"Hurray!" The kids charged up the wooden steps of the deck.

"We're not keeping her!" I called to their disappearing backs.

A week later, I slipped out into the garden by the pond as dawn glowed. I sat by the dark and still water, pulled my sweater close against the chill of the summer morning air as I sipped my morning cup of Irish Breakfast tea.

"Mrrow."

I glanced up as Snowflake jumped down from the pine tree and ambled over to sit beside me, both of us watching the pink and orange reflection of the sky against the surface of the water. When I dipped my fingers into the water, the goldfish came to the surface, and immediately Snowflake was on the alert, eyes glued on the flashing orange shapes.

"Oh no you don't," I laughed, deflecting her paw as she moved to strike at the fish. "Those are my goldfish." She initially resisted, but then relaxed and curled up next to me. As I rubbed her she flopped onto her back, silently begging me to scratch her belly.

When I felt the small swellings, I knew Snowflake was pregnant. Just what I needed—a knocked-up teenager. While I wasn't ready to turn Snowflake into a housecat, well, not my housecat, I couldn't ignore a pregnant cat.

I purchased nourishing food for expectant mommies, and Snowflake rewarded us with her presence every time we were outdoors, sitting with me in the early mornings or following the kids as they played in the yard.

We created a safe place for her to sleep and ultimately have her kittens. Snowflake allowed my children to pick her up and place her in the new bed we'd provided. But as soon as we walked away, she'd hop out and head over to my strawberry bed, through the wire field fence to our neighbor's yard to where she had found a small space underneath one of their many sheds. Our neighbor had many piles of wood, lumber, sheds, and abandoned cars, which made good hiding places for small animals and an even better hunting ground for a determined cat like Snowflake.

As Snowflake became heavier and bulkier, she was content to just sit and watch my children play. One morning, she failed to appear and I worried that an owl or coyote had gotten her. But later Mary ran into the house, face glowing, and announced, "Snowflake had her kittens!"

"Where?"

"Under the shed next to the fence!" We all charged outside and raced to the fence line. Try as we might, we couldn't see far enough under the shed to spy the kittens, but we heard their tiny mewling sounds. For several days, we saw nothing of Snowflake, but continued to hear her kittens. I had hoped my kids could see the kittens as newborns, but I explained to them about Snowflake's determination to protect her little family.

About a week later, my kids and I sat on the porch hulling strawberries. I looked up to see what looked like Snowflake coming through the fence, hopping over the strawberry hills, heading our way. She had something in her mouth.

"Mom! Snowflake is bringing us a kitten!" Mary cried.

The skinny, dirty, bedraggled white cat carried a tiny black and white kitten in her mouth. Snowflake dropped it into my outstretched hand, turned away, trotted across the yard, and through the fence. She reappeared with another white bundle. Five times she came through the fence with one of her kittens held gently in her mouth.

Snowflake's appearance alarmed me. It had only been five days since we had seen her, but she looked awful. Her eyes were dull, and I noticed that her nictitating membranes were not fully retracting. Our new little mother was clearly exhausted. The last time she disappeared through the fence, she didn't reappear.

We stared down at the kittens curled together in a tight mass of black, white, and brown fur, and I suddenly realized that Snowflake had brought her brood to us to babysit. "Jim, go get a box. Mary, there's a towel under the sink in the bathroom." Beth and I stared in wonder at the tiny miracles in my lap. Beth gently stroked between the eyes of one tiny kitten who raised its head to her touch and began to purr.

The kittens nestled together in their box. About four hours later, just as I began to worry that she had left her still-blind kittens for me to raise, Snowflake reappeared. Her movements were more brisk and her eyes were brighter. She was still bedraggled, but she'd made an effort to groom herself.

Snowflake had taken a much-needed nap.

This set the pattern for the next few weeks. Every afternoon after lunch, Snowflake brought her kittens for us to babysit while she took a nap and had a bath. Before dinner, she retrieved her kittens, who had learned to follow her.

Knowing firsthand how tiring pregnancy and childrearing can be, I could only look at Snowflake with admiration. Who could resist such a cat? When time came to find homes for the kittens, we opened our home and our hearts to Snowflake and one of her daughters, both of whom visited the vet to prevent another unwanted teen pregnancy. A delightful addition to our family, Snowflake and her daughter gave us many years of pure love, but no more babysitting duty.

~Kathleen Birmingham

# Stray Cats

*You own a dog but you feed a cat.*
*~Jenny de Vries*

I'm going to jail—directly to jail. I'm not passing GO, and I'm certainly not collecting $200. My crime, you ask? I've been feeding the stray cats in my yard. It seems there's a town ordinance against it punishable by a fine, and since I'm refusing to stop, probably jail time.

No, I'm not a crazy cat lady, although I must appear to be one. In fact, I had never been a pet person in general. When we bought our home fifteen years ago, however, it seemed to come with a built-in pet in the form of a beautiful black cat that lived in the back yard. It will come as no surprise to cat lovers that the little black cat made her way into our home and hearts.

When Toonsie passed two years ago, the balance of power in our yard was destroyed. It became the real life version of the animated film *Over the Hedge*. The cat was away—far away—and every other critter in our yard was vying for the vacant position of head honcho. Ducks began swimming in our pool in spite of massive amounts of chlorine. Chipmunks climbed our screens for sport. But the final indignity came while I was reading a book on a chaise lounge and two squirrels circled me in a mad cartoon-like chase, holding me hostage and quivering in fear that they would hop onto the chair.

"We're not getting a cat," said Prospero. "Don't even ask." He knew that I had been popping into local adoption centers, but he was adamant that we would resume our old life of traveling and having no fur on the furniture. Prospero was absolutely brokenhearted when Toonsie passed, but he was looking forward to the freedom one has in life when there are no pets or children to consider.

Then one day when I went out to feed the birds I found a black and white tuxedo cat huddled under the feeder. She was injured, with freshly dried blood on her paws, quivering and near starvation. Hunting in her weakened condition was nearly impossible, and she used all of her energy trying to get away from me. So I put out a dish of leftover dried food along with a can of food found in the cabinet. I brought it near to where she was hovering, along with a bowl of fresh water.

Tripod, as my husband began calling her since she favored her left front paw, made herself comfortable in the flower bed under the bird feeder, only getting up to eat. After several days she began to heal and within weeks had a shiny coat and fighting spirit. When the cool weather set in, we bought her a heated house to sleep in. Tripod was happy there for several weeks, then abandoned it for reasons of her own.

Weeks passed after her disappearance, but word must have gotten out that there were good eats to be found in our back yard. Stray cats began appearing each day and no one left hungry, including one cat that had a lovely home around the corner. Tiger Lily may not have had a collar, but Prospero and I saw her walking into a woman's house like she belonged there. By this time, all of the strays had names: Phantom had a black and gray mask over half of his face, Midnight was a spitfire of a black cat with a white moon on his chest, and Chestnut had fuzzy brown fur. Even Tripod reappeared and established herself as the ruler of the roost, often chasing the other cats away.

Feral cats are funny creatures though. They never make human contact, disappear for days on end, or you can have a morning like today when everyone showed up at the break of dawn for the breakfast buffet. Prospero and I ran around the yard putting plates of food in various corners so the cats could eat in peace. It's a cat comedy to watch them take a few bites, give each other the stink-eye as a warning to keep away from their food, and then glance at us to make sure we remain securely locked in our habitat. They do love to watch us through the glass door, especially when I'm on my elliptical machine, making me feel like a hamster on a wheel.

It's a win-win situation. Seeing cats in the yard helped us to not miss my Toonsie so much. Prospero was happy that no cats worked their way into the house, which is why he splurged on the heated cat house in the first place. And the cats were happy to have their bellies full of healthy food. Best of all, balance was restored in the yard. The cats chased the ducks out of the pool. The chipmunks kept their distance from the house. And the squirrels stayed in the trees where they belonged.

Only the town officials weren't happy, or they wouldn't have been had they known what I was doing. One day I read in our local paper that an elderly woman had to appear before the judge because her neighbors turned her in for feeding the cats.

"Now madam," said the judge kindly. "You can look at the cats. You can pray for the cats. But you cannot feed the cats; that's against the law in this town."

I felt so sorry for the poor woman. I also realized that I was in deep trouble. Several other articles appeared in the paper regarding the ongoing wars between cat lovers and their bird-loving neighbors, and the bird people always won. Even when I had my beloved Toonsie a neighbor hissed, "That cat is vicious. She kills for the fun of it." Well, she was a cat.

Eventually I'll get caught, but until that time I'm going to continue to feed the stray cats. Is it really so wrong? Anyway, I have a game plan. If I have to go before the judge, I'm going to drop a dime on my neighbor across the street. She keeps two chickens—also against the law—so that her family can have fresh organic eggs every day. The horror! I like her a lot and we really get along. She often gives me fresh eggs. Hopefully, we can be roomies in jail, maybe even form a book club in our cellblock. Or, on the other hand, I can fight this ridiculous ordinance up to the Supreme Court. I always loved a good fight. I'll keep you posted on how this goes down. Until then, the stray cats will eat!

~Lynn Maddalena Menna

# Tax Time

*Man is not like other animals in the ways that are really significant: animals have instincts, we have taxes.*
*~Erving Goffman*

A chill permeated the small bedroom that functioned as my office in our tiny rental house. The single heater that forced weak warmth into the living room and kitchen just didn't have the oomph to reach my feet under the desk. So I wore a second pair of socks and picked up my cat Smudge for extra warmth.

It was tax time and Smudge caught my optimistic mood, his warm belly vibrating on my lap as I laid the last W-2 in a careful stack.

This was my second year of marriage and joint returns. Remembering the previous year, when the refund was large enough to fund a weekend getaway, I eagerly tackled the taxes, anxious to run the sums and send the forms, while imagining all the ways we might spend another refund. We could replace our tattered couch, pay for the next term's books or go to the beach for a few days.

Between each painstaking calculation I stopped to run a hand over Smudge's soft fur that showed up on my clothes no matter what color I wore. Black and white, like a tuxedo, he shed without discrimination, all over me. But that day I didn't care. Dressed in jeans and a sweatshirt, I had no one to impress except my husband and this furry first child who kept me company when I was home alone.

Smudge had come with the house as a kitten, left behind when the previous renter was evicted. I loved him on sight and he rewarded my affection by purring with abandon and catching as many mice as he could leave by his food bowl, as if saving them for dessert. Aside from the mice, he was a model family member.

A great source of entertainment in our television-free home, when we weren't studying, Smudge kept us amused with his antics. We watched him bat ping pong balls around the living room or chase strings across the floor.

But if I wanted to cuddle on the couch and study, he'd settle on my feet or chest and demonstrate his devotion by purring, starting soft then revving until his happy rumbles sounded like an unmuffled motor idling in the street.

The day I did our taxes, Smudge snuggled on my lap, his eyes closed to slits until I slammed my hand on the desk.

"No. This can't be right." I held up the form, staring aghast at the final tally. We owed money. Smudge jumped to the floor, looking at me with reproach.

"Sorry, kitty," I said. I pulled my calculator out and punched in numbers with growing frustration. It was clear I'd figured correctly. We wouldn't get a refund. We had to pay. I wanted to cry. Instead, I gathered the taxes into a sloppy stack and dropped them on the office floor with a thud. Smudge jumped again.

Before he could dash off I picked him up under the belly and cuddled him against my chest like a baby, kissing him between his green eyes. "I didn't mean to scare you, Smudge. Let's forget about taxes until April."

He melted into me, stretching his chin up so I would rub beneath it. I stroked him just the way he liked, relaxing as I watched his eyes close and his mouth fall open. Another purr escaped and I put the taxes out of my mind.

It was a few days before I went back in the office. My nose twitched. I sniffed. We'd been in the house for six months and the room had always had an unpleasant odor, but this day an unmistakable pungency permeated the air.

"What did that cat do?" I muttered as I dropped to my hands and knees and felt the floor inch by inch, searching for the spot I'd need to clean.

The carpet was dry. I sniffed again and reached out tentative fingers. "I can't believe it," I said as I found the source of the smell. I sat back on my heels and shook my head. I couldn't scold the cat when he'd echoed my emotions so effectively. He'd peed on the taxes.

~Jill Barville

# Our Own Incredible Journey

*The language of friendship is not words but meanings.*
*~Henry David Thoreau*

Soon after we moved to a remote parcel of land in the Sierra foothills that hadn't been built on for miles around, we brought in two feral cats, Nosey and Quincy, to keep down the critter population. We had never been cat owners before, and I feared it would be a challenge for our aging Terrier, Lacy, but she became their best friend right from the start. She let them drink from her water bowl, sleep on her dog bed, and I even watched her licking cat food from their fur a time or two. The three amigos formed quite a bond.

As Lacy continued to age, her cat friends stayed close. When we drove up our long driveway coming home from work, Lacy would hobble to greet us, trailed by the cats, even when her arthritis made it hard for her to get off the porch. As her condition worsened, we spent a lot of time at the vet's office trying to find the right medication to ease her pain.

On one of those visits, I questioned the doc. "There are times now when our dog seems disoriented. I know she has suffered some hearing loss, but there seems to be more to her behavior than just that. Am I imagining things?"

"No, you're not." Her reply was unexpected. "Dogs can get a form of dementia," she continued. "It's hard to know if that's happening, but I would suggest that you keep her in for the most part. She could wander off and forget how to come home, especially on all that land around your house, Linda."

I recruited the help of my three teenagers to keep an eye on Lacy. With a house full of teenagers, things tended to get pretty chaotic, but I encouraged them. "We can't let the dog go outside unless somebody goes with her."

They all agreed to keep watch, and they did until one bustling Thursday night. The house was full of their friends, who were hanging out until Youth Group started at church later that night. There were kids coming and going from every door. Just as the last kid left I realized that Lacy was nowhere in the house to be found. By then it was dark, so my husband and I grabbed flashlights and looked all over the hillside. We called for her for hours even though I doubted that she could hear us. We didn't see the cats either, but we figured they were on their nightly prowl around the property. At midnight we gave up our search and decided to we would have better odds during the light of day.

The next morning the entire family joined in the search. We combed the countryside until the kids had to be at school and we had to be at work. That night was a usual busy Friday night, but I kept checking the porch, hoping to see Lacy resting there on her doggie bed, curled up with her cat buddies.

Saturday brought more busyness. My oldest had to be dropped off at work while my son was heading for music practice, and my youngest needed me to pick up a friend who was spending the day with her. As I went out to start the car, I couldn't believe my eyes. Walking up the long driveway was Lacy, alive and well, with Nosey on one side and Quincy guarding the other! The two cats nudged and rubbed against her, guiding her up the driveway.

"Kids come quickly. You have to see this!" I needed witnesses. I wasn't sure I believed what I was seeing!

One by one my children lined up behind me wide-eyed and slack-jawed. We stood there silently until the three animals had made their way onto the porch and were fiercely lapping up water. "They had their own personal *Incredible Journey*," my son commented, remembering an old Disney movie we watched over and over when he was younger.

"I needed you to see this because I knew you wouldn't believe me if I told you what I saw," I agreed.

~Linda Newton

# The Cat Did What?

## That Little Rascal

# The Disappearing Kitten

*You can always tell a real friend: when you've made a fool of yourself he doesn't feel you've done a permanent job.*
*~Laurence J. Peter*

I was living in New York City with my German Shepherd, Greta. Our studio apartment was on the first floor and featured something incredibly rare in Manhattan—our own back yard. It was the perfect place for a bachelor and his dog!

Now and then, friends would ask if it wasn't cruel to keep a somewhat large dog in a decidedly small apartment. I didn't think so. A natural watchdog, Greta spent most of her day on her rug just inside the entrance. I knew even if we lived in a mansion, she would stay at her post near the door. Plus, we took long walks and she had the yard. As long as the weather was nice, I would leave the back door open, so she could come and go as she pleased.

Nevertheless, I was becoming concerned that she was lonely during the day while I was at work. I decided to get a cat to keep her company.

So, one Saturday morning, I paid a visit to the ASPCA. Row after row of cages held cats of all sizes and all colors, all looking for homes.

As appealing as some of the adult and teenage cats were, I thought it would be best to get a kitten for Greta, hoping her maternal instincts would lead her to "adopt" it and become attached to it. After looking at dozens of adorable kittens, I settled on a gray striped eight-week-old female, still tiny enough to fit in a pocket!

When we got home, Greta thoroughly examined her new friend and then lay down on the rug to watch as she ate a little food. When the kitten was done eating, she promptly walked over to Greta and rubbed up against her.

Although her size and coloring made her look a bit like a wolf, I knew Greta was a very gentle lady who had never shown any interest in chasing cats. After a few moments, she put her head down and the kitten collapsed in a fluffy little heap, falling asleep right next to the big dog's face.

Now she needed a name. Midnight, Sweetie, Speckles, Tommy—the names of cats I had known while growing up came to me, but none provided any inspiration. After an hour of mulling over other animal names, human names, names of places, names of colors, names of foods, I was no closer to choosing one for Greta's kitten.

Suddenly, I remembered something from a high school literature class about a mythical goddess—an oracle named Cybele. Instantly, I knew that would be her name! However, I changed the spelling to the more conventional Sybil.

Greta and Sybil became pretty much inseparable. They ate side by side, cuddled together to sleep, and when I'd take Greta for a walk, Sybil would cry mournfully on the other side of the door, begging Greta to come back.

One evening, after Sybil had been with us a couple of weeks, I finished washing the dinner dishes and settled down to do some reading. I glanced at the front door, expecting to see Greta and Sybil curled up together. There was Greta, but no Sybil.

Not really concerned, I started searching the apartment. I looked under the couch and the dresser. I checked the bookshelves and the sleeping loft, in the bathroom and behind the stove and the fridge. No luck.

I rummaged through the kitchen cabinets and the clothes closets. I checked the windows to make sure she hadn't climbed out to the back yard. I looked everywhere and just couldn't find her. Running out of possible hiding places to search, I even opened the front door to see if she'd snuck into the hallway, although I didn't remember opening the door after dinner.

Now I was beginning to feel a little anxious. I sat down on the couch and tried to figure out where she could have gone. What was I missing? Where haven't I looked?

I tried to remember everything I'd done since coming home. I specifically recalled watching Sybil eat with Greta in the kitchen. Then, they had both lain down on their rug, and I hadn't really noticed her after that.

After more fruitless searching, I was really starting to worry. Greta seemed to sense my concern and sat by my side. Stroking her fur, I said, "Greta, where's Sybil? Get Sybil." I guess I imagined she might suddenly turn into Rin Tin Tin and find her kitten. She didn't. It was as though Sybil had disappeared into thin air.

Then I heard it—over in the kitchen area—a faint knocking sound. Greta heard it too, and we both went to investigate. I opened the cabinet, but couldn't see her. I took out all the cleaning supplies and old grocery bags and looked inside with a flashlight. She wasn't there.

Suddenly, the knocking started again. Oh no! Now I knew where she was, but could hardly believe it.

I opened the refrigerator door and was rewarded by a weak little mew. There, huddled in the back on the bottom shelf next to a bottle of soda, was a frightened gray kitten. Apparently, she had climbed in there when I was putting away the leftovers after dinner, and I must have shut the door without looking. Trying to get out, she had been hitting the soda bottle in the dark, and that was the noise we'd heard.

"Sybil, you little dope. Come out of there." Too cold or too scared to move, Sybil just sat staring at me, probably wondering why I put her in such a cold, dark place.

Greta came over and stuck her muzzle into the fridge. That's what Sybil was waiting for! She crept to the front and let me pick her up. I put her down, and Greta proceeded to lick her all over. I think she sensed Sybil was cold and wanted to warm her up.

After a minute, they both went over to their rug. Greta circled a couple of times and lay down. Sybil got so close to her that she was almost hidden underneath the big dog. She began kneading Greta's side and soon fell asleep, contentedly purring. Finally, she was safe and sound, and back where she belonged—with her surrogate mom.

For the rest of the evening, Greta wouldn't let her out of her sight. Sybil would try to explore the apartment, only to have Greta keep nudging her back towards the rug. Finally, Sybil got tired of the attention and arched her back like a miniature Halloween cat and hissed at Greta, who nearly fell over trying to back away from the angry little ball of fur.

Sybil didn't soon forget her scary stay in the cold and dark. For days, whenever I opened the refrigerator, she would hightail it to the rug and watch me with big, wide eyes. I never worried about her getting trapped in the fridge again. Of course, I never stopped checking to make sure of it, either.

~J.J. Crowley

# Let's Make a Deal

*Dogs eat. Cats dine.*
*~Ann Taylor*

Gracie, my mini Maine Coon, likes to dine graciously. She's definitely the tablecloth, flowers and candlelight kind of cat. Unfortunately, her siblings Thomas, Iggy and Maggie, aka "The Vacuum," devour everything in their dish in ten seconds or less, giving a new definition to fast food. The moment they're finished, they're on the hunt for more. Gracie's dish is an easy target.

While Gracie is quite happy to carve her initials into my skin without the slightest provocation, she won't so much as lift a paw to protect a single kibble in her dish. At first I felt sorry for her. I figured her bigger siblings were intimidating her into handing over her food, like the school bully stealing lunch money from smaller kids. Then I realized my little wheelerdealer, far from being a victim, had initiated a barter scheme. She traded kibble for favors.

I can see how it goes down. Gracie sidles up to Iggy and murmurs, "Give me your favorite cat toy for two hours, and I'll let you have three of my kibble." Iggy immediately turns over the catnip-filled scruffy carrot. She swishes over to Thomas with another offer. "Clean my ears and you get four kibble." Thomas quickly sticks his long tongue into her ear before pushing her out of the way to scarf her food. Then she waltzes over to Maggie and whispers, "Let me sleep in the sunny spot on the dining room table this afternoon, and you can have six." Maggie leaps off the table and rushes to Gracie's dish before her brothers even get a whiff of the kibble.

Having belatedly caught onto the conspiracy, I decided to put an end to it. I tried standing guard while she ate, but Gracie likes to take her time eating, rolling the kibble around her dish and savoring each bite. On mornings when I was rushing out to work, I didn't have time to cat-sit and Gracie barely ate three kibble before I had to remove the uneaten food.

Next I tried separating the cats at mealtime by putting Gracie in a room by herself, but she refused to eat at all. She got thin, I got frustrated and her siblings got mad.

So we were back to feeding and guarding, with her siblings prowling around us, glowering at me every time Gracie crunched a kibble. Iggy even started nibbling on my toes in protest.

Since Gracie likes to sleep with me, I decided to shift her last feeding to my bed at night. In my mind, I had it all worked out. We'd both get into bed and I'd toss a couple of kibble in a dish near my pillow. While she ate, I would get in a little bedtime reading. I figured just my presence in bed next to her dish would keep the other vultures away.

As usual when it comes to my cats, I figured wrong.

Maggie, who can hear the sound of a single kibble barely kissing a dish from four miles away, appeared on the bed within two seconds. Three seconds later, with my book barely open, a little brown paw snaked its way towards her sister's dish.

"Oh no, you don't," I said, dropping my book and grabbing her paw. "That's not for you. You're already fattened up for market."

She stared up at me with big round eyes. I swear she even sucked in her cheeks to make herself look thinner.

"Yeah, right. Like that's going to work on me. Remember, I was there when the vet weighed you. Svelte was not one of the words she used to describe you."

Maggie slowly pulled her paw under herself, settled down within an inch of her sister, and sighed. Keeping one hand firmly on Maggie's head, I picked up my book again as Gracie delicately nibbled at her kibble. Twenty minutes later the kibble was gone, I had finished a chapter, and Maggie jumped off the bed, disgusted with the state of the world and me, not necessarily in that order.

By the next night, the word had gotten out. As I walked into my bedroom, I was met with a line-up of all four cats across the edge of the bed. Four pairs of eyes watched me change into my jammies. Four tongues licked their lips in anticipation. Four bodies refused to budge an inch to let me get into bed.

I walked around to the other side and climbed on top. As I reached for the container of kibble, they surged toward me en masse, their gazes ricocheting between the container and my face. Iggy sauntered over to my toes, licked his lips, and then stared at me while the others crowded in closer. I could almost hear their silent communication. "On the count of three, we take her down."

I did what any other cat-owned person would have done. I gave in. "Okay guys," I said, my voice wavering a little, "here's the deal. I give you each a couple of extra kibble and we all live to see another day." Four heads nodded and I removed the lid to the container.

As Gracie nibbled from her dish near my pillow, I tossed kibble into the far corners of the bedroom for the hungry hoard. I figured the energy they expended racing for the food balanced out the extra calories. But you can bet I've slept with my toes safely under covers from that night onward.

~Harriet Cooper

# The Taste of Victory

*One reason we admire cats is for their proficiency in one-upmanship. They always seem to come out on top, no matter what they are doing, or pretend they do.*

*~Barbara Webster*

"Honey, come here. You've got to see this." I stared at the blob resting on our porch rug.

The hard fought battle waged between the boys had been won.

It all started one morning with an abandoned litter of bobtail kittens at the vacant house across the street. After a week of feeding and care passed, one of the neighbors decided to adopt the runt, a tiny female tabby.

That left us with the males. Two stump-tailed balls of fur mewed and tumbled together for hours, perpetually obsessed with outdoing the other. Each of them proved irresistible in his single-minded determination to win.

Before long we noticed several distinct differences developing between the pair. Johnny, a shorthaired marmalade, bore a crisp white bib and mittens. He weighed in at close to double his little mate. A muscle-bound mass of feline energy, he despised being carried, and held cuddling in disdain. If he'd been born of my species, he'd have sought work as a bodybuilding cage boxer.

Nothing pleased him more than a bowl brimming with food. Well, almost nothing. This ruffian's supreme joy remained attacking his smaller sibling from behind—or as he slept or ate or simply breathed. If one looked up the phrase alpha cat in the dictionary, Johnny's photo would run alongside.

Timmy—short for Timothy—seemed cut from different cloth. A long, luxuriant coat the shade of a buttery biscuit clothed his sleek frame. Soulful green eyes gazed out from a face angled with aristocratic lines. His chin even sported a clef.

This little fellow moved with the grace of a dancer, eating only enough to stay alive. An afternoon spent on my lap in front of the fireplace or dozing in the sun suited Timmy just fine. If he were human, I wager he'd grace the cover of a gentleman's magazine. Or perhaps he'd lead an orchestra with his discerning gaze and graceful and precise movements from the podium. Whatever it might be, his career would focus on sharing joy and beauty. Unlike his brother, the big galoot.

Like oil and water trapped in a bottle, the sibling rivalry roiled and churned with every show of affection I offered. For those who argue animals don't possess emotions, I'd invite them to spend an evening with my two. There could be no denying the flashes of jealousy volleyed back and forth.

A couple of months passed as the vying to be Top Cat played on.

Timid, small and endlessly harangued by Johnny, Timmy and I shared his elation when at last he discovered something at which he could beat his nemesis—hunting. Despite, or perhaps because of his size, the little fellow could have caught the wind if he so chose. After a while, a steady flow of little critters were dropped at my feet, accompanied by a sweet meow. And living at the very edge of town, with a river running nearby, the availability of all manner of varmints seemed infinite. Timmy learned to strut and swagger.

Johnny didn't care for that, not a bit. He narrowed his eyes and stepped up his efforts. If a training course in stalk and kill had been offered, he'd have signed up. One way or another, he'd master this skill. He meant business. But disappearing for most of the day, he returned home empty-pawed and disappointed every evening.

My heart went out to the big lug. At times, I almost wanted to say, "Stay quiet and still, then pounce. You're doing it backwards."

At last, through sheer dogged effort, Johnny caught on. Assaults on his beleaguered brother slowed as he strove to outdo Timmy at another task.

And so, one week I might be gifted with a field mouse from Timmy and the next a fresh vole held in Johnny's strong jaw. Gophers and nutria also landed with a soft thud, as the cats cleared the floodplain for us, one rodent at a time.

Timmy excelled at his favorite pastime, but clearly Johnny participated only for the sake of the game. He never fully understood the technique involved, and there were instances where I felt certain he'd brought home an icky critter dead of natural causes. He wasn't fooling anyone.

Worse still were the times Johnny merely stunned the little creatures, releasing them in the bedroom or bathroom for us to deal with. Snakes slithered and terrified mice skittered and ran as David and I struggled to trap them and bring them outdoors. The bat bouncing around the ceiling still gives me nightmares.

Today was even weirder.

There on the floor at my feet rested a large beige lump, about five inches square. Hairless, headless, and legless, I thanked heaven it wasn't moving. The thing didn't look particularly appetizing, but they rarely did. This meat wasn't an animal, at least not in the purest sense. Unless one of the boys moonlighted as a butcher, I might owe one of the neighbors an apology.

Because, this trophy kill was a roast, straight out of somebody's pot or slow cooker. I could almost have served it. "Hurry, honey, or it'll get away," I called to my husband, trying not to laugh.

My husband arrived at the front doorway a few seconds later.

The two of us stood side by side, staring down at the beefy mass. It had put up quite a fight, as evidenced by the chewed spots and claw marks covering it.

I wondered what to make of this most recent prize. "Now, what?"

"Potatoes, carrots?"

I rolled my eyes, focusing my attention on the cut of meat. "I wonder who...?" No kitty hovered over this victim, or beamed up at me with pride. No one claimed this catch.

Just then, Johnny raced up the porch steps, sniffed the sorry Sunday dinner and strolled into the house.

My husband grinned. "Looks like Johnny found somebody his own size to fight. He's the only one strong enough to wrangle something this heavy up the stairs." He grabbed the beef and carried it away for disposal.

I remained planted in place. Something didn't fit—why hadn't Johnny waited for the usual praise? I disagreed with my husband regarding this, the largest offering we ever received from the pets. Crossing my arms and shaking my head, I headed back inside.

At the last second, I turned and scanned the porch railing.

There, hidden just beneath the wisteria's greenery, lay Timmy. A tiny morsel of beef clung to his clef chin, and his lips stretched in the widest Cheshire cat grin ever.

He'd bagged a cow.

~Heidi Gaul

# The Future Is in Plastics

*Chemicals, n: Noxious substances from which modern foods are made.*
*~Author Unknown*

"It's normal for some cats to do that," my veterinarian told me in answer to my anxious questions on the phone. "Most of them outgrow it."

"But will it hurt him? Will he get sick? What if his insides get all plugged up?"

She laughed. "None of that is likely. He'll either throw it up or poop it out. I've never had to operate on a cat whose intestines were all twisted up with bits of plastic wrap."

Only I could bring home a cat who fervently, obsessively, compulsively, searches out plastic of all types to supplement his diet. And it's not just the plastic bags I leave sitting on the counter after a trip to the grocery store.

Little Simon will dig through my purse to find a small plastic sandwich bag I've tucked in there that contains my medications. He will pull all the towels from the linen cubbyhole to get to a disposable shower cap brought home from a motel visit.

One day he ate the plastic wrap off a microwave TV dinner, then followed it up with the plastic window from a box of Christmas ornaments!

He's eaten the bottom out of the thin, transparent produce bag containing zucchini, and then managed to open the kitchen drawer where I store such bags to help himself to a similar snack in the middle of the night.

Bread sacks must be hidden inside the freezer or the oven, because he hasn't figured out how to open either of those doors yet.

I've been so frustrated when I find yet another plastic bag with the bottom chewed off that I even briefly considered just wadding a few of them up and stuffing them into his cat bowl instead of kibbles!

Who knew that green plastic Easter grass, pulled from the basket of silk flowers on the coffee table, could be included in the list of feline major food groups?

I have occasionally found my toothbrush, comb and disposable razor under the dining room table. Thank goodness he didn't manage to swallow them!

But the strangest thing to date was when my fluorescent orange earplugs disappeared. I knew I'd left them on the bedroom bureau, so where did they go?

I noticed that the top dresser drawer was open, but they hadn't fallen inside. I moved the bureau out from the wall to take a look behind when it suddenly dawned on me: Simon!

And yes, after some investigation, I found one of the earplugs under the dining room table, torn nearly in half. Looking for the other one, I found five more earplugs in a hoarded stash behind the recliner in the rec room!

Simon is over a year old now, and it's been nine months since my vet told me that most cats will outgrow their compulsion to eat plastic. Most, but apparently not all.

~Jan Bono

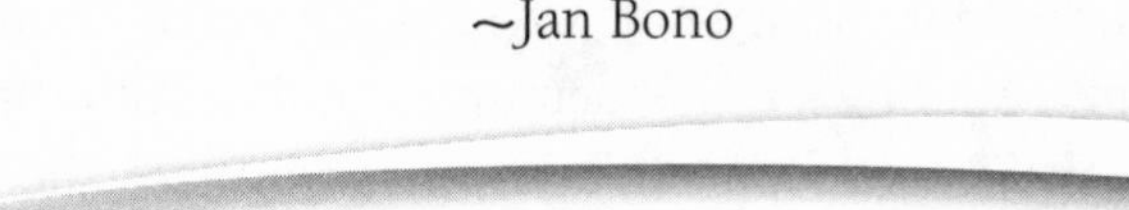

# Hide and Seek Anyone?

*Cats can work out mathematically the exact place to sit that will cause most inconvenience.*
*~Pam Brown*

My son Ben was finally getting a kitten to replace the cat he had to give up when we moved to another state for my husband's job.

"I want the fluffy gray," Ben insisted, as he dragged the blue-eyed kitten from the cage. He tried to cuddle the obstinate character while it clawed its way up his T-shirt onto his shoulder.

Ben stroked the kitten's back. "See how soft he is, Mom. I'll name him Smokey."

Tempted to have him choose one of the friendlier felines, I hesitated. But seeing the content smile on my son's face, I realized this kitten might be just what he needed to help ease the pain of missing his friends. "Oh, all right. Maybe with lots of love and attention he'll calm down."

As we started our twenty-mile drive out of town, I remembered we needed milk. Making a quick detour, we pulled into the parking lot of the grocery store. I flipped off the air conditioner, then realized we couldn't leave the kitten in the car for even a few minutes in the sweltering August heat.

With a raised brow, I zeroed in on Ben. "You carry the kitten, but hold him tight while we shop."

"I will," he assured me as we climbed out of the car.

Ben held the kitten against his chest. But just as we approached the store's front doors, Smokey squirmed his way loose. He leaped to the ground. In a gray blur the kitten streaked to the nearest hiding place—three huge bins piled high with watermelons.

I spotted a furry tail disappear into the pallets beneath the summer display. "Oh no! How will we ever get him out of there?"

My daughter Bethany held a finger to her lips. "Shh… I hear him."

Meows emanated from the melons. Lying on the hot pavement, I tried to coax the kitten out. When he refused to budge, I reached between the wood slats. He tilted his head to one side, gazed at my hand, then scampered under the middle pallet and up into the bin.

Hovered over the boxes we peered into the dark spaces around the fruit, but couldn't spot our fugitive. Moving several melons, we caught a glimpse of a paw. Ben grabbed for Smokey, who skittered to another hiding place. In our frantic search, we removed melons from the box and set them on the ground one by one.

Voices of a gathering crowd began to buzz. "What's going on?" a shopper whispered to the person standing next to them. "I don't know. I think they've lost something."

Using our feet, the kids and I tried to keep the melons corralled. Oops. One melon too many. Like wild horses, they broke free. A downward slope in the parking lot escalated the stampede.

Laughter erupted from the onlookers.

Joe slapped his hands on a melon. "I got it," he shouted as another barreled past him.

Bethany's flip-flops slapped the pavement as she chased a runaway melon. "I'll catch it."

While we scrambled to collect the loose fruit, a courtesy clerk spotted the commotion. He abandoned his train of shopping carts and raced in our direction waving his arms. "What are you doing?"

Sweat dripped down my burning cheeks. "Our kitten is hiding in the watermelons."

The teenage boy rushed to retrieve several grocery carts. One by one, we scooped up melons and loaded them into the carts.

And then Bethany pointed. "There he is."

Ben dove into the box and captured Smokey. With a secure grip on the tricky escape artist, he headed to the car. The rest of us helped the young man reassemble the display.

Exhausted, we left town without the milk. Ben cuddled and talked to his new friend all the way home. That night I looked in on Ben, who lay sound asleep in his bed. Snuggled beneath his chin on his pillow, purred the gray kitten. Smokey became his constant companion and did help Ben adjust to our move.

Unfortunately, the watermelon incident was only the beginning. Always the prankster, Smokey continued his wild antics. We retrieved him from the roof of our house and rescued him from the fir tree in our front yard. But we soon grew to love his smug sense of humor even as he tricked us into endless rounds of his favorite game—hide and seek.

~Kathleen Kohler

# Smokey's Lockout

*Everything comes to those who wait... except a cat.*
*~Mario Andretti*

This was not how the evening was supposed to go. "Darn Smokey," my husband Paul muttered, as he poked the wire hanger into the seam where the window met the metal. But the little Ford lived up to its manufacturer's claims and the wire could not wedge its way against the tightly shut window. Inside the white car, oblivious to the consternation he had caused, our white cat Smokey prowled back and forth.

"Nice kitty, Smokey. Up." Paul coaxed the restless animal to the driver's side of the car for the umpteenth time. Simultaneously he pointed to the lock with what he hoped was a beguiling smile. But the cat, trapped in the vehicle by its own doing, refused to be courted. The animal's pupils were dilated; the normally blue eyes bulging pools of brown. Paul tried again. And again. Each time the beguiling smile got thinner and more forced.

Paul grabbed the door handle at the sound of the lock settling in place. Too late. His black briefcase lay on the seat, the spare key safe in one of the compartments. And the little cat had no clue that anything was amiss.

Smokey had been the house kitten since he was five weeks old. The first time I laid eyes on him I knew I wanted this cuddly white ball of fur with its big blue eyes and tiny pink nose for a pet. He was cloud soft, with a hint of grey to his coat, as if he had just wandered through a haze of smoke. As he grew older, the hint of grey evolved into dark stripes on his tail, haunches, and legs, revealing his Lynx Siamese blood.

The playful cat had developed a love for vehicles, ingrained through frequent visits to the vet, the house in town, and back to the farm, where we were then. The warmth and soft seats of the car felt as cozy as the house.

Paul was growing impatient. He wanted to solve this problem and get to work in the fields while there was still some daylight. "If I can get him to press the left side of the lock, maybe he can flip it up," Paul reasoned aloud. And so began a lesson in English, explaining the concepts of LEFT and RIGHT, with hand motions, to an increasingly bewildered cat. Not that it was without effect. Smokey followed the hand movements, pawing the lock to show that he understood. But while the switch was easy to press in the Lock position, to unlock it called for more pressure than his little paw could exert. Nor could his bemused brain fathom why the usually trustworthy Paul was not letting him out into the sunshine, grass, and meows of his fellow cats.

An hour dragged on. The sun dipped behind the trees and the cold spring air darkened into evening haze. Smokey fell asleep in the driver's seat. Paul finally called the Canadian Automobile Association for help.

"My keys are locked in my car." Then Paul gave his address. The ride from Yorkton to the farm in the south took nearly forty-five minutes. By the time help arrived, it would be over two hours since the lockout had begun.

"Help" turned out to be a tow truck driver, an intimidating-looking fellow of stocky build. He had not asked details about who had locked the keys; presumably it would be the driver or a passenger. A two-legged one. A guffaw burst from his lips as he took in the scene: the cat in the car, the helpless man outwitted by a "four-legger," and a host of other felines glancing warily at their caged friend.

A red-faced Paul looked on, reassured that it would be an easy fix. Armed with an ample supply of picks for various locks, and rods with hooks to catch the locking mechanism inside the door, the driver started his work. First he placed an inflatable rubber-like item in the doorframe. Then he pumped it and the square rubber opened the door a smidgen, just enough so he could insert another rod and get the button that Smokey had punched. Every so often his face twitched. He had never had to use his skills to free a cat that had locked itself in a vehicle. This was an event he'd remember for a long time.

Fifteen minutes later it was all over. The tow truck driver opened the door and Smokey shot out, straight into the haven of an old dark shed. Sheepishly Paul reached for the ignition and rescued the coveted key that would spark the engine to life for his return to town.

~Susan Harris

# Archie the Angel

*The best Christmas trees come very close to exceeding nature.*
*~Andy Rooney*

I tiptoed to the corner of the living room. "Archie, where are you? Come out, come out, wherever you are!" I chanted.

Archie's loud purring had revealed his hiding place behind our freshly cut eight-foot Christmas tree, but he didn't realize we'd located his whereabouts. I peeked through the branches and spotted him rolling from side to side on the red plaid tree skirt—playfully sparring with a tiny tree branch that was touching his tummy. Archie's black fur glistened as he nestled close to a strand of twinkling miniature white lights my husband had just put on the tree.

Suddenly, Archie's purring became louder and he began to twitch and thrust about. Then he sprawled flat out on his back and lay motionless under the tree. I was stunned to watch our lively eight-month-old kitten become subdued and induced into a state of euphoria from inhaling the intoxicating scent of the fresh pine.

I motioned for my husband to join me. "Look at Archie," I whispered, "he's intoxicated from the fragrance of the pine."

"I think pine is the new catnip," my husband teased. "He can sleep it off under the tree."

The following morning, we'd hit the snooze button twice and were trying to steal another ten minutes of slumber. But Archie was wide awake and his noisy purring woke us up when he entered our bedroom. He was back to his energetic self, and leapt upon our bed and began jumping back and forth between our pillows—licking our faces and purring incessantly in our ears. There was no way to coax Archie to settle in with us and take a catnap before breakfast.

As I fed Archie his breakfast, my husband made us omelets. While we ate our breakfast, we compiled a list of things to do that weekend.

Before we left the house to run errands, we looked in on Archie, lying fast asleep in his bed. "He's such a good-natured little guy," I said. "How could anyone abandon such a sweet kitten?"

My husband gave me a hug and said, "Just be thankful he was dumped on our doorstep."

Indeed. I'd never forget that chilly, rainy Halloween night. It was long after the trick-or-treaters had stopped begging for candy at our door. My husband was sound asleep on the couch and I'd settled in to watch *The Addams Family* television marathon. Suddenly, tires squealed, a loud, gruff voice shouted, "Get lost runt!" and a vehicle peeled rubber down the street. Quickly, I turned on the porch light, opened the front door and discovered a soaked and crying black kitten underneath the porch swing. I scurried to grab a towel and scooped him into my arms. As I dried him, he arched his back and purred. After he was completely dry, I gave him a bowl of warm milk. He arched his back and purred as he lapped up the milk. When finished, he arched his back, meowed softly, rubbed against my legs and waited for me to pet him. He was so cute when he arched his back to get my attention—I decided to name him Archie.

Our four-hour shopping expedition that afternoon was a huge success. We finished the Christmas shopping for our parents and siblings, purchased a vintage metal angel tree topper and a red personalized Christmas stocking for Archie. On the drive home, we decided after dinner my husband would place the angel on top of the tree and I'd hang Archie's stocking from the fireplace mantel.

"Archie's probably pacing and meowing by his food bowl," my husband said, pulling into the driveway.

As we entered the back door into the kitchen, the sweet fragrance of pine filled our nostrils. "I love the smell of Christmas!" I said, with no sign of Archie waiting to be fed.

My husband headed for the living room. "Archie's sleeping under the tree. Let's feed him after we unpack the car."

To our dismay, when we returned to the living room twenty minutes later, Archie wasn't asleep in his favorite spot. Apparently, Archie had no plans to leave his new haven, the Christmas tree. Unbeknownst to us, he'd managed to climb limb by limb up the back of the tree. In a matter of seconds, the tree began to sway to and fro against the wall. Then we spotted Archie on a tiny branch in back of the tree, about a quarter of the way from the top of the tree.

"Archie, stop!" my husband shouted. "Don't go any farther!"

But it was too late; the branch made a loud cracking noise and tinkling sounds of tin ornaments rang in our ears as they tumbled to the floor. Archie dug his claws deeper into the tree trunk and the tree began to tilt forward. Fortunately, it was my husband to the rescue. He reached for Archie, tugging hard, forcing him to release his claws, as the tree, laden with lights, vintage tin ornaments and tinsel crashed to the floor.

"What were you thinking? You could have been badly hurt," my husband scolded, stroking Archie's head and shoulders to soothe his frayed nerves.

"The top of the tree was bare, and I believe Archie wanted to be our treetop angel," I chuckled.

While Archie ate his dinner, we lifted the Christmas tree back into the corner of the living room. Surprisingly, there were only a few minor adjustments to make to the branches of lights and tin ornaments—no breakage whatsoever.

After Archie's stocking was hung and the metal angel was placed on top of the tree, we couldn't help but admire our handiwork. "This calls for a glass of bubbly," my husband said. "You grab the champagne flutes."

Unaware that Archie was underfoot, my husband popped the champagne cork into the air and it grazed Archie's head.

"This sure hasn't been Archie the angel's lucky day," I said. "Do you think it's true that cats have nine lives?"

My husband laughed. "I sure hope so. I think Archie's going to need them."

~Georgia A. Hubley

# Murphy's Law

*There are no ordinary cats.*
*~Colette*

Our eight-year-old cat, Murphy, is not just a dimwit, he's also a thief. But he swipes things that no cat with even half a brain would want.

Well, I'm not being fair. Murphy doesn't have half a brain. There should be a sign over his head that reads: "Vacancy."

Nevertheless, he's lightning fast. One night, in a flash, he jumped on the table, grabbed an entire crown of broccoli that was twice the size of his head and raced away with it, all the while scarfing it down so that none of our other cats could have what every cat dreams of: broccoli.

Murphy finds dust balls even when the whole house has been vacuumed and coughs them up for us as gifts. He has an incessant desire to rip tape off UPS boxes. When I extract the tape from his throat, he doesn't notice. Can you imagine sticking your fingers three inches down your cat's throat without him even caring you're doing it?

Murphy's race to eat everything took a disastrous turn late one recent Sunday night. Bob put a pill on the counter for our dog. This pill is so bitter that no pet will take it unless owners disguise it in something with a strong and delicious taste. But Murphy made a beeline to it and ate it.

We called a poison hotline. We were told he needed to get to a twenty-four-hour emergency veterinary hospital immediately. I'm disabled and can't move late at night. Bob rushed Murphy to the pet hospital.

We figured they'd pump his stomach and send him home. We were wrong.

Bob called me from his cellphone after the vet saw Murphy. "He has to stay here three days. They made him vomit, but the toxin is still in his system." He was sobbing. "He could lose all kidney function."

"Did the vet say he could die?"

"Yes."

"Murphy's so innocent," he said, crying harder. "I hate myself for letting this happen."

I felt as much anguish for Bob as I did for Murphy. "Oh sweets, you didn't mean for this to happen. I wish I was sitting next to you." We cried without speaking. Then I said, "Don't drive. Not when you're like this."

Then I called the vet. I asked her for emotional guidance for Bob. She said, "This happens all the time. It happened with me and my cat. He needs to forgive himself. It's impossible to prevent these things 100 percent. Plus I've never heard of a cat who'd want to eat a pill, especially one that tastes so awful."

"Bob's in your parking lot. Would you please go to him and tell him what you told me?" And she did.

Three days later, Murphy came home happy and healthy. When the vet called and asked about him, I incorrectly assumed she knew about Murphy's insane antics.

"He's back to normal. He just presented me with a dust ball the size of a Burger King Triple Whopper! Isn't that great?"

"What?"

"Don't worry," I said, and then cemented myself as a bonehead. "Nobody's getting near MY broccoli again!"

She asked to speak to Bob. I said, "He's busy. UPS came. Bob's racing like a cyclone, ripping tape off the boxes before disaster hits. You know what he's like around UPS tape."

She sounded confused. "Bob?"

I laughed. "Not Bob—"

Before I could explain she interrupted, "Please have him call me."

Bob's role as a caregiver is not a role he asked for, but one he feels blessed to have.

He takes care of me with my spinal cord issues, our old pet duck who's arthritic, our young Border Collie who can never run again because of a genetic spinal problem and our very sick cat Josie to whom Bob administers IV fluids daily.

"How could I be so lucky?" Bob says, every single day of his life.

Yesterday at dawn, as the light gently filled our bedroom, I slowly turned over to see which of Bob's brood was in the protection of his arms. He was cradling beautiful Murphy, who was sound asleep on his back in the crook of Bob's armpit. Bob's eyes were open but I didn't say a word. I knew he was preserving the precious moments for as long as he could before Murphy would wake up.

I watched as Murphy opened his eyes then curled his paw under Bob's chin. I heard him purr when he closed his eyes again, preferring to remain in the safety of Bob's arm for just a little while longer.

And so, snuggling next to Bob, I closed my eyes again too.

~Saralee Perel

# Muffy's Mad Moments

*A cat can purr its way out of anything.*
*~Donna McCrohan*

Muffy was our old, adorable, fluffy, but very useless cat. At twenty years of age and somewhat incontinent, she messed in all the wrong places inside the house. So when the family went to work each day, Muffy stayed outside.

Thursdays was the street's rubbish day. This particular Thursday Mum came home around midday. She was puzzled. Muffy was nowhere to be found. No matter how often she called, no black and white bit of fluff came running—which was unusual because she loved her food. Thus the search began in earnest. Nothing! Questions tumbled out. Had the dog next door at last caught up with her? Was she run over? Had she wandered off and then forgot how to get home? All these worrying thoughts flashed through Mum's mind.

Then strange noises nearby distracted her; they seemed to come from the carport where our daughter's small Honda was parked. She listened closely and heard the noise again, a muffled "miaow." Inside the car? That's impossible, Mum thought. The windows were closed! Down on her knees she peered underneath. Nothing! Yet the noise persisted. Where on earth was that cat?

Just then the rubbish truck came rumbling and clanking down the opposite side of the street. A terrified "miaow" emerged from somewhere near the front of the car. Surely not under the bonnet?

Quickly, Mum flicked the catch and lifted. Two big saucer eyes stared out from a small space behind the engine block.

No matter what was tried, Muffy refused to shift. How she got there was a mystery.

Then the explanation hit Mum. Frightened by the noise of the rubbish truck, Muffy must have scooted under the car, then scrambled into whatever narrow space she could find. Now she couldn't move! She was wedged in, too far back among the grease and coils and wires.

The day was becoming a scorcher, heading towards 40 degrees Celsuis. Scared that Muffy would drop dead from the heat, Mum sought immediate help. Our neighbour Ronda came over to lend moral support, but really nothing else. In desperation, Mum phoned all of us at work. I arrived home just as my daughter pulled up in a taxi. Convinced that her darling pet would soon be in "kitty heaven," she was bawling her eyes out.

I set to work to solve our cat problem. From every angle I poked, pushed, prodded, pulled every bit of fur I could reach, but nothing worked. Muffy was wedged in too tightly. She had twisted her body into impossible and very greasy places. I didn't have a hope in moving her.

We called the RSPCA, but no, they don't do rescuing just investigating. The Animal Welfare was more helpful, suggesting the best bet for a car-related problem was the RAA. So in desperation, we summoned roadside assistance. We waited the usual hour before a familiar yellow van arrived. For five minutes he just stood in silence, exploring the situation, walking round and round the car, shaking his head. Then he uttered words we didn't want to hear: "No go. I won't dare touch it! Call in an air conditioning specialist. He'll have to remove all those pipes and coils before the cat can even be reached. Best of luck!" With those parting words he vanished down the road, heading to the next call, no doubt!

We searched the Yellow Pages again. Another phone call and another hour went by.

To our concern, Muffy had stopped miaowing a long time before.

We pushed tissues soaked in water to where she could lick the moisture. Would she last much longer?

We had our doubts. Fortunately the air conditioning specialist arrived. He took one look, smothered a grin, fossicked around the engine, then set to work.

Leads undone, nuts unscrewed, compressor degassed, pipes pushed aside, all to create space so Muffy could be reached. Three hours after Mum had made the original discovery, and $150 poorer, we arrived at the moment of truth. A greasy, bedraggled, exhausted, very floppy cat was carefully lifted out and placed in the arms of my teary daughter. Still sobbing, she rushed Muffy inside to the lounge room where the air conditioner was on. We followed her in, fearing the worst.

Muffy was gently placed on the carpet. For a brief moment she stood, wobbling, unsteady on her feet, eyes staring straight ahead. She glanced down at the bowl of milk placed right underneath her nose, then lapped it all up. Blinking several times, she stretched and came to life as if nothing had happened. Miaowing loudly and true to form, Muffy then proceeded to wee on our good lounge carpet! She looked back at us with saucer-sized eyes as if to say, "Eh folks, what's the fuss? What do you expect a poor girl to do after spending so much time imprisoned in that hot box? I couldn't hold on any longer."

We just stared in amazement. Then I muttered to my daughter, "That's it! I've had enough. She's used up all her nine lives. Next time she's going on a long trip to the animal home."

With that Muffy walked over softly to where I stood, started purring and rubbed against my trouser leg. I just groaned.

~John McInnes

# Cat Rules for the Multi-Cat Home

*A cat sees no good reason why it should obey another animal, even if it does stand on two legs.*
*~Sarah Thompson*

"So what's another cat?" I heard myself saying, knowing that we had no choice in the matter. We already had four cats, and when my son's wife was told she had to get rid of their cats for her health, we had to take them in. You do things like that for family.

If you own a cat, you know a new warm furry body added to the mix changes things. In our case, it was two new warm furry bodies.

We had to set up new rules, though we knew there was no way we were going to be able to enforce them. We knew how effective rules and regulations would be to cats. Cats simply have no need for rules. You can make as many rules as you want, and you can use repetition and positive reinforcement to try to teach them, but with cats, it just does not work. With six cats, I knew I might as well pack my bags and move to a cheap hotel. Sure, it was my house according to the mortgage statement, but I knew who really ruled the roost.

**My Unenforceable Feline Regulations**

1. Buttercup does not belong in the refrigerator, even when there is leftover turkey on the bottom shelf.

2. Zorro does not belong in my office because he eats paper, but Cleopatra does belong in the office because she is perfectly behaved and likes to pretend she's my secretary.

3. When there is a little snag in the bedroom window screen, Peaches may not pull on it with her nails, even when there is a bird sitting on the ledge on the other side.

4. Smokey must use the litter box, even though he prefers the corner by the fireplace in the living room.

5. Samson does not belong on the back counter because there is a stove that's often hot, and we don't want Samson to burn his cute little nose off.

6. Zorro may think he is a brave renegade who can carve a "Z" with his claws, but he cannot sharpen them on my couch or my bedspread or my carpet or my jeans.

7. If Smokey is eating, because Smokey doesn't always have a big appetite and, in his old age, is getting very skinny, none of the baby cats may disturb him. Even Buttercup cannot push her little kitten face into Smokey's bowl, not even just to see what it is he is eating.

8. If one cat is asleep in a sink and a bigger cat comes along and wants the same sink, adult humans will not interfere with the decision-making process, no matter how loud Buttercup screams, unless it wakes us up. Then no one gets a sink and the bathroom is closed for the night.

9. Smokey may know how to open closet doors, but he may not teach the baby cats how to do this until they are old enough to not eat expensive fabrics or dry-cleaner bags or pull on hanging threads.

10. When Mommy has a client in the office, Buttercup and Zorro may not come in, unless the client loves cats and wants one or two on his lap.

11. Visa receipts and checks are not cat food.

12. When Mommy and Daddy have company, cats do not belong on the dining room table, but when there is no company, cats may walk on the table as long as they walk around the plates and not through them.

13. Buttercup may not take Mommy's glasses and hide them behind the washing machine because Mommy can't see well enough without them to find them.

14. *Scrabble* tiles and *Monopoly* pieces are not cat toys. Neither are pieces of jigsaw puzzles or Legos.

15. Zorro is not allowed in the bathroom when someone is taking a bath unless he promises not to try to swim ever again.

16. The only time Buttercup, Zorro, Peaches, Samson, Smokey, and Cleopatra are allowed outside or in the garage is when they are in their travel boxes on the way to the mean old vet.

17. Cleopatra may only sit on homework after it has been handed in and graded.

18. Cats may not investigate electric appliances. Humans are responsible for putting all electrical appliances in drawers or, at least, pulling their plugs.

19. Cleopatra may not stretch her body out on the wall where the on/off switch to the sink disposal is.

20. When Mommy and Daddy are asleep, cats may not come up on the bed to kiss their faces, but when cats are asleep, Mommy and Daddy may pick them up and do anything they want to them because they are just so cute when they are asleep and there is such a thing as equal time.

~Felice Prager

# The Cat Did What?

## Four-Legged Therapists

# Family Counselor

*Mirth is God's medicine. Everybody ought to bathe in it.*
*~Henry Ward Beecher*

The stress of working and raising our hyper four-year-old son, Trig, had put a strain on our marriage like nothing else could. Life had become a day in and day out feat until one day Trig came running into the house carrying a dose of sanity. "I caught a cat! I caught a cat!" Folded over Trig's palm like a rag doll was a tiny black, caramel, and white calico kitten all ruffled up. It had come from the field beside our house. My first thought was: Oh great, it's sickly. What has he gotten us into this time?

But, because Trig seemed so happy, Steve and I let him enjoy his discovery for a while before insisting he put the poor little thing down. But Trig would not have it! He carried that poor cat all evening with the lower part of her body swinging gently left and right. Unbelievably, the cat seemed to enjoy it.

We explained to him in no uncertain terms that when we got ready for bed, the cat would go outside. Tomorrow, he could keep her on two conditions: she would need a clean bill of health from the vet and she would be an outdoor pet. It was enough that we already had two dogs that demanded a lot of attention. We didn't need any more stress in our house.

So, when it got dark, Trig finally followed orders and went to the back yard to put the kitten down. But she refused to be left and followed him all around the house. He danced around her and she tried to trip him with every step. They had bonded. Trig said her name was Sammy and she was determined to stay inside.

Steve smiled for the first time in what felt like months and put his arm around me too. "Looks like we have ourselves a pet cat!"

A pet cat? How could that be? I had never had a cat. My parents didn't like cats. The only place I had ever even seen kitty litter or a litter box was on television commercials. So, prior to going to bed that night, some friends gave me a crash course on cat food, catnip, the kind of toys kittens like to play with, litter and litter boxes and how to house-train a kitten. We were embarking on a new, amazing adventure. I was reluctant until I realized what was happening. In an instant, Sammy had brought happiness back into our home.

I thought back to a time when a marriage counselor told Steve and me that in order for a couple to survive raising small children, they had to learn to laugh together. Sammy is the answer. She keeps us laughing constantly. We get more than enough entertainment just out of the various awkward places she decides to nap: in a cardboard box, inside the cupboard, inside the dryer, in the dish towel drawer, or on top of the new package of paper plates. My personal favorite was the day I found her sleeping face-first on an oven mitt.

This may sound crazy, but even the dogs seem happier. They wait patiently, letting her eat before they do and allowing her to walk in front of them when I let them out.

They adore Sammy and she, in turn, loves teasing them. They play with her roughly but carefully. If Sammy ventures outdoors, the dogs round her up by gently pushing her back towards me or towards the back door, similar to the way certain dog breeds herd cattle. They do not take their eyes off her for a second, as if to communicate that they do not want to go back to life without her.

Sammy has taught me to live in the moment. Computer time has become mom and cat quality time, and is no longer about efficiently writing a bestselling novel. Also, exercising is not something I rush through like I did before. Because if I'm not enjoying my workout session, Sammy immediately interrupts it by refusing to give me enough space on my mat—and laughter quickly ensues. These days it is more important to me to be around my family and Sammy's soothing purrs than it is to accomplish everything on my to-do list.

Steve is smitten too! Nothing makes him happier than to discover that Sammy has killed yet another pesky mouse. She becomes a tiny hero to my big, strong husband. Even though this is what cats do, Steve makes a big deal about it for days.

Adopting Sammy has done wonders for our family. Steve is always laughing and smiling. Trig is less hyper. My nineteen-year-old son, A.J., feels comforted by Sammy at night while the rest of the world is sleeping and he's juggling college and working the night shift.

I used to believe cats were dirty and useless. They couldn't fetch or swim in the lake. They weren't smart and they couldn't bond with their owners. Of course, my problem was I had never owned a cat!

Some would say a lonesome kitten roaming around a huge field discovered by a four-year-old little boy was just a coincidence. I choose to believe that God knew we needed a cat and knew Sammy was the one for us!

Up till now not a single one of us has ever seen another cat in that field. Why Sammy was there that particular day is a mystery. And every time she brings a smile to my face, I think about how lucky we are that an ordinary cat brought happiness back into our home.

~Melisa Kraft

# A Friend in the End

*The opportunity for doing mischief is found a hundred times a day, and of doing good once in a year.*
*~Voltaire*

Tess, our beautiful twelve-year-old calico cat, was sad. She had recently lost her best friend, Sheba, our sixteen-year-old cat, and was spending most of her days moping around the house. Tess and Sheba had eaten side by side, slept side by side, and groomed each other every day. It was time to get Tess a new friend.

We named him Murray, a gentle sounding name for a kitten, or so we thought. At first, this black, little fur ball delighted us with his typical kittenish behavior: racing after mouse toys, chasing toes that moved beneath blankets, or lying in wait to pounce on unsuspecting passersby. He even had the adorable habit of sleeping upside down on my husband's stomach, purring ever so softly.

But our hopes for a loving companion for Tess were dashed. Murray wasn't interested in being her friend. He much preferred to scare her. It didn't take him long to find the perfect hiding places where he could lie in wait for her to stroll by. Leaping out, he would chase her from one end of the house to the other.

Tess, to her credit, still tried to bond with him. One day when Murray was asleep in a circle of sunlight on the back of the couch, Tess, seeking companionship, or perhaps warmth, crept up ever so gently beside him and curled up as close as she dared. When Murray didn't move, she inched up a bit further. And then a few inches more.

Murray slowly opened one eye, leaped up, and lashed out at her. Tess never approached Murray again.

As the months passed, Murray grew into a strong, muscular cat who preferred his own company. Instead of stalking Tess, he now simply ignored her. His desire for solitude overcame any need for human or feline companionship. The basement became his haven. He ate his meals primarily at night when the house was quiet and everyone was asleep. In the daytime he sought places that were secluded and free from interaction with others.

Not only did he find Tess an annoyance, but he began to act as if we had done him a disservice by adopting him. He hissed and scratched when he was held and swatted anyone who gave him a pat on the head. If I tried to give him sweet talk, he would ignore me, then slowly turn his head and give me that who-do-you-think-you-are look. Murray was fast becoming a curmudgeon.

He was also a slob. In the morning I would walk into the kitchen to find bits of wet cat food clinging to the walls, the cabinets and the sides of the stove. Murray ate with his paws. Scooping one paw into his dish, he would fling the food into the air as though he were catching mice. His water bowl, for whatever reason, would be in the middle of the kitchen, its contents spilled across the floor.

"That's it!" cried my husband one day, after sliding across the kitchen floor from the spilled water. "Back he goes to the shelter! He is a monster!"

Over several days we discussed this option. But we knew it would not happen. We were responsible for Murray. And who would take him—this antisocial, ornery rapscallion who had horrible table manners and who terrified every living thing that came within reach? No, Murray was ours, for better or worse. And all the while, Tess grew lonelier.

We began searching for another cat for Tess. She was such an affectionate cat and she deserved the love and companionship of a friend. But during that time we began to notice a change in her. She was limping a great deal and seemed to be in pain. A trip to the vet revealed the grim news: Tess had a tumor on her spine and had only a few months to live.

"You'll know," said our veterinarian, "when it is time to let her go. But don't wait too long."

These are the words every pet owner dreads hearing. Our hearts were broken. As the weeks passed, we watched Tess grow weaker and weaker. She soon stopped eating and lost all interest in everything. Most of her days were spent wrapped in warm blankets on the couch, with us carrying her to the litter box. It was shocking to watch the change in her each day. But it was not as shocking as watching the change in Murray.

During the last few days of Tess' life, Murray left his basement sanctuary and began to make appearances in the living room. He would sit and stare at the couch where Tess lay. He might sit for fifteen minutes and then disappear, only to return again after a few hours, each time moving closer to the couch. His look and his demeanor suggested to us that he knew we were losing Tess.

I called the vet's office on a warm May morning. It was time. The sun was bright, the air was clear, and the day seemed too beautiful for such sadness. Our appointment was for 4:30 in the afternoon, closer to the end of office hours when we would have more privacy. Placing her on the living room couch, I wrapped her blankets closer and told her that soon she would no longer be in pain. I told her that I would be with her and that I loved her. As I sat stroking her head, Murray appeared and jumped onto the couch. Tess opened one eye and gazed at her visitor. After sniffing Tess' head and blanket-wrapped body, Murray circled twice and lay down beside her, pressing up close to her body. Here he stayed for the entire day, getting up but once to use his litter box and then returning to her side.

Shocked by Murray's actions, I left them alone, coming back into the room every now and then. Murray still lay beside her. Sometimes he would be facing her, staring into her eyes. Other times he would be lying close to her side or stretched across her back legs, keeping her warm. Tess lay perfectly still. Her breath came in gentle waves and her eyes remained glued on her new "friend." She began to purr.

It's been two years since Tess died. Murray is still with us, and he still ignores us. I still spend too much time scraping cat food from the walls and cabinets. And I continue to curse whenever I feel that familiar puddle of water seeping into my socks in the morning. On occasion when his behavior is too much, we bring up the subject of the shelter. But that's about as far as it gets.

Why Murray went from monster to angel is a mystery. Why he remained by Tess's side in the end, we can only guess. He may be a curmudgeon and a cantankerous recluse; he may test us with his sloppy ways; he may spurn our attempts at affection. But we will never forget the comfort he brought to our Tess, who simply wanted a friend. For that, we can only be grateful.

~Gretchen Nilsen Lendrum

# Oliver's Ministry

*But ask the animals, and they will teach you.*
*~Job 12:7*

Oliver was next on the list at the local shelter to be euthanized. An irresistible tabby with markings that looked like thick black mascara outlining his friendly green eyes, he was doing his feline best to attract the attention of my sister and her pastor husband. They fell for his charms and took him home to their church rectory where he was free to explore the large rooms, spacious yard, and cemetery next door.

One hot summer day, the church door was left open as a funeral got underway. Oliver took the organ music as his cue to check things out. He went up the wide stone steps on little cat feet and sat in the doorway listening to the service. As the pastor read the part of the eulogy that described the deceased as an avid animal lover, Oliver padded down the aisle, all the way to the front row of the church, where he approached the grieving granddaughter. He sat at the end of the pew and stared up at the little girl. She stared back at him for a moment and then invited him to hop up and sit with her. Oliver accepted the invitation, curled up on the child's lap and stayed there until the closing prayer, as if in tribute to the dearly departed. His mere presence offered a comforting distraction to those in mourning. When the service ended, Oliver left the way he had come.

Parishioners often talk about visiting the cemetery and the graves of their loved ones and finding Oliver there at just the right moment, purring, looking for a scratch behind the ears, ready to offer a gentle rub up against a mourner's leg. Oliver can sometimes be seen perched serenely on a monument, as a reminder that we are watched over and not alone.

But something was different this time. The hearse had already pulled away from the graveside and the casket, draped with flowers, was resting on racks waiting to be lowered into the ground. There sat Oliver as usual, present in the moments that can be the saddest for family and friends. He seemed once more to provide a pleasant, even hopeful, distraction from overwhelming grief.

Suddenly, Oliver flicked his tail and dove into the hole under the coffin just as the lowering device was switched on. My sister gasped, "Oh! Get the cat!" The pastor sprang into action, his clerical robes billowing white around him. He reached out in the nick of time to grab Oliver by his hind legs and haul him to safety.

As people chatted and milled about, chuckling over Oliver's narrow escape, he wound his way through the legs of the crowd and settled at the feet of the widow. She bent down to pick him up. As she stroked and Oliver purred, she looked him in the eye and whispered, "You stay with him now and I'll be back soon to visit you both."

~Jo Yuill Darlington

# How Did He Know?

*Cats are a tonic, they are a laugh, they are a cuddle, they are at least pretty just about all of the time and beautiful some of the time.*

*~Roger Caras*

My wife Carol returned from a Guide Leaders' retreat bearing a furry object in a cage. The squawking, urine-soaked animal, cringing on the floor of the metal carrier, was a black and white cat.

The cleanup revealed he was a handsome American shorthair, glossy midnight black from head to tail, with a black moustache, white chin, throat and belly and four white socks. He had an intelligent face with wild white brows arched above luminous yellow-green eyes. A black velvet nose tipped a muzzle that sported an impressive display of ivory whiskers. When he tilted his head and presented a bright pink tongue, even my heart melted. He looked like he was wearing a tuxedo. The name stuck.

Tux had been twice passed along, making us his third home. Our veterinarian estimated his age at about four years, updated his shots and pronounced him healthy. Tux immediately started to amaze us.

We soon discovered that he had two very un-cat-like quirks. Far from finicky, he was a voracious eater. Also he could not meow; he squawked! As a result we never again needed an alarm clock. Every morning Tux would sit on Carol's bedside table and emit a sound like the incorrect answer buzzer on a television game show.

This was the signal for one of us to rise and fill his food bowl. He would keep squawking until someone did. And if ever you couldn't find him during the day, a noisy shake of his dry food container would bring him running. When we had company and dinner guests moved to the table, unfinished hors d'oeuvres disappeared and he followed up by actually begging at the table during the meal.

As the years passed Carol and I became empty nesters with a now "senior" cat we loved dearly. Then Carol was diagnosed with breast cancer.

The surgery was successful, but chemotherapy left her exhausted and feeling very ill. Somehow Tuxedo knew. The morning wake-up calls ceased. Following treatments when Carol lay on the couch, sick to her soul, Tux would come to her. Nuzzling her chin, he would whisker-tickle her nose, tilt his head, look into her eyes and purr as if to say, "It's alright, I'm here," then snuggle as close to her as possible.

Shortly after one of Carol's treatment cycles I underwent knee replacement surgery and returned from hospital bandaged from thigh to calf. Then a week later we found Tuxedo splayed on the floor, crying in pain.

Our vet was truthful and not hopeful. Tux had a very large mass in his belly, possibly malignant. Now a senior cat, perhaps it was time to say goodbye to our friend. They did an exploratory and removed a baseball-sized tumor and a portion of his liver. If Tux survived the night, he might make it. It was heartbreaking to see him in an incubator, lying on his side, his head resting on his curled front paws. A dark red incision, held closed with knotted black stitches crusted with dried blood, stretched from his chest to his pelvis. Each forepaw had a shaved area hosting an intravenous port and one was connected to a fluid bag. He lay deathly still. Carol scratched under his ear. Tux's eyes opened a little and he purred. The next morning he was still stable and the morning after that Tuxedo ate his food and squawked for more. After that, we knew he would make it.

After Tux came home I ended up back at the hospital with an infected incision in my knee. An antibiotic was administered intravenously and another was ordered for later in the week. No problem! A nurse was due that week to administer Carol's next intravenous dose of cancer meds, so I was added to the house call. When she arrived, Tux, still recovering, was sleeping by the fireplace. What a trio!

Carol and I sat side by side in our easy chairs; the nurse hung the fluid bags from the overhead lamp between, and hooked us up. Then Tuxedo padded over. He lay down between us, rolled on his back, put four paws in the air and displayed his shaved and still sutured tummy as to say, "Where's mine?" The nurse just shook her head and smiled. Carol and I started to laugh.

Carol recovered fully and Tuxedo—he restarted his morning wake-up calls. We'll never know how he knew when we needed him to be a caregiver, and when he could resume being his normal, noisy self.

~John Forrest

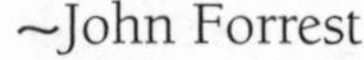

# Let the Cat into the Bag

*Lettin' the cat outta the bag is a whole lot easier 'n puttin' it back in.*
*~Will Rogers*

Skunk was six weeks old when I picked him up from a friend. He was tiny, with black and white markings—a dark black fur coat with a white stripe bib and stomach. He looked like an inverted skunk, had some of the same mannerisms of a skunk (minus the smell), bobbing his head as he sniffed at his new surroundings, padding around my apartment.

But Skunk was all kitten. He'd race around, climb up the curtains, chew on shoelaces, claw at the couch, chairs, mattress and anything else he could get his paws on (including my hair as I lay in bed).

A few weeks after I got Skunk, a census-taker showed up at my door. "I'm here to complete the remainder of the long forms, as was explained in the package we sent out to you," she stated.

When I looked puzzled, she flipped over a sheet on her clipboard and showed me the appropriate form, pointed out the appropriate box. "You agreed to this follow-up, when you ticked that box there."

So I had.

I always try to help out my country when it comes to statistics. And since they weren't tax forms, no balance owing, I showed the young woman inside.

Her name was Abigail. She looked to be in her early twenties, the part-time census job probably a way to help pay for college. And being in her "serious twenties," she hid her nervousness about questioning strangers in their homes behind a cool, brusque air of efficiency.

I showed her to a chair at the dining room/card table and asked if she'd like something to drink. "Soda? Water?"

But she was all business. "No, thank you." She placed her clipboard down on the table and took a pen out of her purse. "I won't take up much of your time." She put her purse down on the carpet.

I took a seat across from her at the table.

And that's when Skunk made his appearance, poking his furry head around the hallway corner and looking into the dining alcove. When he saw the new person in the apartment, he instantly narrowed his big yellow eyes, raised his head and sniffed at the air, his wet, black nose twitching.

And then he spotted Abigail's purse on the floor—a large, off-white canvas kind of bag—and his eyes widened again. Something new he could really sink his claws into!

He hopped forward on his little legs, over to Abigail's purse. He sniffed at it, tentatively swatted at it, playing it cool cat. Then he grabbed onto the side with his front paws, rolled onto his back and kicked at the bottom with his back paws.

"Oh, I see you have a cat," Abigail commented, looking down at Skunk attacking her purse.

"Skunk," I replied. "I mean his name is Skunk."

"Hmmm. He's, uh, quite playful, isn't he?"

She reached down and kind of poked at the air with her pen, trying to shoo Skunk away from her purse. He happily jabbed back at the pen.

I nodded. "Yes. He's only nine weeks old."

Abigail frowned, Skunk not taking the hint. "I used to have a cat… when I was a child." She said it like pets were something you outgrew as you matured.

She brought her pen back up to the census forms and looked at me across the table. "Anyway, we're just about done," she said seriously, bearing back down on her rather boring work.

But Skunk wouldn't be put off. Because the only thing more fun for a kitten than getting into mischief is getting into mischief with an audience. Skunk enjoyed putting on a show.

Skunk put on a show, growl-mewling at Abigail's purse and chewing on the canvas as he clutched it with his front claws and pedaled with his back claws.

Unlike me, Abigail was not amused. She reached down and grabbed her purse off the carpet. Skunk rode along with it, clinging to the side and bottom.

Abigail glared at me, holding up the purse and the attached kitten accessory. I grinned with embarrassment, half stood up, reached over and grabbed onto Skunk's furry little torso, and pulled. He held onto the purse with teeth and claws.

Abigail tugged on her bag in the opposite direction I was tugging on Skunk. The bag and the kitten held together, suspended in mid-air. Until, finally, detachment was achieved with a rendering sound like Velcro as claws were torn off canvas.

"Sorry about that," I said, holding the squirming kitten against my chest.

"Well… I guess there's no harm done," Abigail said dubiously, patting the slightly striated and pinholed side and bottom of her purse.

Abigail looked at me. I knew what I was supposed to do. "Bad Skunk," I said sternly.

She carefully placed her purse on the seat of another chair under the table, for safekeeping. I dropped Skunk back down to the floor with a plop. The census taking proceeded, in a most professional manner.

"Thank you again for your assistance, sir," Abigail concluded soon after, meticulously aligning the forms on her clipboard. "Your government appreciates it." She stood up.

"And I sometimes appreciate them," I joked.

She stared at me.

I escorted her over to the door. She left.

I blew out my cheeks and looked around the living room for one small kitten. No Skunk in sight. Probably off burrowing around in the fresh laundry I'd put away/dumped on the floor of my bedroom closet.

I stretched out in my easy chair to watch some football on TV. I was only mildly surprised Skunk didn't come racing out to jump and claw at my socked feet when I smacked the button on the side of the chair that shot out the footrest. That particular sound seemed to be practically Catlovian.

Ten minutes and two series of football plays later, Abigail suddenly reappeared at the screen door. I scrambled to my feet.

She was actually smiling when I opened the door. "I'm afraid I accidentally took something of yours with me when I left," she said.

I didn't understand.

She gently swung her shouldered purse around to the front and opened up the top. A little black furry head with tiny ears and whiskers popped out.

"I was at one of your neighbours," Abigail explained, "when I reached into my bag for my pen and felt something… lick my hand." She blushed, carefully plucking Skunk out of the warm, cozy confines of her purse and handing the purring kitten back to me. "I don't know how he managed to jump up that high—onto the chair, and get into my bag."

"He likes you."

Abigail's grin widened. "There, um, aren't any other friendly kittens from Skunk's litter still available, are there? It gets pretty lonely in an apartment all by yourself."

I grinned back at Abigail.

Skunk happily batted at the twist-ties on my sweatshirt, and then gnawed on them.

~Laird Long

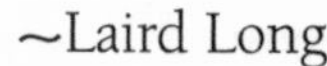

# Mandrake

*Cats are kindly masters, just so long as you remember your place.*
*~Paul Gray*

Mandrake was a never a "here kitty, kitty" kind of cat. Black as midnight, it was clear from kittenhood that this cat had channeled more of the wild, dominant genes than those of his more domestic ancestors. He tolerated us as a family. We were, after all, his main source of food. But he made it clear from Day One who was King.

My parents brought Mandrake and a black Lab puppy, Sugar, into our home the day I turned one. We were a formidable trio, but Mandrake established the pecking order early. The wiry, black kitten ruled. Sugar and I gave him a wide berth. This "live and let live" philosophy pretty much governed the rest of Mandrake's existence. A few years later, when my sister and then my brother arrived, Mandrake still ruled. Even my dad held no sway when Mandrake was around.

The first time we realized how fearsome our black cat was, our family had run out to the front yard in response to strange sounds. The neighborhood terror, a large aggressive German Shepherd, was a biter of children and pets. Now he was whining and running out of our yard at a full sprint. We stared in astonishment at the bully's uncharacteristic behavior. Soon we saw the cause.

Mandrake sat crouched on all fours on the Shepherd's back, riding the dog out of our yard. Seeing Mandrake repeat this performance became a monthly ritual. He perched on the fence leading between the front yard and back. When unsuspecting large neighborhood dogs passed by on our property, Mandrake, self-appointed defender of our land, jumped on their backs, dug in his claws and rode them off our land.

Through the years this pattern continued. Mandrake defended our property, purposely walking widely around Sugar and the rest of us, and ignoring us as if we didn't exist. That changed one night. Twelve-year-old Sugar disappeared. She had not been looking her normal spry self. Gray whiskers mingled with the black. Her walking had become labored.

We set off around the neighborhood calling for her. When we looked back, Mandrake was following, twenty feet behind. We walked a good mile before we located Sugar, belly down in a ditch. Her sad eyes looked up as we carried her home. Mandrake followed us, still twenty feet behind. We set up a comfortable bed for Sugar and wrapped her in blankets.

As soon as we closed the door, Mandrake went wild. He scratched. He yowled. He climbed the screen. When we opened the door, Mandrake, the cat that loved no one, climbed in the bed with Sugar. No amount of moving him would make him leave. We put him outside. He yowled and waited until the door opened. Then he headed back to Sugar's bed. For two days, Mandrake refused to leave Sugar's side. He wouldn't leave for food. He didn't leave for water.

The time came when Dad said the end was near. We gathered around our sweet dog. Mandrake left his recent home curled up by Sugar's belly. He walked over to Sugar, lay down by her head, and placed his nose on hers. Mandrake gently rubbed his nose on Sugar's as she closed her eyes for the last time.

Mandrake was old and fierce and independent. After Sugar died, we got a new dog, Rocky. Mandrake went back to his old ways, riding neighborhood dogs out of our yard, ignoring us and our new dog. Anyone watching him would have said he didn't care.

We all knew better.

~Julie Reece-DeMarco

# Of Yancy & Me

*It often happens that a man is more humanely related to a cat or dog than to any human being.*
*~Henry David Thoreau*

A feline framed in a windowsill
A portrait of poise, standoffishness
Nary a muscle moves
as the world moves around him
But for his hourly arch
and his paw Pilates
he could be a cutout silhouette
pasted to the drapery
Another friend
behaving this badly
would surely lose his status
with me
I'll tell you why he's allowed to stay
Yancy and me, we're of the same ilk
Kindhearted, yet aloof
Loving, from a fair and reasonable distance
Affectionate, on our own selective terms
We don't play that well with others
But oh when we do play
It's part greed, part gusto!
We're darn good cuddlers

If you don't mind that we plop down
and don't move until
shooed
Yancy gets me
far better than most of his
two-legged rivals
We communicate without ever
raising our voices
We share space
yet manage to honor one another's privacy
We don't try to be anything we're not
And maybe that's the simple beauty
Of Yancy & Me
He, comfortable in his own fur
I, in my own skin
Deign to be together
That's the end of our story
(and a happy one at that)

~Lisa Leshaw

# When It Mattered

*Touch has a memory.*
*~John Keats*

We found Scooter at the ASPCA in New York City when he was about a year old. He looked at us from his cramped cage with such a look of desperation. We knew instantly that this calico tabby would be ours.

Jack and I were newlyweds. Neither of us had taken care of a cat before. We were still learning how to take care of each other. Sure, I had cats during my childhood, but Scooter would be our own responsibility. He would be our first child.

On a tight budget, we went to the store to get all the cat essentials: a bag of dry cat food, kitty litter, a few little balls that jingled when you rolled them, and, of course, the obligatory catnip mouse. We placed everything in a discarded shipping box and proudly carried them home to our tiny apartment. When we got home, we emptied the box. Jack methodically cut the top off and I lovingly arranged a towel inside.

The day we brought Scooter home we were anxious to see how he would react to our apartment. It was less than six hundred square feet but it was a railcar layout so Scooter would be able to run the length back and forth. We assumed he would run crazy, jump for joy, and meow with high praise and gratitude. After all, tiny to us would be a mansion to him, after living most of his life in a cage barely large enough for him to turn around.

His reaction was anything but excited and happy. He did run, but it was for cover, behind the sofa bed. He stationed himself behind it, only coming out for food and bathroom breaks. He was scared and apprehensive.

Months went by and we hoped he would be more receptive. We finally reconciled ourselves to the fact that Scooter was not the cuddling type.

A year later we moved to a one-bedroom apartment in the suburbs of Connecticut. With the newly added commute back into the city and our long working hours, we felt guilty leaving Scooter alone for so long. We decided it was time for a second child. We made a visit to the local shelter and found a tiny bundle of gray and white fur and named her Yaicha.

Before we brought Yaicha home we read numerous articles on the proper way to introduce a new kitten to your adult cat. The general consensus was that to ensure the most success in any sibling-cat relationship, we should bring home the kitten and present her to the established cat. Little human contact should occur with the new kitten. The senior cat would adopt the kitten as its own and only then could we interact with the new kitten.

Sounded like a plan.

Yaicha could not have been more than eight weeks old when she left the shelter with us. We brought her home wrapped in a towel. We found Scooter sequestered behind the living room chair and placed Yaicha, still wrapped in the blanket, in a shallow box for him to discover by himself.

After a while he came out from behind the chair. He passed right by us with a look of contempt and entered the bedroom. I do believe if he could have slammed the door he would have.

This went on for several days until I couldn't take it anymore and picked up poor Yaicha, who I felt was longing for the attention she had not received from Scooter.

Months passed and Scooter tolerated Yaicha. He was never mean or aggressive, just nonchalant about his feelings towards her as he had been with Jack and me.

One day I received a call. It was my father telling me that my childhood friend had died. Tommy and his fiancée had been murdered in their apartment over the restaurant that Tommy and his family owned. The same restaurant where Jack had sung and I had worked as a waitress. The same place where we had met and fallen in love.

The realization as Pop relayed the horrific details of their deaths turned me numb. I remember my legs giving out as I fell to the floor. I can't remember how long we spoke or all the details of the call. I do remember hanging up the phone while a hot flash ran through my body, making me nauseous. Then the tears started.

I started to sob louder and louder. I couldn't breathe. I couldn't comprehend. I was in such a state of shock, of disbelief. I had experienced the loss of loved ones and friends before, but this was different. This was so unreal, unnatural, unfair. It was so senseless and yet every part of my body was telling me that their deaths were to be a part of my life forever. For it was because of Tommy and his family that I had my own family.

I was half leaning against the couch, half sprawled out on the floor as I sobbed. Minutes earlier I had been sitting on our new couch admiring our new carpeting and thinking about how far we had come from our tiny New York apartment. How much we had already accomplished in our lives, Jack and I. We were living! We were growing as a couple with great careers and a loving friendship and marriage. We had it all!

When I finally started coming out of my stupor I looked up and saw Scooter standing in the doorway between my bedroom and the living room. He uncharacteristically began walking towards me. He stopped about two feet from me and watched me cry. He observed me as I tried to cope with what I had just heard. Eventually, he walked up to me and put his front paws on my arm. He lifted himself towards my face and gently licked my cheeks, removing some tears before they could fall from my chin. His paws seemed to embrace my arm, feeling like he was trying to hug me. Then he slowly removed his paws and lay down next to my legs.

With that, Yaicha came out of her box and lay next to Scooter. He did not fuss; he just let her, let us… be. I don't remember how long we sat there together, the three of us. Long enough for me to absorb what my father had said. Long enough for me to catch my breath.

As the months passed, Scooter began to allow Yaicha to lie next to him. It seemed that during the day they went their separate ways, Scooter roaming around the house and Yaicha chasing bugs outside. But when nighttime arrived, they could usually be found lying side by side, quietly purring to each other, confirming that there was comfort in the closeness of family.

~Jeanne Blandford

# Cinnamon Spices It Up

*If we treated everyone we meet with the same affection we bestow upon our favorite cat, they, too, would purr.*
*~Martin Buxbaum*

Dr. Henderson's report concerning our seventeen-year-old cat, Almond, was not good. Her lack of appetite and resulting weight loss were due to kidney failure. Sadly, my husband and I made the compassionate decision to end Almond's pain. Her basket, carrier, and toys were donated to a local shelter. We vowed not to take another cat into our lives, but a call from Dr. Henderson several months later caused us to reconsider.

Aged clients of Dr. Henderson were moving to an assisted living complex where cats were not welcome. The owners were heartbroken about giving up their pet. Dr. Henderson said the cat, Cinnamon, had received lots of love and gentle care, just like our Almond. He thought we would be a good match.

My husband and I agreed to meet Cinnamon and her owners, Margaret and Bill Sheppard, at the veterinarian's office.

We shared the story of how our recent loss had left an empty spot in our hearts. As we chatted, Cinnamon meandered across me and settled on my husband's lap. We looked at each other and nodded, promising to give Cinnamon a permanent, loving home. Little did we know that this decision would give a new focus to our lives.

After Bill and Margaret were settled in their assisted living apartment, my husband and I took Cinnamon for a visit. She was a big hit with the residents. When we saw how her presence brightened their day, we began to make frequent trips to the complex. The Sheppards and their many friends began to look forward to our visits.

Cinnamon enjoyed all the attention and soon learned that when the carrier came out, she was headed for special treatment. Hugs, ear scratches, and treats were generously given and gratefully received. A new toy often awaited her arrival. Cinnamon always wore a colorful ribbon attached to her collar, looking like the pampered cat she was.

Cinnamon became our life changer, opening up a new world to us and adding spice to our lives. Our days were filled with purpose. Our visits gave us a sense of accomplishment, introduced us to interesting people, and Cinnamon got all the loving strokes and kisses a cat could ever want.

We began volunteering for special events and introduced a few friends to the joy of interacting with the senior residents.

Adopting Cinnamon and opening our hearts to yet another cat became a fulfilling experience for the Sheppards, their neighbors, Cinnamon, and most of all, for us!

~Mary Grant Dempsey

# Crazy Cat Lady

*Most beds sleep up to six cats. Ten cats without the owner.*
*~Stephen Baker*

I have three cats, so naturally people like to buy me cat-themed gifts, especially oversized mugs. It is a truth universally acknowledged that a woman in possession of a good number of cats must be in want of a good cat mug. Whether earthenware or bone china, these mugs all tend to feature frolicking felines with such captions as "Knit One Purr Two," "I've Got Cattitude," or "Chairman Meow."

I'm not sure if these gifts are intended to say, "Here's something I think you'll like," or, more likely, "Honey? You are one cat shy of being declared a crazy cat lady."

So how many cats does it take to tip you over the threshold? Five? Ten? Twenty-seven? When do you cross over the border between pet lover and crazy cat lady?

Just like the famous judge who said, "I know pornography when I see it," I can spot a crazy cat lady when I see one, and I've seen my share at the annual cat show at County Center. They're the women decked out in dangling cat earrings and cat-themed sweaters, hawking the homemade kitty condo towers covered in organic tree bark. It's not a far leap to imagining them lounging at home in a squalor of cats and uncollected newspapers, wearing puffy chenille bathrobes, cramming down Kit Kat bars and watching old Tom Selleck movies on the Hallmark channel.

Crazy Cat Ladies are such a cultural cliché that Amazon even sells a crazy cat lady action figure. She "has a wild look in her eye, offers all the fun without the allergies, and comes with six cats." There's even a Crazy Cat Ladies Society. According to their webpage, their mission is to appropriate the term "crazy cat lady" for themselves as a way to combat stereotypes about cat-loving folks. Their attitude: "You say crazy cat lady like it's a bad thing."

Isn't it strange that you never hear about crazy dog ladies? And who said cats are the sole province of women anyway? In Key West, Florida, Ernest Hemingway, that most manly of men, is fondly remembered as a famous collector of cats.

Hey, it's not as if I'm taking my cats out for a walk on a leash. I don't let them eat at the table with us often. (Kidding.) It's not as if I'm feeding the ferals down the street. Sure, I frequently forward cute cat videos. I've referred to our three cats as my "furry children." I confess to keeping a Kitsch Kittens calendar on my desk. I've posted a picture or three of my cats to Facebook, and maybe I've even been known not to answer a phone because I didn't want to disturb the cat sleeping on my lap. But when people try to tempt me with terrible tales of strays in dire need of homes, I always refuse. I'm not about to upset the cat equilibrium of our household. You know what they call a woman who houses twenty cats? A hoarder. But you know what they call a woman with twenty kids? A reality TV star.

In our complicated household, cats are the comic relief. They lower my husband's blood pressure, keep our autistic son company, and generally amuse and delight our human family of four. To have and to hold them, in sickness and in health… when all is said and done, our cats are family too.

One night at the dinner table my husband started to hiccup badly. Our son looked up in consternation. "Dad?" he asked. "Are you having a hairball?"

Clearly, we're all a bit invested in our cats here.

But please: keep the cat mugs and refrigerator magnets to yourself. Stop calling me a crazy old cat lady.

Because I'm not old.

~Liane Kupferberg Carter

# All about the Balloon

*It is a happy talent to know how to play.*
*~Ralph Waldo Emerson*

If you look up the word "curious" in the dictionary, you really should find a picture of my cat, Palom. He was the inspector general of the household, checking on the contents and flavor of every grocery bag, prying open cupboards with a swipe of his paw, and inspecting every bit of the Christmas tree.

I loved him to bits, but quite honestly, his relentless nosiness drove me bonkers. If I heard any strange noise in the next room, I knew to yell out, "Palom!" because he was bound to be into mischief.

As part of his curious nature, Palom was also an extremely social cat. He met everyone at the door. He scrutinized purses and shoes like a judge on some fashion reality TV show. When my son Nicholas's therapists arrived, Palom presumed he was the reason for their visits. Many times, he dove into a session and stole toys, causing me to chase after him or grab a broomstick so I could knock a plastic figure out from beneath the couch.

Even though Nicholas had grown up with Palom and his sister Porom in the household, he almost completely ignored their existence. When he did notice them, it wasn't in a good way. Nicholas's autism made him highly sensitive to loud sounds, so Palom's brash yowl of greeting made him cover his ears and cry. I could only coax Nicholas to pet the cats if I did it with him, hand over hand.

It made me sad to see my first kids—my cats—exist in a separate sphere from my son. Porom is an introvert and didn't mind being ignored by Nicholas. But Palom always meowed hello to Nicholas, or curled up in his bed, or attempted to groom him. Sometimes, I felt like I had to break them apart like squabbling siblings.

Palom had many obsessions—his beloved shoes, his cardboard box—but he had a special interest in balloons. As I drove Nicholas home from a dentist appointment, a reward balloon bobbing in the back seat, I worried about what would happen.

Palom would do everything possible to get that balloon, and if it popped, the sound alone would drive Nicholas into a panic. Plus, I was always worried about Palom trying to eat one of his "kills." I would need to keep a close eye on things.

That first day, the balloon drifted along the ceiling. Nicholas was content to stare up at it. So was Palom. The cat pondered his prey, tail lashing in anticipation.

The next morning, when I brought out the balloon it had lost enough air that it hovered at about four feet. The string dragged on the floor.

"Balloon!" shouted Nicholas. He grabbed the string and spun around.

Palom galloped in and sprang at the string. I opened my mouth to call out a warning to Nicholas, but I froze at an unexpected sound.

Laughter. Gales of laughter. Nicholas almost doubled over in hysterics as he made eye contact with Palom. He jerked on the balloon. Palom bounded after it. For once, Nicholas wasn't terrified of the big cat. He twirled in a circle. Palom's white paws pounded after the small tail of string still on the floor. Nicholas heaved in giggles and danced forward.

Tears filled my eyes. I did what any mom would do in such circumstances—I ran for the camera.

The next fifteen minutes passed in a happy blur as Nicholas and Palom played together for the first time. The barriers of autism had crumbled, all because of the hilarious determination of one tabby cat. Palom leaped, and dashed in circles, and chased Nicholas from room to room. The sound of laughter rang throughout the house.

Whenever Palom had too strong a hold on the string, I intervened, but otherwise I let them do their thing. Nicholas couldn't stop laughing. Palom couldn't stop his pursuit. He meowed and pirouetted and had the grandest of times.

All too often, I'd scolded Palom for his nosiness and apologized to guests for his aggressive friendliness, but those very same traits had created this beautiful moment.

Soon enough, Nicholas was distracted by a book. He curled up in a chair, his face red and sweat-soaked. He didn't give Palom a second glance. I grabbed the balloon and set it to drift from the top of a bookshelf. Palom followed me with a querulous meow.

"Sorry," I said. "I don't want you to pop it. Maybe you two can play again later." I couldn't help but smile. These two loves of my life had connected. Maybe they could connect again.

Resigned, Palom curled up in his box a few feet away from my computer desk. I sat down and stroked him with my foot.

"You did good, Pal," I whispered to him. "Just keep on trying."

Palom yawned as if to shrug off the praise, his ribs vibrating in a purr. One amber eye squinted as he monitored the balloon up high.

When it was playtime again he would be ready.

~Beth Cato

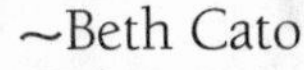

# The Cat Did What?

## What I Learned from the Cat

# La Chatte

*I love cats because I love my home and after a while they become its visible soul.*
*~Jean Cocteau*

I have a left-handed cat. Her name is La Chatte, and my husband and I acquired her by default three years ago, when I was a new stepmother and was in bending-over-backwards mode towards my husband's children, who live with their mother and stepfather on the other side of town.

In a fit of romantic display, my sixteen-year-old stepson had arrived at his paramour's door on her birthday carrying a fluffy, black kitten. The birthday girl's mother was less than enchanted; one is either a cat person or one is not, and I've found that when it comes to cats, there is no middle ground. Wanting to thwart the possibility of her daughter's attachment, the mother spun my stepson around and pointed him in the direction of his car, kitten in hand.

What happened next was a domino effect: my stepson went back home with the kitten, which he handed into the willing arms of his eight-year-old sister who formed a bond with the ball of fur within seconds. Promptly, their mother arrived on the scene followed by the family's four curious dogs. Barking, jumping and general pandemonium ensued, and it didn't take long for their mother to make an executive decision: there would be no kitten living underneath their roof and that was the end of that.

When the phone rang at our house, my husband spent the following half hour trying to soothe his precious daughter, who sobbed and wailed that all was lost because she couldn't keep the kitten. My husband looked at me with desperate eyes so I gestured for him to hand me the phone. "Tell me about the kitten," I said, and by the end of the day we were the guardians of an appeased eight-year-old, and the permanent caretakers of a nine-week-old black kitten.

Suffice it to say, La Chatte has changed the dynamic of our home, and we have adjusted our lives to accommodate her. She is large on personality, whimsical and capricious. She is aloof until it doesn't serve her, at which point she'll capitulate. She is primarily an indoor cat, but she likes to dart outside should one of our screen doors fall off the track. She never goes very far; she typically just hangs around on the front porch evading us when we give chase and sauntering back inside when it suits her. Rather than being frustrated, I have cultivated an essential patience and am now in the habit of waiting indefinitely to do her bidding.

The reason I know La Chatte is left-handed is because she uses her left paw to get my attention. When we are seated at the dinner table, she positions herself on the counter behind me and reaches out with her left paw to tap me on my shoulder. This is her way of saying that she wants to join us for dinner even though she has already been fed. If you were to have asked me four years ago if I'd ever envision myself inviting a cat to dinner, I would have told you the idea was preposterous. Yet I have changed my mind completely and I cave every time she taps me, because the gesture is so endearing.

La Chatte is exceedingly vocal for a cat, having figured out quickly that one well timed meow will spur me to action. "What is it, La Chatte?" I say, springing to her command. She'll meow again for good measure just to make sure she's got me, then lead me to the kitchen where her green food bowl with "The Cat" written in white block letters awaits—because we couldn't find one written in French.

I am the reclining sort, as in I like to lay prone on the sofa while watching movies. For years I had the exercise down with a soft pillow and throw blanket strategically appointed, but all that changed when La Chatte moved in because she's the affectionate kind who doesn't take no for an answer. She simply insinuates herself onto my chest and all the king's horses couldn't dissuade her, so I have amended my ways to include her. Now no movie would be worth watching without La Chatte's Zen-like presence on my chest.

I have learned that in order to live harmoniously with a cat, you have to accept their premise: they are mysterious little creatures with whiskers, claws, flexible bodies and searing eyes. They are curious, elusive, independent, and fundamentally beyond the reach of human influence until they decide there is something they want from you. I have learned that sometimes in life it's best to suspend judgment and embrace the entire package, even if you never went in search of it. I have learned all this and more. And now I know that sometimes the virtues of patience, acceptance and unconditional love arrive by default in a warm black bundle that purrs.

~Claire Fullerton

# The Marks of a Lasting Love

*To bathe a cat takes brute force, perseverance, courage of conviction— and a cat. The last ingredient is usually hardest to come by.*
*~Stephen Baker*

It was Mom's fault. She got the ball rolling with one simple, crazy declaration: "WT needs a bath."

Imagine my surprise. WT had been with us for a full year and had shown no symptoms of being especially grimy. I tried to put up a good fight, for her sake and mine.

"What are you talking about?" I asked. "Cats clean themselves. Constantly. WT doesn't need a bath."

Mom was insistent. "It's been a year. She needs a bath."

It's not that I had any objection to having a clean cat; it was just that I was perfectly happy with WT the way she was. Once more I tried to avert an obvious mistake. "Have you ever tried to give a cat a bath? You know how cats feel about getting wet."

I thought this salvo of good sense would move Mom away from her madness, but she remained adamant. "It's been a year. She needs a bath."

Against such obstinacy the gods themselves strive in vain. Mom's mind was made up: WT had a date with the kitchen sink.

WT had arrived in our lives exactly one year before—on my twenty-first birthday, no less, which made her arrival extra special for me. And over the ensuing twelve months, WT revolutionized our lives.

You see, we had never had a cat before. It had been a long time since we had had any pets. Our most recent pet had been one lonely goldfish with a penchant for jumping out of his bowl; he had made his final flop a couple of years before, and our home had been pet free ever since.

Then our landlord finally relented and gave us the okay to get a cat. So, while I stayed on the couch and celebrated my birthday by watching playoff baseball, Mom and my sister Paula went to the shelter and picked out our new kitty.

Very quickly, our new friend earned the name "Wild Thing," a moniker that was inevitably shortened to her more dignified initials, WT.

WT instantly became the joy of our lives. Everyone doted on her, all day every day: constant petting sessions, countless snapshots to capture her every mood and move, hours of playtime with balls, string, and dozens of toys. Each day of that first year seemed to bring some new delight. A first cat is always a source of endless surprises. You never know what crazy thing kitty will do next—or, as it turned out, what crazy ideas she'll inspire in her human companions.

Like, for instance, the idea that a cat needs a bath.

Crazy or not, that afternoon the three of us herded WT into the kitchen. Before she knew what was happening, we were able to grab WT and get her into the kitchen sink, where Operation Clean Kitty commenced.

The first part of the job went smoothly enough. WT, though profoundly unhappy, favored us with quiet, begrudging, squirmy cooperation. The trouble only truly began when we got the reluctant target of Mom's enforced hygiene routine out of the water.

Paula and I made every effort to dry her off, but—as you can imagine—WT was most interested in beating a hasty retreat. Our hit-and-run attempts with the towels left WT dry enough that I was ready to call it a day.

Again, Mom had other plans. "She's still wet," Mom said, declaring her dissatisfaction. "She needs to be dry."

"She's as dry as she's going to get," I said.

"She's unhappy enough as it is," Paula noted.

"She'll get sick if she's not dry," said Mom.

This, of course, was absurd. "It's almost 90 degrees outside," I said, in mounting exasperation. "She's not going to get sick. The heat will dry her off soon enough."

"She will get sick," Mom insisted. "She needs to be dry."

Again: obstinacy… gods… striving in vain…

And then came the fateful moment. I honestly don't remember who suggested using the hair dryer. In hindsight, an obviously crazy idea. But—as is always the case whenever things really go off the rails—it seemed like a good idea at the time.

So, while my sister got the hair dryer from the bathroom, I kept WT corralled within the kitchen. Soon enough Paula was ready, standing by the kitchen table with the hair dryer plugged in and ready to go. Then I made my move: I grabbed WT and hastened into position, a few feet in front of my sister. I held WT out in front of me, the same way a person holds a baby who has done terrible things in her diaper.

"Hurry," I advised. "I won't be able to hold her like this very long." Truer words were never spoken.

Paula held up the hair dryer, pointed it at WT, and flipped the power switch.

The results of that fateful action were, literally and figuratively, electric.

The instant the hair dryer roared to life I found myself holding a furry tornado. WT spun around in my hands, like a cartoon Tasmanian devil, in a frenzied and ultimately successful attempt to escape the hair dryer's fury. In the process, her rear claws raked my left forearm, slashing a series of angry-looking gashes from the base of my thumb to halfway down to my elbow. As I howled in shock and pain, WT leapt down to the floor and scrambled away, her revenge already turning bright red along my forearm.

And with that, our "bathe the cat" project came to an abrupt end.

Having done her damage, WT vanished into some faraway hiding place. She got away clean, you might say.

I was not so lucky. Again I spent part of my birthday watching playoff baseball—this time sitting in a chair in the local emergency room.

My wounds, as it turned out, looked impressive but were not particularly dangerous. A bit of professional cleaning, some sterile coating, and a tetanus shot covered my medical needs. All in all, not much damage despite those few seconds of high drama. I would make it home again alive and in one piece.

The funny thing is, I never really blamed WT for the damage she did to me. After all, she had not meant to hurt me; she just wanted to get away from our clumsy attempts at cat grooming. Even if she had scratched me on purpose, she was probably justified. No court in the land would have convicted her.

But something deeper was at work. Later that night, as I sat on the couch holding up my arm, studying the red streaks that traced the paths of WT's claws, feeling the throbbing ache within those scratches, I knew that I loved WT too much to ever hold such a trivial thing against her. In fact, that incident sealed the deal for me: I was "all in" on being a cat person. A year with WT had shown me the delights that come from letting a cat into your life; a few flesh wounds were a small price to pay for such a blessing.

It has now been ten years since WT passed away. Gus, our family's equally beloved second cat, is also gone and sorely missed. Today, our Maxi holds the office of beloved family cat. These days, I also get to enjoy an extended feline family: a stable of wonderful kitties I know through my cat-sitting clients, plus the numerous cats I've helped prepare for adoption through volunteer work at a local animal shelter—many of whom have gone on to join families and change others' lives in the same way that WT changed my life.

All of the joys that cats have brought to my life began with WT. And those scratches on my arm turned into a set of scars that I have come to cherish. They are not just the physical evidence of a moment when WT literally touched my life; they are also a permanent reminder of WT's legacy, of how she changed my life in so many ways. The scars on my left arm are truly the marks of a lasting love, and I will treasure them until the day I die.

~Stephen Taylor

# The Bond of Sisters

*Help one another, is part of the religion of sisterhood.*
*~Louisa May Alcott*

Puma and Kovu were tabby cats with soft gray and black fur that striped and swirled in unique patterns. My sister adopted them both, as they were sisters from the same litter. They lived in an apartment along with my cat, Dakota. Dakota was a beautiful orange male tabby. We decided we'd better get Dakota fixed but it turned out we were too late. Three or four weeks after Dakota's procedure, we realized Puma was getting big around the middle. Another week later we knew she was pregnant. We got things ready for the kittens and highly anticipated them for weeks.

I woke up in the early hours one morning to Puma meowing softly and nudging my hand. It was time! Puma was very clingy and tried to get as close as she could to me. I had to keep taking her out of my bed and putting her into her pet bed, which she only stayed in when I sat next to it. Eventually the first kitten came.

To watch a birthing process is amazing. How the instincts of the animal kick in and they seem to know exactly what to do. Once the first kitten was out and getting licked by mom, Kovu and Dakota were right there, curious as to what was going on. I was scared they would hurt the kittens, so I shut them in my sister's room while she slept. When I walked back into my room, Puma was meowing and walked over to the closed door the other two cats were behind. I picked her up and put her back in her bed as well as the kitten she had in the middle of the room; however, she wouldn't stay. She kept going back to the closed door, meowing. And as in answering her, Kovu was meowing and reaching her paw under the door.

After several times carrying Puma back to her bed and trying to get her to stay there with her newborn kittens, I gave up with a huff. "Have it your way!" I opened the door and Kovu shot out straight to her sister. They meowed at each other, then Puma led the way into the pet bed and curled up with her kittens, which now totaled three. She touched each one with her nose and looked at Kovu like she was showing them off. Kovu lay down next to the pet bed with her head inside and began to lick one of the kittens. She probably would have crawled right in with Puma, but there wasn't enough room. That is how the rest of the morning went: Puma had four more kittens. She was exhausted and focused on birthing while Kovu stepped in and took over the chore of cleaning each kitten dry.

As the kittens grew, Kovu was in the bed as often as the mother of the litter. She enjoyed keeping them warm and giving each kitten a bath when Mom needed a break. She let the kittens suck on her too though she most likely wasn't producing milk, but neither of the parties seemed to mind. When Puma came back and crawled in, Kovu jumped out. It was a joy seeing the kittens grow up and interact with their mom and aunt.

To this day, I realize just how important it was to Puma to have her sister share that special moment with her. And how important it was to Kovu to be there and help out when her sister couldn't continue doing what she needed to do. They were there for each other. That is a true sister bond that survives through all the years, no matter what.

~Alicia Penrod

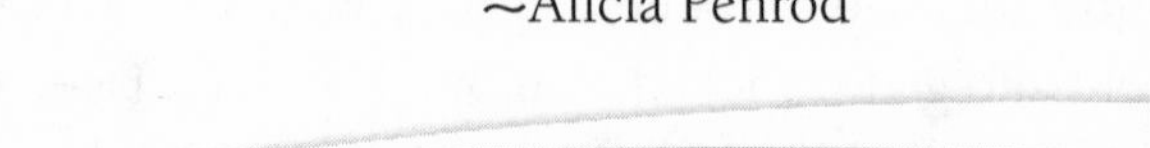

# Peanut the Pioneer

*In a cat's eye, all things belong to cats.*
*~English Proverb*

Learning that my wife was pregnant? Jubilation. Shopping for the lengthy list of necessities at baby stores? Slightly overwhelming. Knowing how those products work? Quite the challenge.

"Honey, not to sound clueless, but I'm completely in the dark about what some of these products do," I told my wife, Joy.

"Don't worry. We will learn it together," she responded happily.

Following our baby shower, I wore out the asphalt on the driveway carrying in a plethora of boxes of all different sizes with objects that were "foreign" to me inside. In a matter of minutes, we had a mountain of gifts in our living room. How on earth were we going to figure out how to use all these things? Our cat Peanut was eyeing the gifts with some curiosity. Why not let him test some of these products for our soon-to-arrive bundle of joy?

Peanut was an extraordinary feline, and I often wondered if he truly was an invertebrate. He could twist and turn his body in the most peculiar positions that would make even gymnasts and acrobats grimace and gasp. If he was any longer, he could be the reigning champ at *Twister*.

The first item we tore into was a BabyBjorn, (which I finally learned to pronounce after several failed attempts). This thing is designed to hold the baby in front of the parent's torso so that the parent doesn't have to constantly hold the baby. When it was time for Peanut to showcase this item for us, he came scrambling toward us with no idea what we planned. As I picked him up, I whispered into his ear, "Big guy, you are going to be rewarded with many snacks for helping us out."

Trembling a bit with excitement and nerves, I lowered each of his cooperative hind legs into the two openings of the contraption. Once he was in it, he actually looked very tranquil. Joy and I laughed at the sight of Peanut getting an aerial view of our living room while in the BabyBjorn. After I took a few laps around the coffee table with my fluffy friend, we suddenly heard a loud, booming sound coming from him. Indeed, he was purring loudly.

"Unbelievable! He loves it! This thing really must be cozy for babies and… cats. This gift is a keeper," Joy said enthusiastically.

Feeling positive about our first experiment, we decided Peanut should try the play station. From a child's perspective, this was like Disney World! It included colorful shakers that made gentle sounds, a flexible, vivid sun that was as soft as cotton, and realistic farm animal sounds with a simple press of the button.

Shortly after it was assembled, Peanut meandered over to us, as if on cue. He took a seat in the play station and starting jabbing at the plastic sun like a boxer, turning it this way and that. "Unbelievable! Even Rocky Balboa would be proud of Peanut's moves in there," exclaimed Joy.

After the sun was literally down for the count, Peanut swiveled around to his next victim: the shakers. Sniffing each one carefully, he slowly tapped one of the three oddly shaped objects, which produced a high-pitched noise. Unfazed by the sound, he quickly moved over to the other two noisemakers, but seemed bored by them. Without hesitation, he moved to the station that made realistic animal sounds that included a cow, cat, dog, and pig. Since he appeared baffled by what to do, I pressed the cat noise first. His reaction was hilarious! He twisted his head to the side and stared at the speaker intently. I pressed it again with the same result. As I was going to press it a third time with my eyes focused on Peanut, my finger must've slipped and I pressed the dog, which sounded like a St. Bernard barking. Without hesitation, Peanut's ears went back, and his whole body started to squirm like a worm. Understanding that he was terrified of this sound, I immediately took him out.

Joy and I concluded that Peanut liked moveable objects more than noisy objects. It took a few minutes for him to come back into the room, but when he did, I generously gave him a small handful of meaty treats. All was forgiven.

Shortly after Peanut graciously tried out some of these gifts, my son was born. Fortunately for us, he was not allergic to cats. After passing that hurdle, we wondered how Peanut would react to our son, Colin. It didn't take long for that question to be answered.

On the first night that I gave my son a bottle of milk using the Boppy, a plush feeding pillow, Peanut wandered over to the rocking chair where I was nervously sitting, suspiciously licking his chops. Peanut touched the Boppy a couple of times and then started licking Colin's feet. I couldn't believe it! He had accepted Colin.

Peanuts involvement didn't end when Colin was a newborn. Several months later, as I put Colin into his crib, I grabbed Peanut, nuzzled him, and plopped him on the Boppy the way he liked it best—inverted. I rocked him and said how much he helped us through this new experience by teaching us to be patient and to understand someone else's feelings through careful observation. As he lay there on the cozy Boppy, I noticed something on his chin. As I brought him over to the light, I detected what I feared. Like butter on bread, pureed green beans were spread all over his fur. It made sense since I didn't clean up the unwanted portion of vegetables from the table. But never did I think Peanut would dive into it. I was wrong. It appears that he wanted to try out everything that we brought home, even the food.

Curiosity might not kill the cat, but it sure makes things a bit messy.

~Austin Tamillo

# The Wonder of Birdy

*It always gives me a shiver when I see a cat seeing what I can't see.*
*~Eleanor Farjeon*

From the moment she was born I knew that she was destined for greatness. I can recall holding her in the palm of my hand watching her wiggle and meow, announcing her arrival to the world. I knew that she would be a very independent young feline eager to explore her territory. From the enormous lynx tips on her ears to her silky brown tabby coat, she was everything that I could ask for in a Maine Coon kitten and I was in love. She was addicted to play and would spend countless hours in hot pursuit of all her favourite toys. She especially loved her cat treats and would wait patiently each day for me to serve her allotted share, always hoping I would spill the bag and she would score extra goodies.

As a very young kitten she would climb to the top of her cat tree and stare out our picture window at the antics of the birds swooping past her vantage point. The sights and sounds she witnessed outside seemed to mesmerize her. It was usually impossible to break her gaze once she focused on an object.

Perhaps it was because of this quirky trait she earned the name Birdy. I delighted in watching her grow into a beautiful young feline with countless energy, eagerly anticipating every event tossed her way. I knew that our Birdy was one special bundle of fur but what I didn't know was that she was destined to save us from a near disaster.

Birdy's special powers were put to the test one chilly November evening. My husband and I had just started to watch our evening television programs when I noticed Birdy perched on top of our upright piano. Her eyes were locked in a death stare with the wall thermostat. She was a cat with a mission and no amount of coaxing would entice her to relinquish her post. I rattled a bag of her special treats and still she would not move. I thought if anything would catch her attention it would be food, but to no avail.

I sensed that something was very wrong and motioned to my husband Tony to lower the volume so we could hear what captivated our little cat.

"Tony, there is something the matter with Birdy. She won't move. I have tried everything and she won't budge."

"Can you hear the hissing noise?" he exclaimed.

Once we were beside her we saw small flashes of light bursting from the baseboard heater thermostat—the real possibility of fire was not far away.

When my husband removed the cover of the thermostat he discovered electrical arcs sparking from the thermostat cover to the mounting box. We flew into action, shutting off the power and removing the thermostat from the wall. The wooden cedar strips beside the electrical box were severely burned. It terrified us to think that, by the evidence of the burns, the arcing had been happening for quite some time.

The experience left us shaken, overwhelmed and very grateful to our little cat for her perseverance.

"Tony, what if Birdy hadn't heard this? We could have been away." I shuttered. What a marvel our little Birdy was!

Birdy insisted upon staying by our side during the whole ordeal. Her gentle purring only served as a reminder of the unconditional devotion and love our furry felines provide us. I couldn't have been more proud to be her "human" mom.

Quickly new materials were purchased and installed, making sure that all the wire connection terminal screws were tightly in place. We felt quite sure that we would never experience the problem again.

Birdy has since passed away. I truly believe that if it hadn't been for one curious little cat and her fascination with the world around her, our home might have succumbed to the devastation of a fire.

~Gail Sellers

# Shut Up, Boycat!

*Cats are a mysterious kind of folk.*
*There is more passing in their minds than we are aware of.*
*~Sir Walter Scott*

Boycat always had something to say about everything! Whether the subject was a startled lizard, a passing bike rider, the next-door neighbor's children, or his empty food dish, our gorgeous, loving Siamese made sure he let us know about it. And of course, we were always glad to listen. Or, at least, most of the time!

But as much as we enjoyed his exuberant cuddling, his playful antics with our three young boys, and his very serious efforts to guard his home and family against threatening butterflies—all the while keeping up his "cat-ter chatter"—we did look forward to having some quiet. At nine each evening we tucked in our three bubbly preschoolers, kissed them, and turned out the light. Peace at last—with Boycat staying with them as self-appointed babysitter.

That way my husband Don and I had a chance to clean up, chill out, unwind, and head to bed ourselves.

Then one night our peaceful sleep was shattered with a jump on our bed—and very loud meowing. Blinking, I turned on the light. "Boycat! What's the matter with you? Quiet down!"

Instead, he pawed at the covers and moaned, then meowed again, nonstop.

I was furious. Jumping out of bed, "Shut up, Boycat! Stop it!"

As I lunged for him, he leaped off the bed and ran out the bedroom door, still meowing at the top of his lungs. I jumped up and ran down the hall after him. Man, was I ready to teach that ornery cat a lesson!

That's when he ran into the boys' room and leaped straight up onto my son Chat's bed.

I turned on their light. Oh, no! Why did Chat look so strange?

Touching his forehead, my heart sank. He had a raging fever. And was barely breathing.

That's why Boycat was so loud. He knew one of his beloved playmates needed help—and needed it fast.

And Chat got it. After several hours in the emergency room, he finally returned home with antibiotics. Waiting for him at the front door was Boycat, meowing a loving welcome.

And we didn't care how loudly he did it!

~Bonnie Compton Hanson

# Sugar Magnolia

*Miracles are not contrary to nature,*
*but only contrary to what we know about nature.*
*~Saint Augustine*

On Easter weekend 1997, my daughter Jessica was home from college. I had flown to Philadelphia to join my husband for a "dog and pony show" arranged by the company attempting to recruit him.

In the middle of my first night in Philly, we received a call from Jessica. She was frantic. An F3 tornado had struck Chattanooga. Our newly built home was destroyed. Our cat Sugar Magnolia was missing! We flew back to Chattanooga the next morning.

We had rescued her from a shelter as a kitten. My daughter named her Sugar Magnolia (from a song by the Grateful Dead). She grew into a magnificent cat—fluffy, long orange fur, golden eyes, and the best disposition ever. She graciously allowed us to live with her and she made our home a happier place.

The devastation of our home was total—everything ruined or blown away. Emotions ran high. We were thankful to be safe and that the storm had claimed no lives. But where was Sugar Magnolia? As pet lovers know, these critters become an integral part of families and we had lost a family member.

For three days we searched through the rubble. For some reason, the local and national media picked up our story and gave daily reports on our family and our search for our cat. On the fourth day, the bulldozers were scheduled to clear the land. That day, only Jessica went back to what we now called "The Site." We had not found Sugar Magnolia and feared all we might find was her body.

Later that same morning, as my husband and I watched *Oprah* in our hotel room, the program was interrupted by a news bulletin announcing, "Jessica has found Sugar Magnolia!" We were stunned and thrilled as we listened to how Jessica had found her just before the bulldozers started. She was alive and miraculously uninjured, having been buried three days under the rubble in an air pocket.

Sugar Magnolia became the celebrity of Chattanooga and lived happily with us for many years. We had lost her. We had found her, and although now, many years later, she has gone to Kitty Heaven, we will never forget her or stop loving her.

For me, the whole tornado experience was a jolting reminder and reinforcement of my basic philosophy of life: The glass is half full. To this day, I keep a picture of "The Site" in my living room as a daily reminder that "things" don't matter—only lives—even if animals.

~Janet E. Lord, Ph.D.

# And Baby Makes Six

*Kittens can happen to anyone.*
*~Paul Gallico*

She strolled up the steps of our deck, her tiny yet powerful pink nose tracking the scent of salmon sizzling on the grill. Skinny as a rail, this far-from-finicky feline had no time for gracious invitations. She was on a mission to fill her empty belly.

"What a beautiful kitty," I whispered while stroking her coat, a patchwork of dirty white, gray, black and brown.

She slid her body along my leg, anxious to bond with the suspected source of the tantalizing smells that wafted through the air.

"Looks like trouble," my husband teased.

He's an animal lover too, but for him common sense usually wins over sentimentality.

"I know, but look how skinny the poor thing is," I said as I scooped her into my arms, cradling her like a baby against my chest.

Then something caught my eye: the telltale signs of a soon-to-be-nursing mother cat.

"Oh no, she's pregnant—look at her nipples!"

"You're kidding," my husband said as he placed the salmon on the table. "I guess we'd better get her a plate."

Our guest perked up in anticipation of the impending feast. With no time for manners, this hungry little hobo practically inhaled the little mound of salmon we'd placed in front of her. Afterwards, she stretched out on the warm wood of the deck, soaking up the sun while licking her paws clean.

"A kitty!" cheered my six-year-old son as he raced into the back yard just in time for dinner. "Can we keep her?"

"I don't think Chelsea would be too keen on that idea," I said, referring to the reigning queen of our castle, a fat and happy feline with no desire to share the attention of her human subjects. The last time we introduced a potential playmate, she snarled and hissed and left a special "surprise" for me to clean up.

"And we don't need a house full of kittens," my always-practical husband pointed out.

"Kittens!" squealed my son, his eyes lighting up like Fourth of July fireworks. My husband rolled his eyes, obviously wishing he'd kept his mouth shut.

If this cat birthed her kittens outside, I thought, they would be feral and unadoptable—another sad statistic in the growing problem of homeless strays.

As the evening wore on, our diminutive dinner guest ate up our undivided attention. In the hustle and bustle of clearing the dinner dishes, she disappeared like a shadow into the night.

I hope she has a warm place to sleep, I prayed.

During the next few days, I learned that this wandering waif, dubbed Lucy by one neighbor, had dined and dashed at houses all along our street. I imagined her as a weary, cross-country traveler, stopping only to recharge and refuel at convenient truck stops along a dark and lonesome highway—and I worried about the future of her babies.

I guess it's in Mother Nature's hands, I told myself.

A week later, Lucy reappeared. Although a little rounder in the belly, the rest of her body was still much too thin for a pregnant mother.

"What if we keep her in the laundry room until she has the kittens?" I asked my husband. "Then we'll find them good homes."

A tall order I knew, even for an eternal optimist like me.

Surprisingly, my husband agreed. My son jumped for joy.

Quarantined in the laundry room, Lucy was safe and well fed; but she wasn't exactly content. Accustomed to roaming the streets, this free spirit was used to doing what she pleased. Now she found herself trapped by the unwelcome responsibility of impending motherhood.

Despite her objections, our makeshift maternity ward offered privacy, protection and plenty of space for her to stretch her legs while we waited for the big day to arrive.

Periodically, we let her roam the house when "her majesty" was fast asleep in the upstairs bedroom. During one of these adventures, Lucy became strangely fixated on my husband, meowing and pawing at him. He repeatedly shooed her away but she kept at it with a frantic, almost desperate look in her eyes.

The light bulb of female intuition switched on in my head.

"I bet the babies are coming!" I exclaimed and we rushed Lucy to her birthing suite: a laundry basket lined with old baby blankets.

"What's happening Mom?" my son asked, his eyes wide as her body contorted with contractions.

"She's giving birth, honey," I answered softly. "We need to be as calm and quiet as possible because this is a big job for her."

In a matter of minutes, Lucy squeezed out a motionless bundle of bloody fur—ugly yet amazing.

"What's that?" My son looked like he was about to lose his lunch.

"It's her baby," I said. "And I think there are more on the way."

Lucy licked each newborn until tufts of fuzzy, down-like fur appeared, then leaned into the next set of contractions without a sound. I stroked her softly, marveling at how calmly she performed one of the most daunting duties of motherhood.

"Is it a girl or boy?" my son asked, anxious to find out whether he had a new sister or brother.

"We'll have to wait and see," I said.

Exhausted after this maternal marathon, Lucy and her new family fell fast asleep.

The next day, the unsteady siblings—one girl and four boys—inched around on weak, wobbly legs in search of milk from mama's belly.

"Why can't they open their eyes?" my son asked.

I appreciated his eagerness, recalling the first time I gazed into my own baby boy's eyes as I held him in my arms.

The kittens seemed to double in size overnight, as did their curiosity. They explored every nook and cranny of the laundry room, clumping through their food dishes and digging feverishly in the litter box while dust clouds puffed into the air. They squeezed through narrow passages behind the washer and dryer, played hide-and-seek in a stack of paint trays, and wrestled in piles of dirty clothes. This once plain and practical space became a playground of endless fun and fascination for them.

Day after day, Lucy dutifully tended to her babies' needs. Then one afternoon, she made a break for it.

I spotted her from the kitchen window, a flash of fur sprinting across our back yard. It didn't surprise me: what mother hadn't fantasized about making a mad dash from reality? But I wasn't about to become a surrogate mother to five little felines.

I acted fast, running to the laundry room and gently holding one of the kittens up to the open window while he mewed frantically. Lucy stopped short then bounded back to comfort her crying baby.

A wanderer's soul is no match for fierce maternal instinct.

I soon found good homes for all five kittens—and for Lucy. My son cried when one adoptive mother chose his favorite, the one he'd hoped to keep as his own.

This feline family not only touched our hearts, but also taught us some important life lessons about giving to those in need—and about letting go.

~Margrita Colabuno

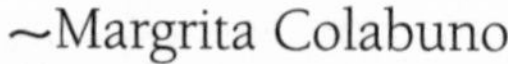

# How to Calm a Skittish Cat

*A cat can be trusted to purr when she is pleased,*
*which is more than can be said for human beings.*
*~William Ralph Inge*

First you breathe. Not a casual inhale-exhale, there I'm done. Rather, a long, slow, conscious, deep-from-the-belly breath, even counts on the in and out. You don't need to be in bed, but it helps. Begin sitting up, breath now even, and sigh audibly, vocalizing softly from the top of your range to the bottom. Repeat as needed. Wait for cat to approach.

Note: This technique is not aimed at the extroverted cat. The extroverted cat will eagerly choreograph a Twyla Tharp ballet of twists and poses, circles and dips. She will tell you what she wants. You need only listen.

But a skittish cat won't tell you. A skittish cat will arrive tentatively, squat just out of arm's reach, and stare. Your job is to stare back, gently, not wide-eyed, and smile a Buddha half-smile. For now, do not move your body, just your facial muscles. This is essential in creating a safe, nonthreatening atmosphere. Remember, your cat wants love but she is afraid, untrusting.

Once she meets your gaze, which may take a moment, slowly lower and raise your eyelids as if you're nodding off. She will mirror you. You are now eye-kissing. Continue for as long as you like. To deepen the mood, you may add a delicate, sympathetic furrow of the brow. Keep breathing.

When you feel ready, add the following: extend one hand, palm and fingers curled downward, soft and close to the covers. Repeat the audible sigh. Add smooching sounds if you wish, no louder than pianissimo and only if you feel comfortable. She'll know if you're not. She will continue to stare, curious but wary.

Next, scratch the covers lightly with your fingernails. At this point, unless your cat was irreversibly traumatized as a kitten, in which case she might flee, she will move toward you. Thank her. Not verbally, because calming her is not a verbal thing. Breathe.

Now unfurl your fingers and invite your cat to push her head into your hand. Begin to stroke her head, first along one jawline, sweeping behind one ear in circles, then switch sides. Then with one continuous motion press your fingers against her nose and massage up to the brow, traversing the skull, and trace a line down each furry vertebra, gently swooping the tail, and release. Let her control the pace and the pressure. She will tell you, if you listen. She wants you to listen.

Over time, as you repeat the encounter, she will lie down beside you. This is your cue to progress. Slide a palm firmly along her chest, up and down, scratching the belly, kneading the underarms, even skittling the tip of the nose. If she responds, try alternating rhythms and pressure, perhaps graduating to a two-handed back rub. Expect purring.

When you have mastered these techniques, you may proceed to the final phase. Position yourself beside your cat, stretching out fully, your front facing her back. Inch closer, then curl into her, spooning tightly. Move your head and hands as desired, nuzzling, petting, smooching, sighing, humming, breathing long and deep.

And if your cat stays still, and if she purrs, and if you yourself were not irreversibly traumatized as a child, you will experience your heart open, pulsing with boundless gratitude.

And if you can love in this way, you can love in every other way too.

~Deborah Sosin

# Healing Hands

*If you would know a man, observe how he treats a cat.*
*—Robert Heinlein*

The wipers beat against the driving rain, echoing the thump of my heart. I slowed as a wall of water splashed over the roof of my Jeep as it hit a deep puddle. I was trying to hurry and drive safely at the same time, which was only sort of working.

My husband had called me at work just as I was packing things up and preparing to shut down my computer. The stray pregnant cat that had been hanging around our property had given birth in the cold spring rain on an open hillside. Four of the kittens were alive; two didn't make it. He was in such a panic that the remaining kittens would die if not kept dry that he grabbed the four surviving ones and put them in a towel-lined laundry basket with a milk jug full of hot water. This move escalated the crisis because he couldn't catch their mother.

I told him I would be right home and bolted from the office to make the thirty-six-mile drive home. We had to catch the mother, a feral stray, so the kittens could nurse. I understood why he moved the newborn kittens inside, but I wasn't sure it was the best decision. The mother would have moved them, I reasoned, as my Jeep splashed through another enormous puddle.

On my way home, I met my husband at our veterinarian's office to purchase kitten formula, bottles and a catch and release cage. In the event we couldn't catch the mother, at least we could feed the kittens.

By the time I pulled into my driveway, the rain had slowed. I dashed inside to inspect the four orange kittens huddled around the warm jug. The vet had recommended this to my husband. The kittens would snuggle against it when they were cold and they would move away from it when they became too hot.

I threw on an old coat and went outside to try to catch the mother. The cold rain soaked all the way to my bones and I knew she had to be as miserable and scared as I was. We baited the cage with tuna, hoping the aroma would lure her. We found one of the lifeless kittens in a dry spot under the pine trees, but the mother cat kept running away.

After half an hour of pursuing her, I went inside to try to mix formula and get the bottles to work. The kittens had been born three hours ago and needed to eat. The bottles were just as frustrating to figure out as was trying to catch the mother.

We followed the directions and poked needle-sized holes in the nipples, but could not get the formula to drip out. We tried to make the hole wider using a thumbtack. I held one tender little orange kitten that refused to eat. I dribbled formula on its lips hoping it would lick it and give me a chance to slip the nipple into its mouth, but no luck.

I placed the kitten back in the basket and leaned against the wall. We couldn't do this. We couldn't feed the kittens or catch their mother. If the kittens weren't returned to her, they were all going to die. I decided that releasing them was their best chance.

Back upstairs my husband was peering out the window. The mother cat was standing on our covered porch with one of her limp kittens. We both stepped outside and she ran, leaving behind the tiny soaked mass of fur. My heart ached.

"Get rid of it," I told my husband, the harsh words surprising even me. I was done. We had managed to rescue thirteen felines in the eight years we had lived here. We lost this time.

He bent down and scooped up the kitten that was smaller than his hand. Peering closely at it, we took in its tiny whiskers, itty-bitty paws, folded ears and closed eyes. I reached out and touched the cold little body, swallowing hard against the lump in my throat.

"Get rid of it," I whispered.

My husband, still mesmerized by the kitten, placed his other hand on top of it. When he moved his hand the kitten's paw flexed.

"Did you see that? It's alive," he said and placed his hand on top again for a minute, then removed it. The paw moved every time he did this. I wasn't convinced, but looking into my husband's eyes I saw a man who was going to fight for this kitten's life.

The urgent race was back on! We dashed into the house and wrapped the kitten in a kitchen towel. I threw my adult cat's buckwheat bed warmer in the microwave. Once heated we placed the kitten on the bed warmer and the kitchen towel on top.

My husband instructed me to keep rubbing the kitten in a circular motion to get its blood circulating. He went back to preparing bottles. He remembered seeing on Animal Planet that if kittens are born too quickly, the mother doesn't have time to lick all of them to get their blood circulating.

I rubbed and rubbed, still not convinced we could save this little guy. Every now and then his paw would flex. As I rubbed, my thoughts drifted back to the mother cat outside. She was in a state. She was soaked and had given birth and her babies were swiftly taken away. Despite all that, she trusted us because she brought this baby to us.

The kitten moved its mouth.

"It's alive!" I nearly jumped out of my chair. My husband rushed to my side and took over kitten revival duties.

He covered the kitten with his hands. Pretty quickly, it was impossible to tell the kitten had ever been lifeless. It was very much awake and hungry.

I had given up, written the kitten off. But my husband never lost hope. With determination and a heart full of love for that tiny kitten, he used his healing hands to restore life. I didn't need another reason to love him, but there it was.

My spirits lifted. We could do this—we could catch the mother cat and we did.

I fell into bed that night exhausted. Mom and babies were reunited and sleeping soundly in the laundry basket. And it turned out my husband's decision to rescue them was the best decision after all.

~Valerie D. Benko

# Who's in Charge Here?

# Our Secret Society

*There is, incidentally, no way of talking about cats that enables one to come off as a sane person.*
*~Dan Greenberg*

Cat owners always recognize one another by a quick glance at our hands. Our hands are soft and caring hands that feed our cats, stroke their fur, and cradle them when they're nervous—loving hands, but often covered in scratches.

Our non-cat people friends don't seem to understand and ask, "Why don't you have your cat de-clawed?"

This may be a good option for other cat owners, but I simply can't bring myself to put my kitty through a surgical procedure strictly for my benefit. Besides, what would I do with that brand new scratching post I bought last week?

Non-cat people just don't understand us cat people. I know that the marks on my hands were earned through love, as my fuzzy friend and I played with the fraying gray toy mouse he so adores, or as we had a tug-of-war over a bit of string. The marks happen innocently enough, like when I turn my cat on his back and rub his tummy. At first he closes his eyes as I roll him from side to side, then he extends his neck and opens his mouth just enough to reveal the tip of his pink tongue. Then he grabs at my hand with all four paws simultaneously, claws extended. I've been trying to perfect my tummy rub technique so that I remove my hand before the grabbing part, but I haven't quite mastered that maneuver yet.

My doctor doesn't understand either. During a recent visit, he examined my hands curiously, and then questioned me about the origin of the marks.

"They're from my cat," I told him.

He looked at me with his eyes in an odd squint. "And how long have you had this cat?" he asked.

"Three years."

"Uh-huh. I recommend a tetanus shot for you," he said as he reached for the serum and syringe, "and some discipline for your cat."

From the look on his face, I'm convinced I was about one claw mark away from my doctor also recommending an intervention. I sense he is a dog person.

Ah, but my friends the cat people, they understand. I came across another cat-loving comrade as I waited on line at the supermarket the other day. This time, I didn't even need to glance at her hands to know she was a cat person. The two bottles of hydrogen peroxide that sat atop the mountain of tuna cans in her shopping cart were the only clues I needed.

"How many?" I asked.

"Four."

"Four cats!" I exclaimed. "You're my hero."

She looked down at the supersized bag of kitty treats I had placed atop the belt. She nodded her head in its direction. "You too, huh?"

"Yup, me too." Then in the special handshake of our secret society, we both raised our scabbed hands and did a triumphant high-five.

~Monica A. Andermann

# Blur of Fur

*I don't think it is so much the actual bath that most cats dislike; I think it's the fact that they have to spend a good part of the day putting their hair back in place.*
*~Debbie Peterson*

"Some cats actually enjoy being bathed," my friend Bruce told me. Owner of a local pet supply store, Bruce had successfully bathed his cat, Fluffy.

He recounted how his curious kitty had batted some bubbles in his bathtub water and how he had gently lowered his blue-eyed beauty into the tub. "All went well," he assured me, "until I had to chase Fluffy around the living room with a blow-dryer, equipped with only a four-foot cord. Other than that, it was actually fun."

Inspired by Bruce's story, I decided that my two-year-old Siamese mix, Oscar, should also be "cleaned." He'd rolled in something stinky.

But how would I do it? First I checked out a copy of *Complete Cat Care Manual* by Andrew Edney, B.V.M. M.R.C.V.S. Armed with those impressive initials, Edney provided a "simple" seven-step procedure for bathing a cat.

"Make sure you get everything ready beforehand," he advised. Further: "You may need to enlist the aid of an assistant who can help you keep the cat calm and reassure it while it is being bathed." Sure. Right.

Step four advised me to "handle the cat firmly but gently. A cat does not like getting his fur wet and may try to scratch or bite. Talk to the cat to reassure it." (That word "reassure" kept popping up and was starting to bother me.)

Under step seven Edney advised: "If the cat is not frightened, dry it thoroughly with a hairdryer." (Now the word "if" was starting to bother me.)

Since Edney's advice seemed a tad scary, I decided to pursue option two—purchasing helpful items to alleviate hazardous duty. I found a pricey item in a pet supplies catalog—the Bath 'n Carry, a "pet-friendly restraint [that] comfortably slips over your cat to secure him without trauma." That seemed like something that might safely immobilize Oscar.

Bruce's store also afforded some useful "backup" items, such as Quick 'n Easy Cat and Kitten Shampoo that didn't require dipping, Quick Bath with five pre-moistened wipes, a Quick Fit Muzzle, and some stress-reduction pills for Oscar (or me).

But it was option three that won out. Always one to savor new adventures, I opted to bathe Oscar the old-fashioned way—shampoo and water, in the shower.

Weighing the situation, I concluded that Oscar had the advantage of quickness, cunning, claws that could remove all skin from my body, and a lack of concern for human life. I had the element of surprise, strength, and the advantage of battlefield selection.

So I chose a fairly large bathroom with a shower enclosed by a sturdy glass door. I needed a small manageable area for the skirmish, ruling out shower curtains that cats can shred.

I next assembled my special wardrobe for the occasion—a long-sleeved jacket, sturdy overalls tucked into my high-top boots, heavy gloves, and (just for "fun") my bullet-nicked Belgian army helmet.

I began by nonchalantly scooping up Oscar, as if to transport him to his food dish. Since Oscar wasn't fashion-conscious, he hardly noticed my attire.

With everything carefully laid out in the bathroom, I moved inside and, in one liquid motion, shut the bathroom door, stepped into the shower enclosure, shut the glass door, dipped Oscar in the running water, and squirted him several times with shampoo.

It's difficult to describe the next sixty seconds, since Oscar had soapy fur and no handles. He was more or less rinsing himself in a blur of fur.

Oscar next required drying—something quite simple actually, since he was semi-permanently attached to my right leg. I dragged him out of the shower toward the electrical outlets so I could blow-dry him. Drying out just a bit and leaving a trail of smoke, Oscar scurried out of the room to hide and plot his revenge.

I rinsed the blood off my face and arms, recalling that riveting scene from the film *Psycho*. Oh, well. Oscar did smell a lot better and I—I still had my pride.

My arm scratches faded, the red marks on my right leg were barely noticeable, and my partial hearing loss subsided in time. It looked like I'd beaten the odds.

Fellow cat custodians: heed my advice. Unless you loved Alfred Hitchcock's shower scene in *Psycho*, never put your kitty in the shower.

~Robert J. Brake

# Rabbit Food

*Cats seem to go on the principle that it never does any harm to ask for what you want.*
*~Joseph Wood Krutch*

Before adopting my two kittens, I did a lot of research. I wanted to make sure I gave them the best possible start in life. One of the things I read was that, while dogs are omnivores, cats are true carnivores whose diet should simulate what they ate in the wild, where they hunted their own dinner.

After I brought my new kitties home, I quickly weaned them off the kibble they had been fed by their foster family and onto a raw diet of free-range beef, turkey, chicken, and the occasional fresh fish with vitamin and mineral supplementation. They both thrived on their new regimen.

Seeing how well my cats were doing "in the raw" prompted me to overhaul my own diet too. I had read a lot about the benefits of a raw diet for humans, so I tried to incorporate more fresh fruits, uncooked vegetables and raw nuts into my meal planning—but left the raw meat to my feline companions.

Every night I'd make a huge salad for dinner. When I took my salad ingredients out of the fridge, both cats would jump on the kitchen counter to see if it was for them. They were very interested in anything I did on the counter, since that's where their meals were prepared. Misty, the more aggressive eater, would run toward me meowing, then stop and sniff the veggies, turn up her tiny pink nose, and strut away.

But Stormy, who was usually shyer and less interested in food, was fascinated. She'd perch close by and look on with interest as I washed and chopped my vegetables. She gradually became bolder, moving closer and closer, and meowing at me when I tore bite-sized pieces of greens into my bowl.

"Do you want a piece?" I asked her one day, amused by this behavior. I figured if she realized it wasn't cat food she'd lose interest. I held out a small leaf of spinach for her to sniff. She hesitated a second, and then to my surprise she yanked it out of my hand and ran away with it. I laughed at the little imp and went back to making my dinner. Out of the corner of my eye I saw her across the room munching it. I smiled to myself, sure that when she was done playing with her new toy she'd leave it for me to clean up. But when she was done, she came back for another. "Stormy, do you like spinach?" I asked, amazed, and gave her another leaf to test her interest. Again she ran off with it in her mouth and ate the whole thing. She kept returning; she was insatiable.

This became a ritual, with the sound of the salad spinner acting like a dinner bell that called her from wherever she was in the house. When I didn't have spinach one day, I apologized: "Sorry honey, we're out of spinach. This is romaine." She didn't seem to understand and looked at me expectantly, so I gave her a small piece to illustrate the difference. But darned if she didn't eat that too! It turned out she liked just about any kind of green—all forms of lettuce, spinach, kale, etc.—but spinach was her favorite. I even gave her some other categories of vegetables, and while she tried them, most ended up masticated to death on the kitchen floor.

Over time, even Misty adopted vegetarian ways. I attribute this to her great love of food of any kind. (She appears to be a true omnivore—meat, vegetables, shoelaces, carpeting...) Now they both crowd me on the counter as I make my salad, and if I don't immediately indulge them with some leaves, they will put a paw on my arm to get my attention. Their MO is usually to sit patiently nearby and wait for me to hand them each a piece, then grab it with their teeth and shake vigorously. I assume this is an inborn feline response—to shake their prey once they catch it to stun it. Then they trot off a short distance and hunker down on the counter to eat it before returning for more.

Where did this interest come from, I wondered. Could they have imprinted on me, as their human mom, and adopted my newfound enthusiasm for salads?

I'm afraid I've created a monster. Two, actually. Once, when I turned my back to get something from the refrigerator, Stormy stuck her head in the salad spinner and pulled out a piece almost as big as she, carrying it off into the family room to eat. Another time I caught Misty eating directly out of my salad bowl. "I don't eat out of YOUR bowl," I scolded her. But she just looked at me and cocked her head, probably wondering, "Why not?"

We eventually settled into a dinnertime routine. I would feed them their raw meat nuggets first, before preparing my own dinner. Then, in the European manner, they would have a salad after their main course. All was fine, but in the back of my mind I remembered my research about a cat's optimal diet and was a little concerned because of the volume of greens Stormy would eat, given the chance. So at her next physical, I mentioned this unusual behavior to our holistic vet. He looked at me over the top of his glasses and said in a serious tone, "You know what this means, don't you?"

My eyes got wide and I swallowed with difficulty. I shook my head no, worried that her behavior might indicate some underlying nutritional deficiency.

He said, "It means..." and then his face crinkled into a smile, "that she was probably a rabbit in her last life."

I certainly hadn't been expecting that response!

~Susan Yanguas

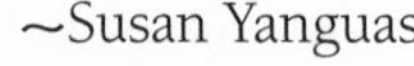

# The Stare Down

*Never try to outstubborn a cat.*
*~Robert A. Heinlein*

My days always wind down with the same routine. Dinner has been cooked and eaten; the dishes have been washed and put away. I grab the newspaper and the television remote control and lean my tired body into the cozy corner of my living room sofa. Then I curl my legs under me as my little black and white tuxedo cat, Chuck, takes his place in front of my seat. It's a Norman Rockwell moment of domestic bliss—until the staring begins.

Chuck sits on the floor in front of me as still and straight as an ancient sphinx, fixes his glowing yellow eyes on me and stares. And stares. And stares. I ignore him as best I can, lifting the newspaper at just the correct angle to block out his hypnotic gaze. Though I resolve to concentrate on reading an article, I continue to sense his unnerving presence. I flip through some advertisements and peer over the newspaper's edge. Chuck is still there, his eyes firmly fixed on me.

I lay down the newspaper and give good ol' Chuck a tickle between the ears. He doesn't move. "C'mon Chuck," I say, "let's watch some TV. I'll put on Animal Planet." Though he shows no interest in my generous offer, I flick on the TV anyway and focus my attention on the show, hoping he will follow suit. He does not.

Within a few moments I hear some stirring in the other end of the house and, heralded by the sound of the television, my husband soon joins us at his seat on the opposite end of the sofa. Chuck still doesn't move a muscle. Or his gaze.

"Will you look at this?" I say to my husband. "Chuck is staring at me again."

My husband gives me a noncommittal grunt and I poke him in the shoulder, "Hey! How come Chuck never stares at you?"

He yawns. "Chuck's just not that into me."

The top of my head starts to pound and I feel the heat rise in my face. I bend down to stare back at Chuck. Maybe a dose of his own medicine will stop him. He never even blinks. Can cats blink? I wonder as I move forward for a closer inspection. Chuck doesn't flinch. I lean back into my seat and lift the newspaper before me again until the heat generated from Chuck's laser eyes burns a hole through its pages. I toss down my smoking paper.

"That's it! You win!" I tell him as I spring from my seat. "The sofa is all yours."

Chuck makes one swift bounce onto my warmed spot, curls up and starts to purr.

I, on the other hand, stomp into my bedroom and close the door behind me. From there I hear an odd staccato sound: not quite meow, not quite purr. I take a deep breath and turn my head toward the living room for a closer listen. From where I stand, I could swear Chuck is laughing at me.

~Monica A. Andermann

# Tuna Time with Ida

*Essentially, you do not so much teach your cat as bribe him.*
*~Lynn Hollyn*

Ida was sick. She'd been wheezing off and on for a few weeks. But since she seemed to feel well otherwise, we'd ignored it. Then suddenly, it seemed, she became extremely lethargic, lying around the house. Her usually robust "meow" had become a whiny "mew."

Sure that she was on her last legs, and overcome with guilt for not doing something sooner, I placed a panic-stricken phone call to the vet. "Bring her in this afternoon," they said. Ida is by nature a very strong-willed kitty, and no one holds her still if she doesn't have a mind to. But that Tuesday afternoon, Ida had very little fight in her for the vet. She was poked, prodded, and even had her temperature taken with barely a mew. My daughter Beth and I exchanged looks that said, "This can't be good." The vet couldn't find anything conclusive: no fever; lungs and heart sounded good; the wheezing seemed nasal. Maybe they would do some blood work or even surgery if antibiotics brought no improvement. "Give this to her twice daily and come back in two weeks."

Antibiotics twice a day—the vet even demonstrated how to force Ida's jaws open to wedge the medicine dropper between her teeth. Not feeling overly encouraged, we brought Ida home to try the antibiotics. My husband Dale felt we should call our son Daniel at college to let him know Ida was sick. As I said, we weren't feeling very optimistic about things.

When we got home, I filled the eyedropper and Beth took hold of Ida. Beth grabbed her jaw just like the vet had shown us, and I held the eyedropper against Ida's clenched teeth, waiting for them to open. It didn't happen. We traded places to see if I'd have better luck. Nothing doing—Ida was not going to allow those antibiotics to pass her little kitty lips.

"Oh great," I thought, "the cat's going to die because we can't get her to take her medicine." I seriously considered calling the vet to ask if we could bring Ida by twice a day for the next ten days so they could give her the antibiotics.

Suddenly a light came on. Tuna fish. I had some cheap watery tuna in the cupboard—maybe I could disguise the medicine with that. I put a little tuna on a plate, stirred in a dose of antibiotics, and prayed as I carried it up the stairs. I set the plate down on the bed next to Ida. She looked it over, suspiciously sniffed at it, gave it a cautious lick, then proceeded to lap it up as though she couldn't believe her good fortune. For the next couple of days I brought tuna and meds to Ida where I'd find her lying upstairs with no energy to move.

By day three Ida had dramatically improved. She started to look forward to her twice-daily treat, following me around the house when the time drew near, getting underfoot whenever I walked into the kitchen. It got so I could just say, "Ida, come on—it's tuna time," and she would run into the kitchen for her treat.

Well, Ida finished her meds quite some time ago. And she was soon back to her old self, racing around the house, playing with the bunny, meowing at full throttle.

It's four years later now, and every evening between 8:00 and 9:00, I'll be sitting on the couch and feel as though someone is staring at me. I'll look up and there will be Ida, looking expectantly at me as if to say, "Come on, it's tuna time!" And it is!

~Laurie Carnright Edwards

# Whose House Is It Anyway?

*Cat people are different to the extent that they generally are not conformists. How could they be with a cat running their lives?*
*~Louis J. Camuti*

"My living space is shrinking," I lamented to a friend over coffee. "I used to have a fairly decent-sized rec room, with plenty of space to entertain my friends, but now..." I slowly shook my head. "Now it's nothing more than a Romper Room for cats."

My friend, also a cat person, smiled and knowingly nodded. "How many cat condos do you have in your rec room?"

"Cat condos?"

"Carpeted cat trees," she clarified.

"Oh those," I said. "Never heard them called condos before." I paused, wondering if my response was going to be judged as too many or too few. "As of last week, there are three cat trees in the rec room."

"Only three?" she inquired, her eyebrows raised.

Clearly, she expected a larger number. "Three trees for two cats," I explained defensively. "Three is quite enough."

"Says you, or say the cats?" She grinned mischievously.

I glowered at her. "For your information, my cat trees are in three different colors, shapes, and sizes. The small one is brown, the medium is blue, and large one is beige."

"And you say they're all different shapes?"

"The tallest one goes clear to the ceiling and has four platforms. There is a cozy, carpeted basket at each level. The shortest has a coiled hemp post and just a single platform on top. And the middle one is, well, mid-sized—it's about as tall as my shoulder—and has three fuzzy perches."

She took a sip of her coffee. "Three trees for two cats doesn't seem like it would take up all that much space."

"But..." I hesitated to tell her the rest of the story. "I also have three cat beds, also of various shapes and colors, strategically placed on two chairs and a couch, plus their food and water dishes are in the room, and their cat box, of course."

"Of course." My friend clucked her tongue and shook her head sadly back and forth. "Sorry, honey. You can't apply for membership in the Crazy Cat Lady Club until you get a few more."

"A few more cats, trees, or beds?"

"All of the above."

I can't imagine ever bringing any additional feline companions into my home. The two I have are driving me nuts as it is. Up all night, running the length of the hallway that ends at my bedroom door, then streaking back down the hall at amazing speeds. I don't know what kind of game they're playing at 3 a.m., but it sure is noisy.

She peered at me over the rim of her cup. "I thought you assured me a year ago that you were a one-cat-at-a-time person. Didn't you tell me that two cats were twice the trouble?"

"They are! Oh believe me, they are!"

"So why'd you bring the second one home?"

It was a long story, beginning with me going in to make my annual end-of-year, tax-deductible donation to the Humane Society, but the bottom line was that I took one look at the furry little guy with big eyes and the huge 90-degree kink in his long tail and fell instantly in love.

"The gal at the desk caught me in a weak moment," I replied. "And I decided cat number one needed a playmate to keep him company when I was not at home."

"Uh-huh."

The way she said it immediately put me on the defensive once again. "Seriously! I didn't bring home another cat for me—I just got my cat a companion, that's all!"

"You got a cat for your cat?"

"It was the day after Christmas, and my resolve faltered." I sighed. "And now they've claimed the entire rec room as their own personal living space."

"It sounds like they've got it pretty sweet," agreed my friend. She shrugged good-naturedly. "And it could be worse." Her eyes twinkled. "By now they could have taken over your entire house."

I laughed. "I suppose you're right. I suppose I'm lucky they let me live with them."

"Darn straight!" she replied, enthusiastically striking the table with her now-empty coffee cup. "That's exactly how I feel about my seven."

"You have seven cats?" I asked incredulously.

"Yes, and if I had known when I got the first one that I'd end up with seven diverse little feline personalities, I'd have started right off naming them after the seven dwarves." She laughed, paused, then asked, "So what are your two named?"

"Well, they're both shorthaired orange tabbies, so they're kind of chipmunk-colored with striped tails," I began. "When I brought the first one home, I named him Alvin, and number two became Simon."

"No Theodore?"

"No Theodore," I replied, adamantly shaking my head. "Nope. Not in this lifetime!"

She howled in mirth. "Wanna bet?"

No, I didn't want to bet. But this year I've decided to mail my annual donation to the Humane Society and not stop by for a visit. I'm not about to take any chances.

~Jan Bono

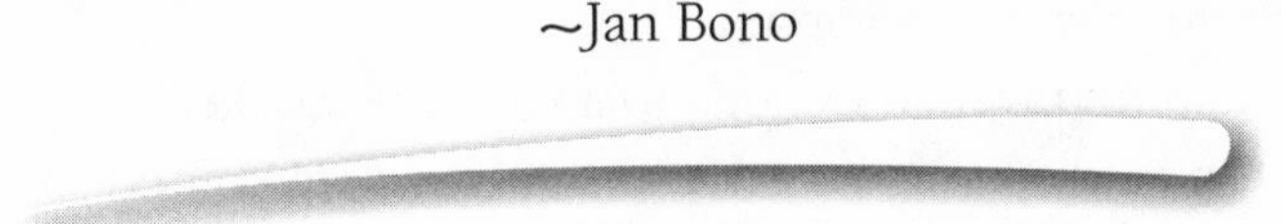

# The Boys Take a Vacation

*No man needs a vacation so much as the person who has just had one.*
*~Elbert Hubbard*

The smoke drove me to it. Southern Oregon summers are hot and parched, and when dry lightning arrives, one storm can produce over 1,000 strikes. Several will find their mark amid thirsty tinder, and our surrounding forests and wildlife suffer the ensuing fires. Though we weren't in harm's way, the wind fed us a choking supply of lingering particulates. The DEQ had declared our air hazardous for a couple of weeks when I'd had enough. I figured my boys felt the same. That's when I decided.

My boys are two extra-large male cats. Oliver is an eighteen-pound tabby with expressive, almost human, green eyes. He loves his vittles and a window seat. Cassidy is a gunmetal gray shorthair who can hold his own with Ollie despite a lame hind leg. His disability doesn't prevent him from galloping, leaping and sliding across the wood floor with exuberance. He flirts with me by slowly batting his eyes and purring. Cass wakes me from nightmares with one paw softly to my lips.

They had given me so much companionship; I wanted to repay them by taking them on a lark, a much needed change of pace.

"Do the boys want to go on a trip?" I asked them, not realizing it was the same tone of voice as "Do the boys want treats?" I took their eager faces for yes and began planning.

I wanted to travel far enough to escape the smoke, certainly, but with as little road time as possible since they weren't used to the car.

I decided Klamath Falls would be perfect, just a little over an hour away and with a nice inn, reasonably priced and pet-friendly. I naively made reservations for two nights.

"We're going to have a weekend of solid fun, boys!"

Cat translation: So, where are the treats she keeps talking about?

I enjoyed bagging up their bowls and things, and smiled as I remembered packing my daughter Emily's baby items so many years ago, a thought I wouldn't share aloud.

Each stout fellow had his own carrier. I tossed a favored toy inside and, after loading everything else into the car, gently but firmly shoved each reluctant traveler inside his cozy conveyance. That's when the duet began. Either they'd figured out how much fun we were going to have and those were exclamations of "Goody! Hooray, a change of pace!" or not. I spoke words of comfort.

"We're going to have fun, boys. Just relax and enjoy the ride."

After hoisting them into the back of my Civic coupe, no small feat, they continued in tandem. I offered up a prayer for help and drove away from our comfortable, smoke-shrouded home sweet home.

A particularly vicious string of yowls, punctuated with what came across as feline sailor talk, caused me to turn and look aghast at Oliver, who clenched the cage door with his teeth. I kept calm, turned the radio on low, and refrained from sticking my fingers through the bars to pat his head.

After about eight miles of pleas and threats from the back, they simmered down along with my blood pressure. There was only an occasional plaintive wail when Bob Dylan or Janis Joplin came on the radio. My boys weren't fond of harmonicas, apparently. They enjoyed the operatic tenor on the classical station. That's when I howled, but we compromised.

"Isn't this fun, guys?" I smiled big, but they were merely resigned.

When we arrived at The Cimarron Inn, the friendly clerk said, "Oh yes, you have the cats."

"Yes." I smiled at the others checking in who smiled back. People traveled with their dogs all the time, treating them more like children. Dogs were some folks' children! So, why not bring my cats? I would learn the answer.

At this point, I may have judged that publicly unloading the giant litter box was the worst of it. I carried our equipment into the comfortable and spacious room, setting the boys' carriers on their very own queen-sized bed. When I was a kid, my first response would have been to test the springs with a good jumping session. Not these boys. Cassidy commenced hyper-exploration while Oliver made a beeline for the darkest corner behind the bed. I thought only mice or gerbils could flatten their bodies like that, not a sumo-cat. I could feel his furry head with my fingertips and he wasn't coming out.

Cassidy seemed delighted to discover all the amenities of home. He kept making the circuit, visiting each station: food bowl, water, and litter box, if only to paw up dust. He seemed satisfied that the world was as it should be, but kept making sure.

I worried that Oliver crouched, psychotic and staring, behind the bed until I heard snoring from his cave.

I made myself at home on the bed, demonstrating what relaxation looked like. Cassidy would flit back to me, lie down briefly, and then take off on another tour of the accommodations.

I got up, grabbed my ham sandwich from the mini fridge, and waved it at the entrance to Oliver's lair but he didn't budge. I ignored him until curiosity won out. Out he stalked, low and slow, on high alert. Whenever anyone walked by the door, jingled their keys or sighed too heavily he ducked for cover.

Nighttime came, and I thought the mood had mellowed and we were all feeling darned cozy. I had my book, TV, and popcorn. I was set for a weekend of low-key fun with the boys. When both cats joined me on the bed, I breathed a sigh of relief, confident that my plan was a good one after all. Nope. Not as far as my two insomniacs were concerned.

Cassidy hopped off and on the bed about eighty-two times during the night with Oliver right behind—their heads jerking when a neighbor yawned or flushed. They finally fell asleep, at 6 a.m. I did not. Refreshed, cat-free people began slamming trunk lids and sliding van doors just outside, causing my head to jerk. Meanwhile, Ollie resumed his snoring. My neighbor must have thought that it was me. Would it have been any less humiliating to explain that it was, in fact, my cat?

So, I hauled myself out of bed not caring if I woke the sleeping giants. I headed for the free breakfast and many cups of coffee.

I could have kissed the desk clerk when he said calmly, "Of course you can cancel the second night. Just be checked out by noon."

"No problem," I said through watery eyes. "The cats didn't have a very good time and I didn't..." That was nutty cat lady talk right there. I stopped the flow.

I checked for other humans before hoisting the litter box outside and into the trunk. With the three of us situated, I pointed the Civic toward home.

I think I read Cassidy's meows as, "Why did we do that, again?" I didn't have a good answer so I turned the radio to the operatic channel and kept my mouth shut.

I was disappointed that it hadn't been the cozy family trip I'd envisioned, but at least I learned something; cats don't like vacations.

~Peggy Dover

# At Your Service, Miss DeCarlo

*The way to get on with a cat is to treat it as an equal—*
*or even better, as the superior it knows itself to be.*
*~Elizabeth Peters*

Where felines are concerned, I have two long-held policies: 1. One cat at a time. 2. Male cats make the best house pets. Don't get me wrong; I love all animals. I support the movement to save the whales and would rather carry a stray ant out of the house than flatten it with the sole of my shoe. It's just that in my experience male cats have made the best companions. So how is it, then, that I share my home with a little girl now?

Well, a few weeks after my husband Bill and I experienced the loss of our sixteen-year-old cat Chuck, we set out to our local animal shelter in search of a new pet. We had every intention of selecting a rough-and-tumble male, the type of cat who is just a regular guy. Yet the day's offerings revealed themselves to be a bit more rough-and-tumble than we would have liked. While Dennis flung himself from the floor to the rafters in feline fits and starts, Eugene howled non-stop. Harvey had a scared female cornered behind a litter box while sporting a creepy leer, and when my husband stooped down to pet Stefan, he leapt at him and sunk all four claws into his arm.

"We find our cats calm down considerably after they get into their 'forever homes,'" Kathy, the shelter adoption coordinator, explained as she extricated Stefan from Bill's bloody limb.

Bill and I looked at each other and headed for the door.

"They're all great cats," I said, lying through my teeth, "but I'm just not feeling any of them."

"Me either," Bill added, rubbing his forearm. "I think we'll come back another day."

Then, as we moved forward, I spotted her—a delicate, long-legged white cat with a black mask and black tail sitting serenely at one of the windowsills. She was so different; the most girly cat I had ever seen. So girly, in fact, the thin outline of black fur around her mouth made it appear as though she were wearing lipstick. Oh, this cat was something special, all right—and I had to have her.

"Wait," I called to Bill. "What about this cat?"

He nodded and walked over to where I stood holding her.

"That's Marlo," said Kathy in a dubious voice, "but she's a female."

Indeed she was. Soft and warm, I cuddled her head close to mine. I took in the scent of her. I swear she actually smelled as though she'd been daubed with perfume.

A few days later, after our references were checked and our new cat was given a clean bill of health from the shelter vet, Marlo entered our home. Out of the carrier she came, one cautious step at a time. First, she sniffed at a wicker chair and shook her head. Then she tested the cat perch stationed at the front window and squinted her eyes. Next, she walked toward the kitchen. She held one paw above the linoleum floor and placed it back down on the carpet as though such a material was meant only for the feet of the lower masses. Marlo looked at me disdainfully. Clearly, she would not be taking her meals in that room.

Bill raised his eyebrows. "What a diva."

As if on cue, our little diva returned to the dining room and took residence atop one of the upholstered chairs as if to say, "This will do for now."

That evening, Bill and I went about Marlo-izing our home. We laid a soft towel on the cat perch and placed three litter boxes strategically around the house with the intention of allowing our new pet to select her favorite location. Then we set a plastic placemat down next to the dining room table with two bowls, one each for food and water. Marlo checked the setup, turned her head and yawned. I held the food bowl up to her nose. She grimaced and slid to another chair.

It seemed as though nothing we provided for this cat could meet her lofty standards. The food we served her, they way we petted her, even the collar we had chosen on her behalf—pink leather with multi-colored rhinestones—all seemed to displease her. Truly, this cat raised the term "diva" to a whole new level.

From deep within the recesses of my imagination, I imagined her backstory. My cat, Miss Marlo DeCarlo, had once been a famous Broadway star. After becoming a feline of advanced age, parts started to dwindle until the offerings finally dried up altogether. Unwilling to relinquish the opulent lifestyle to which she had become accustomed, she spent her savings hastily. She was then forced into bankruptcy, evicted from her Park Avenue apartment and found herself, the once famous and adored Miss Marlo DeCarlo, on the street. There she remained until Animal Control found her wandering aimlessly one cold, rainy night, wearing nothing but her fur coat. To her horror, she was rudely captured and brought to live with a sorry collection of common strays and alley cats.

Suddenly, I saw Marlo in a new light. "Miss DeCarlo," I called, as I offered her some cat food, "you must eat. You must once again become voluptuous for your adoring fans and your return to the Broadway stage." She ate what I gave her and meowed for seconds.

From there, I grabbed a pillow and placed it atop her cat perch. "Miss DeCarlo," I said again, "your cushion is ready." She sashayed across the floor and hopped onto the perch.

It seemed as though I was on to something. "Good girl," I said as I scratched behind her ears. She nipped my hand. "Oh, would Miss DeCarlo prefer a back massage?" I asked. She purred and I petted her back in long, smooth strokes until she fell into a sound sleep.

Since then, Bill and I and the famous Miss Marlo DeCarlo have entered into an understanding. She is the star and we are her adoring servants. We are expected to change each one of her three litter boxes after every use and she has indicated she prefers them to be outfitted with vanilla-scented litter box liners. Dinner is brought to her in the dining room on a tray and water is drunk only from her "goblet," a delicately patterned ceramic bowl located on the porch under the shade of a majestic silk ivy plant. When she saunters into the living room and sings in her high soprano, we know she expects cat treats to be hand-fed to her one at a time. And, most recently, our pet has taken to answering only to her more sonorous nickname, Marletta. She is a diva of the highest order. And she is fabulous.

Do I still think male cats make better companions than female cats? Well, maybe. Bill and I continue to lean toward adopting a male next time the occasion arises. Yet, we're hoping that won't be for a long, long time. For right now we're having too much fun being entertained by our star, Miss Marlo DeCarlo.

~Monica A. Andermann

# When You're Not the Favorite...

*For a man to truly understand rejection, he must first be ignored by a cat.*
*~Author Unknown*

My husband Gabe, our daughter Melissa, and I are all sitting around watching TV when Princess, our seven-year-old gray tabby cat, marches into the room. Princess immediately makes a beeline over to my husband and jumps onto the couch. Then she proceeds to march onto his stomach and lie across his chest. My husband, the "chosen one," talks to Princess as he scratches behind her ears.

"Did-oo scratch-oo head?" he coos.

I'm okay with it. I mean, Gabe has always been Princess's favorite. Not me. I can deal with it. Really.

Then Coco-Puff, our five-year-old tortoiseshell, wanders into the room. I quickly pull the thick quilt around me in case Coco-Puff jumps up, so her claws won't dig into my bare legs.

"Coco-Puff! Coco-Puff!" I say, patting the quilt invitingly.

Coco-Puff ignores me. Instead, she looks at my daughter Melissa and meows.

I know what that meow means. It means Coco-Puff is announcing her intention to jump into my daughter's lap.

"Oh no!" Melissa groans. "Coco-Puff wants to sit with me again, and I'm trying to play my DS and it's so annoying!"

"Yeah," I say, trying to sympathize.

Then Coco-Puff jumps into Melissa's lap and proceeds to knead and nuzzle. She even pretends to drink milk out of my daughter's arm, like a kitten.

I observe their bonding, convincing myself I'm not jealous. After all, being jealous is petty and I'm a mom. Moms aren't allowed to be petty.

I calmly listen to the sounds of super loud purring and silly cat talk going on. Suddenly, I feel so… catless. I also feel sort of silly, sitting here with this big quilt over me, expecting a cat that never came.

It wasn't always this way. We used to have a cat named Cherry. I was Cherry's favorite. And when I say favorite, I mean that cat was crazy about me! We had such a bond, that cat and I.

We would have long conversations (okay, so I did most of the talking) and gaze soulfully into each other's eyes. Whenever our family walked through the door and I was last in line, Cherry would always look for me with a worried expression (my husband reported). Then, once she saw me, her eyes would light up and she would be happy again.

It's not that Princess and Coco-Puff don't like me. Of course they do. After all, I'm the one who feeds them, refills their water bowl, and rubs catnip into toys for them during the day when no one else is around. I talk "cat talk" to them, pet them, and turn on the bathroom sink for them.

Plus, I clean out the litter boxes. I don't know if they appreciate that, but they should.

So yes, they like me well enough. Coco-Puff, in particular, will jump on my lap and cuddle and nuzzle and purr… when my daughter isn't around, that is.

I try to convince myself that second best is good enough. Yet, let's be honest. It's always a bit of an ego boost to be "first best."

Sometimes I'll get really into a bout of string wiggling with Coco-Puff or slip some deli turkey to Princess, thinking Ah-ha! Who's your favorite now?

But then my daughter or husband will walk into the room, and

BOOM! Fast as you can say, "Hasta la vista, baby," the cats and I part ways.

I guess I just have to accept it. The Cherry Days are gone. I'm no longer a favorite—no matter what exciting activities or secret treats I provide. It's sort of frustrating, but there's nothing I can do about it.

The cats have chosen.

Maybe I'm just trying too hard. Kind of like with people. When you come on too strong, you just scare them off. They smell the desperation.

So the other day, I conducted an experiment. I sat on the couch while Coco-Puff was on my daughter's lap. I was cool, nonchalant. I pretended I didn't care. I ignored them. I casually flipped through a magazine.

Cat? What cat? I don't see any cat.

I did not put the Coco-Puff quilt over me. Then I sneaked the quilt over my legs, as though I suddenly caught a chill (despite the fact we're in the midst of a heat wave).

Well, wonder of wonders… it worked! Next thing I knew, Coco-Puff was off my daughter's lap and marching onto mine. Amazing… reverse psychology in action.

"She only did that because of the quilt, you know!" Melissa pointed out.

"Don't be jealous!" I admonished. "It's so petty."

Two seconds later, Coco-Puff was off my lap and back onto my daughter's lap. Oh well. It was worth a shot.

Of course, my husband is still Princess's favorite, and always will be. For some reason, that cat just prefers men.

Sometimes we understand why a cat picks a favorite. But other times, it's a total mystery. Maybe it's the same reason certain people are drawn to each other. It's just a chemistry thing, often elusive and difficult to understand.

So, as I sit many nights on the couch, catless, with that dumb quilt over me even though it's 90 degrees out, I take comfort in my memory of Cherry—the cat who "chose me." I tell myself it's okay I'm no longer a favorite. A close second is good enough.

Besides, I am the favorite during the day, when no one else is around. I console myself with these thoughts as I sit there sweating under that thick quilt.

Although, we could always get a third cat, so I'll have someone to sit with at night too…

~Nanci Merczel

# Zorro and Rocky

*No one ever really dies as long as they took the time to leave us with fond memories.*
*~Chris Sorensen*

Our Ragdoll cat, Zorro, was just the sweetest, most laid-back kind of guy you would ever want to have snuggle with you or lick your hand. Sadly, he's gone now. He passed quietly one night from a common feline heart condition called feline hypertrophic cardiomyopathy, often referred to as "the silent killer."

My husband and I were devastated. Zorro was only eight years old, and he showed no signs that he was ill. It took a while before I could even talk about him. But now our memories of Zorro are comforting.

One story that always makes me smile happened when we moved to our condo situated on a hill above a Nevada desert golf course. During the early days in our new home, we were pleasantly surprised at the different types of wildlife that passed by our patio, clearly visible from our French doors. To our delight, a roadrunner, which we named Rocky, had already staked out our patio as part of his territory.

I met Rocky for the first time one morning as he pecked a greeting on one of our French doors. There's nothing like a friendly knock to say, "Welcome to the neighborhood." I was fascinated by this primitive, scary-looking bird who appeared to have no fear of me. When I went over to the glass to get a closer look at him, he cocked his head and mimicked the same once-over that I was giving him.

I called Zorro, curious to see how he would react. He arrived with urgency, claws clattering on the tile floor. Unfortunately, he misjudged his ability to stop on the slippery surface and slid, with an embarrassing thud, into the glass door. His smoky gray tail waved furiously after he righted himself and began to pace in front of the doors.

The adversaries were face to face now and both appeared uncertain. Rocky's body language and black, beady eyes seemed to shout, "Who are you and what are you doing in my territory?" I witnessed a stare down of epic proportions and tried not to laugh.

Being a smart guy, and not quite confident about the situation, Zorro did what any cat would do. He cocked his head at me with a look that asked, "What IS that thing?"

Much to my surprise, Zorro suddenly threw himself against the glass and began to pound on it with his paws. Rocky reciprocated by jumping back at Zorro on the other side. Their curiosity had turned into a boxing match!

Eventually, Rocky tired of the game that offered him no satisfaction and got back to the business of looking for his favorite breakfast—lizards. From his command post on top of our patio table, he scanned the landscape and every once in a while looked back at the glass door where Zorro held his ground. When Rocky eventually zoomed away in typical roadrunner style, Zorro began to rub against my legs as if to say, "You're safe now, Mom." He had, after all, protected our turf.

As the weeks wore on, Rocky would make an appearance several times a week. He would usually peck on the door to announce his arrival and Zorro would charge to greet him. After a while they figured out that shadow boxing against the glass wasn't much fun. So they would just sit there and stare at each other before Rocky moved on to the serious business of lizard hunting.

Our female Ragdoll Zoe grieved as we did when Zorro died. She's much better now and ready for a new feline buddy. As luck would have it, we walked into our vet's office and were greeted by a sleek, black shorthaired fellow looking for love and a home. Although he already had a name, we weren't crazy about it. My husband suggested the perfect alternative—"Rocky," of course.

~Diane Quinn

# The Cat Did What?

## Meant to Be

# The Thousand-Dollar Cat

*People who love cats have some of the biggest hearts around.*
*~Susan Easterly*

The black kitten appeared out of nowhere on Halloween afternoon, only hours after we laid our sixteen-year-old dog to rest beside the old farm pond. I didn't want the scraggly fur ball to stay because getting attached to another animal was simply out of the question. I fed her and hoped she'd find her way back to wherever she came from.

I noticed her watery eyes and the slight nasal wheezing noise as she gobbled down the kibble. Afterwards she sat on the porch near the front door washing her face and watching my every move, making no effort to leave. The evening grew chilly, so I decided she could stay inside overnight in the guest bathroom since she appeared to have caught a cold. I did not want her to come in contact with my other two house cats, Levi and Baby Bee, in case she was contagious. I called her Elvira because a black cat appearing on Halloween should have that name.

Next morning, I opened the bathroom door only to be greeted by a throaty meow and crusty eyes. I made phone calls to neighbors to see if any claimed her. No one owned up to it so I loaded Elvira into the carrier and took her to the vet. One hundred dollars later she sat comfortably in that same guest bathroom munching her kibble and purring. For ten days I would give her an antibiotic twice a day.

"Okay, Elvira, when you get better you must go live with the barn cats. I already have two felines in this house," I told her as I closed the door for the night. However, as I was about to learn, she had different ideas.

Ten days later her eyes were clear, but she still wheezed. Another $100 trip to the vet netted more antibiotics and another two weeks of inside care. By the time those days ended, Elvira had already escaped the confines of the bathroom and made friends with Levi and Baby Bee. The three of them romped through the house like racehorses, but Elvira's wheezing persisted.

A third trip to the vet brought more tests. This time a chest X-ray revealed chronic bronchitis. The vet wanted to try a different antibiotic. That trip cost $150, bringing my total investment to $350 for a cat I did not ask for, not to mention another ten days of required bed rest.

Bed rest? Did that include trips up the curtains, or hiding underneath the bed and swatting my toes when I got too close? Did it include trying to catch birds through the kitchen window as they ate at the feeder outside? Did it include using the house as a racetrack and a tumbling mat as she and the other two chased and attacked each other? None of that fit my definition of bed rest. The only thing that even closely resembled it had something to do with Elvira taking over Baby Bee's favorite bed in the corner chair of the den.

The third round of antibiotics seemed to do the trick. She was wheeze-free for a week after the medicine ran out, so the coast was clear for me to put her outside. But first I wanted to have her spayed. I didn't want any more mouths to feed in case Elvira decided to hang out indefinitely with the barn cats. Another trip to the vet added an additional $125 to my ever-growing Elvira tally, which now amounted to $475 not counting food and flea and tick treatments. The spaying also brought another week of indoor living to the already spoiled-rotten cat.

Finally I was able to say to her, "Okay, Elvira, I think it's time for you to make your way down to the barn. You can bunk on the top hay bales along with the other outside cats."

As I reached down to pick her up for the trip to the barn, she sneezed. And then she sneezed again. She sat perfectly still and looked me in the eye, then sneezed a third time. If she could have talked, I'm sure she would have said, "Okay, I'll go to the barn, but this cough of mine could get worse out in that dusty hayloft."

"All right, Elvira, one more day inside, but only one. Do you understand?"

She gave me her famous look of contempt and sauntered off to the bedroom, where she immediately attacked the curtains and knocked over an antique lamp.

Next morning her sneezing spasms grew more frequent, only this time green mucus came from her nose. Another trip to the vet brought news that she needed to stay overnight because she had a fever and her chest was tight with infection. She also needed fluids. I left her there.

That evening Baby Bee and Levi walked in circles looking for Elvira. They checked their favorite playground underneath the skirt of the armchair. They checked under every bed and in all the closets for signs of their playmate. They eyed me suspiciously as though I had done something with their little buddy. My heart sank. Had we all become hopelessly attached to evil little Elvira, the demon she-cat who dominated the house with her fearlessness? I had to admit the house was too quiet without her chasing people on the TV screen and climbing to the top of the ficus tree in the corner of the den. Even the birds at the feeder outside the kitchen window didn't appear happy now that they had no one to taunt through the glass.

A call from the vet the next day brought grim news. Elvira had advanced pneumonia. She was seriously ill and needed to remain isolated at the vet's office. I had to choose whether I wanted to pay for her hospital stay and treatments or euthanize her. The vet could not guarantee she would pull through.

What kind of choice was that? The little heathen cat had somehow stolen my heart when I wasn't looking. I looked down and saw her catnip mouse, the one she carried in her mouth like a security blanket. Tears welled in my eyes as I realized at that moment just how much

I loved her. Without hesitation, I told the vet to do what he could to save her. As I hung up the phone, it seemed that Levi and Baby Bee knew exactly what I had done. Within minutes the sounds of them running and chasing each other filled the house as though they were trying to keep in shape until Elvira returned.

Two weeks and $525 later Elvira came home, ready to do battle with the opposing forces. As I write this story she is in the chair with me, or rather I am in HER chair. There is no danger whatsoever of Elvira ever being relegated to the barn unless, of course, I make a bedroom down there for myself. My thousand-dollar cat has become priceless to me.

~Carol Huff

# A Humble Hero

*Cats conspire to keep us at arm's length.*
*~Frank Perkins*

Everyone agreed; Kiki was strange. He acted strange and he looked strange. Even from the get-go, the little tabby born in our home to a stray who sought shelter looked more like a fuzzy orange caterpillar than a newborn kitten.

The only birth resulting from that pregnancy, our strange Kiki preferred the company of his mother to that of his human family. In fact, mother and son were inseparable. The two were a comical sight really; Kiki mimicked the older cat's every move, eating when she ate, sleeping when she slept, and playing when she played. So, that winter my family resigned ourselves to the fact that fate had made us a four-person, two-cat family.

However, warm weather arrived early that year, bringing with it a case of spring fever for the mother-cat who we named Elsa. The warmer the temperature and the brighter the sunshine, the greater were Elsa's attempts to reunite with the freedom of the outdoors. Though we tried in earnest to sequester her, Elsa managed to escape one day, leaving just as abruptly as she had arrived.

Kiki was devastated. For days the kitten sat by the back door awaiting his mother's return and there he remained, hopeful, forgoing all other activities. We, his human family, tried our best to step in and take the place of his mother. However, Kiki would accept no substitute. He was heartbroken.

In due time though, Kiki ended his vigil, seeking refuge in the one place where he felt safe without his partner—under our living room sofa. From there, he would survey the comings and goings of the family and indulge us an occasional reach underneath the furniture to pet the top of his head. Day after day, Kiki remained in his spot, leaving only when there was no human in sight, coming out just long enough to visit his food bowl in the kitchen or take care of his more personal business in the litter box. Afterward, our kitty would quickly scamper back to his lair where he remained until nature called once again.

That's why it seemed so odd to me one summer afternoon when I heard Kiki tapping insistently on the back window as I sat outdoors sunbathing. He even meowed a few times when I turned away from him, something he was rarely wont to do. Yet, I had my own agenda that day. Dad was at work, my brother was at summer camp, and Mom was at the supermarket. For a few precious hours the house was all mine, and my teenaged plan of suntanning while munching on a bowl of freshly popped popcorn was being rudely interrupted by one annoying tabby. Still, this behavior was so out of character for our pet that after a few minutes of his insistent pawing, I put down my snack to see what was bothering him.

As the screen door slammed behind me, I heard Kiki jump off the windowsill and hit the floor. His toenails clicked against the linoleum and I followed the sound to where he stood in the kitchen—directly in front of the stove. There, perched on his hind feet with his front paws leaning upon the cabinetry, Kiki pointed out the problem.

Before the popularity of microwave ovens, popcorn was made the old-fashioned way—in a pot on the stovetop. I thought I did what I always did when I popped corn: empty the contents of the pot into my favorite bowl, place the hot pot on a trivet to cool, and shut off the heating element. But I hadn't. In my haste, I'd left the empty pot on the stove with the element still turned on. The coil had turned a fiery orange-red as cooking oil smoldered inside the pot. Another moment, perhaps, and the remaining grease might have caught fire.

Quickly, I moved the pot away and shut off the unit. "Kiki," I said as I turned to him, "you saved the day." Yet, with his mission accomplished, Kiki had already returned to his post underneath the sofa. I followed him to his special place then reached down to pet him, but after a few moments he backed away, not interested in my accolades—a humble hero indeed. However, Kiki's heroics were never forgotten and from that time forward whenever Kiki returned to his food dish in the kitchen, he always found an extra treat left for him there.

~Monica A. Andermann

# The Greatest Gift

*It isn't the size of the gift that matters, but the size of the heart that gives it.*
*~Eileen Elias Freeman,* The Angels' Little Instruction Book

Anybody who's ever had an outdoor cat is probably familiar with the concept of "gifts." I don't mean the kind of gifts that come in sparkly packages. I mean the "Ew, there's a dead thing on my porch!" kind of gifts. No matter how well fed an outdoor cat is, chances are he'll still enjoy the occasional hunt... and he'll want to share the spoils with his family.

As a nature lover, it was never easy for me to find a limp field mouse or a wounded bird on my doorstep, but I accepted these moments as part of country life. If I wanted to feed the neighborhood strays, I'd have to put up with their good-natured attempts to repay me.

I dealt with the "gifts" as best I could, giving swift burials to the dead and medical care to the injured. Over the years, my parents and I had some interesting patients: blue-tailed lizards, star-nosed moles, even a crayfish. I didn't think I could be surprised anymore by what might be waiting outside our door.

I have to admit, though, that I was scratching my head the first time I found a stick on the porch. The twig was about four inches long. It hadn't come from a pine—the only kind of tree near our house—but I figured it must have blown in from somewhere. I tossed the stick away and forgot all about it... until I found another one a few days later.

The second stick was short, like the first—and again, definitely not from a pine. Over the next few weeks, the mystery deepened. More and more sticks appeared. Some were short and stubby; others were long and bowed. Some had bark, some didn't. And oddly enough, they were all lying parallel to the door. Like they had been placed there. Deliberately.

Frankly, I was getting a little freaked out. Strange possibilities flooded my mind—everything from cryptic alien messages to a really ambitious ant colony. But even my wildest imaginings couldn't prepare me for what I saw one afternoon on my way to the barn.

I was halfway down the driveway when I heard the distinctive, eager mewing that cats often make when they've caught a small animal. I started to run, hoping it wasn't too late to save the poor creature. But as I rounded the corner, my eyebrows shot up: our fuzzy orange barn cat, Panic, was trotting down the lane, and he was indeed carrying something—but it wasn't a mouse, or even a lizard.

The object in his mouth was, unmistakably, a stick.

"You!" I said. "You're the one who keeps leaving those!"

Panic dropped the stick and rubbed against my legs. I shook my head and scratched his chin, my eyes never leaving the stick.

In hindsight, I probably shouldn't have been so surprised—after all, Panic had never exactly been a "normal" cat. He even looked different than other cats, with his bowed legs, unusual sea-green eyes, and a face that was more Ewok than feline.

Another thing that set Panic apart was his behavior. For starters, he wasn't afraid of dogs. Or lawnmowers. Or even cars. The one thing he was afraid of: mice. Once, I actually saw him jump back in terror as a small field mouse approached him.

As far as other cats went, Panic loved them and the feeling was mutual. Aggressive tomcats didn't even blink when Panic wandered onto their territory. Kittens joyfully followed Panic around like he was their mother. Even our oldest and crankiest cat, Molly, could frequently be seen snoozing peacefully beside Panic.

There was just something utterly benign about him; even tiny mice seemed to know he would never harm them. Maybe, on some level, Panic realized this too. Maybe he knew he just wasn't cut out to hunt live prey. Maybe that's why he started bringing sticks.

All I know is that once he got the idea in his head, he never gave it up. He was shy, at first. If anyone caught him carrying a stick, he would immediately drop it. The earliest photos I took were blurry, because I had to jump out from behind trees to catch him off guard. As time passed, though, Panic grew bolder. Eventually, he proudly deposited sticks right at my feet, as if to say, "Here—I caught this for you!"

When he was hunting, Panic's head would turn right and left, his green eyes scanning intently for that one special stick. At times, the search could take over thirty minutes. Once he'd "captured" the perfect prize, he'd hold his head high and swagger back home.

In summer, Panic would bring us as many as ten sticks a day. Sometimes, he'd carry two or even three sticks in his mouth at once. When the weather turned icy, the hunting would stop for a while. But as soon as the snow melted, he'd be at it again, showering us with a Dr. Seuss-worthy variety of big sticks, little sticks, soft sticks, brittle sticks.

Eventually, I stopped photographing them because there were just too many. Dad started grumbling about having to pick up sticks every time he mowed the lawn, and Mom stopped exclaiming whenever she spotted Panic carrying a ridiculously enormous branch. We all learned to casually sidestep the numerous twigs littering the walkway.

Then, one evening, I saw a car stopped on the road, right near Panic's favorite hunting spot. My heart froze for just a moment—then I caught sight of him, healthy and unharmed, trotting along with his latest treasure. A woman was leaning out the car window, snapping a photo of him. As I heard her exclaiming over my cat, realization stung me like a smack to the cheek: Panic was special—truly one-of-a-kind—and lately I'd been taking him for granted.

That night, I scooped Panic up and scratched his chin.

"She probably put you on Facebook," I told him.

Panic's throat rumbled.

The next day, I started taking pictures again. I even managed to record one of Panic's hilarious "hunts" on video. I mowed lawns to earn money for his vaccines, and always gave him an extra snuggle at feeding time, just because.

When Panic didn't show up for dinner one night, I assumed he'd wandered off to cuddle with one of his many friends. It was Mom who made the terrible discovery the next morning: our fuzzy orange cat with bowed legs, lying stiffly by the roadside.

I felt like I'd been stabbed. Tears half-blinded me as I walked out to the road and gently lifted his body off the rough gravel. I dug the grave under a tree, where I knew many sticks would fall. And even as the ache tore right through me, stealing my breath as I tried to choose some of Panic's favorite twigs to place on the mound, I couldn't help but feel grateful too.

After all, there was only one "stick cat" in the whole world. Just one. And I got to take care of him. I got to be with him every single day—playing with him, scratching his chin, laughing at his silliness.

And that was the greatest gift of all.

~Gretchen Bassier

# The Hero Cat

*I have studied many philosophers and many cats.*
*The wisdom of cats is infinitely superior.*
*~Hippolyte Taine*

She showed up one day on our front porch. "Don't touch her, Joshua," I warned. "She might be sick. She probably has fleas." This skinny, beat-up, stray cat found her way to us.

Well, to my six-year-old son Joshua at least. I should have known that moment it was too late. Joshua thought she was beautiful. He fell in love with her and started sneaking her food. Truth be known, I kind of liked her and felt sorry for her too. I encouraged Joshua to feed her until we figured out where she belonged.

Josh was sure that she was a boy and named her Gary. Mostly because he wanted a boy cat not a girl cat. The rest of the family thought this was a good name and it stuck. Well, Gary progressed from sleeping on the porch to the entryway, and then to the living room, kitchen and the rest of the house. She grew and her fur filled in as she regained her health. Gary became friends rather quickly with our dog Patch, a little Jack Russell Terrier. Patch was the kind of dog that everybody loved. She had been with us for years and we considered her a full-fledged family member. The two of them would chase each other around the house, share food, and nap in the sun in the back yard.

I was cleaning the kitchen one morning as Gary slept in the hallway. My kids and Patch were playing in the front yard. Suddenly, there was a commotion outside—kids were screaming, dogs were barking and I ran toward the front door. Not believing what I was seeing, I couldn't move or make a sound. In through the open front door, at top speed, ran Patch with the neighbor's Pit Bull close behind. Out of nowhere came Gary. She stood up on her hind legs and emitted a gut-wrenching growl that I have never heard before or since from a cat. The terrified Pit Bull tried to stop and slid at least ten feet across the tile as he turned and fled through the door. Gary, not missing a beat, ran right behind him all the way to the neighbor's porch, growling and hissing.

The kids and I could not believe what we had just witnessed. Joshua grabbed Gary and hugged her. "Gary, you are so brave. You saved Patch's life!" We had a celebration dinner that night for Gary the "hero" cat.

Several years later Patch died. Our family was heartbroken. We buried her in our side yard and marked her grave with a memorial cross. That afternoon I was missing Patch and went to the side yard with my coffee. There was Gary, lying on the fresh grave, sleeping. She missed her friend too. I sat with her for a while and smiled as I remembered the time she had defended Patch, taking on a Pit Bull without a second thought. I am so thankful for the day that a skinny, beat-up, stray cat found her way to us.

~Lori Bryant

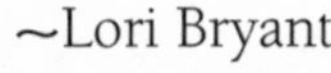

# Cats Are Excellent Dog Trainers

*The family is one of nature's masterpieces.*
*~George Santayana*

My three children, ages two, three and five, had just finished breakfast and made a run for outside when I heard them exclaiming over something on the front porch. When I went to investigate I was greeted with cries of, "Can we keep him? Please, please!" The "him" was a small, brown puppy about the size of a croquet ball that was shivering and crying in the corner of the porch.

Before I could make a judgment call, our mama cat Mits and her five kittens arrived on the scene. Mits examined the pup from one end to the other, looked back at me, and took the pup away with her kittens, who were approximately the same age. From then on Norton was part of her family.

We operated a bird-dog training kennel at that time and Norton was the only dog that was allowed to run loose in the yard. His constant companions were Mits and her kittens. One of the males, Oscar, became his particular buddy.

Mits took her maternal duties very seriously and decided Norton needed a lot of training to meet the standard she had set for her kittens. At that time she had the litter Norton's age and four almost grown kittens from a previous litter. When Norton was about three months old I noticed Mits and the kittens had formed a circle in the yard with Norton in the center. When I went to investigate I discovered he wasn't alone. There was a field rat in the circle also. As the rat would try to escape the cats would turn it back towards Norton. When he got the message and killed the rat, all of the cats got up and went on about their business. Lesson learned.

As they got older, Norton and Oscar spent more and more time together. We had a row of multiflora roses, a vine used to stop erosion in open fields, running across part of the pasture. Norton was sleeping on the porch when Oscar began to summon him loudly. I followed Norton as he headed for the barn. Oscar was waiting at the end of that row. As soon as Norton arrived they stood facing each other, noses just inches apart and apparently decided on their method of attack. They then got on opposite sides of the line of bushes and began systematically working the cover, hunting rats.

On cold days, a pile of cats would appear on the porch. If you looked closely, Norton would be at the bottom of the pile keeping their feet warm while they provided a warm place for him to sleep.

Over the eighteen years he lived, he never developed a friendship with another dog, but every cat we had considered him a very close relative. Over and over, especially when he was still a pup, I would see a cat correct him if he didn't follow correct cat procedure in a situation. Mits oversaw his training for the first three years, and as cats came and went, others imparted their knowledge.

I'm sure you've heard the old adage, "You can't train a cat," but Mits and her descendants proved a cat can do a very good job of training a pup.

~Charlotte Blood Smith

# Finding Crimson

*You can keep a dog; but it is the cat who keeps people, because cats find humans useful domestic animals.*
*~George Mikes*

In high school, my daughter was given a beautiful tortoiseshell kitten she named Crimson. Crimson liked both indoor and outdoor living and we loved spoiling her.

My daughter began college and Crim-Crim, as she called her cat, stayed with me. One day Crim-Crim went missing. I did everything but have her put on milk cartons trying to find her. Finally, I sadly figured she had taken off looking for my daughter.

Weeks later, driving down our road, I saw Crimson about six houses away from mine, lolling on her back on the sidewalk sunning herself. Two elderly sisters that lived there stood by watching Crim-Crim adoringly.

I stopped and stood at the end of the sidewalk calling "Crim-Crim!" She ignored me in that way that only cats can do. Finally, after I called her name repeatedly, she stopped wallowing and looked sideways at me.

The look was one only a cat can pull off. It said, "Who are you, and why are you calling me Crim-Crim?"

The sisters looked at me, each other, then the cat and back at me. "Oh, is this your cat?" Sister Number One asked me, verging on panic.

I reached to pick up Crimson. She growled at me and gave her best confused look followed by scratching.

"Yes, I was keeping her for my daughter away in school," I answered, trying to look natural while being mauled.

"Well, she is just the cutest thing!" gushed Sister Number Two. "We adore her! We didn't know she was anyone's cat."

Sister One chimed in. "Yes. We love her. She sprawls on our couch and beds. And, I hope it is okay we have been feeding her home-cooked fish and chicken. She practically devours it."

Sister Two jumped back in. "We didn't know she had a name. We just call her Sweetie Pie."

Sweetie Pie? Really?

The ladies swooned while extolling the uncountable virtues of this cat who was acting like I was trying to return her to a cage of starving wild dogs. My arms and hands cursed me for not putting Sweetie Pie down.

"We understand if you want her back, angel that she is," Sister One said rather sadly.

Sweetie Pie sprang from my arms and streaked for their house with a "won't somebody save me?" look on her face as she glanced back at me.

"Oh well, she seems to love you two so much. I would hate to yank Sweetie Pie from her happy home," I said, applying pressure to my brachial artery.

The sisters did a little jig and clapped their hands together. They practically hopped to their door to let Sweetie Pie in. It was probably time for her shrimp and caviar lunch.

~Linda Nicely Cheshire

# Christmas Kitty Miracle

*Cats can be cooperative when something feels good, which, to a cat, is the way everything is supposed to feel as much of the time as possible.*
*~Roger Caras*

When my husband Randy and I were newlyweds, we adopted a very precocious gray kitten from one of my coworkers. At the time, we were living in a rented duplex that really wasn't supposed to have pets, but I was young and every cat I'd ever had before had been very well behaved, so I figured this new one, who I named Dink, wouldn't be a problem.

I couldn't have been more wrong. Apparently, Dink felt she should have been an "outdoor" cat because she made it her mission to climb at every opportunity. She'd run up the door frame with all the grace of Michael Jordan making a jump shot, digging her claws in at the top for a couple of seconds before releasing, tumbling to the floor and running up again.

Doorframes weren't her only means of exercise. She also practiced her climbing on the curtains—which belonged to the landlord and were made from a weave that pricked very easily. I'd hear a scuffle in the bedroom and, upon investigation, find her perched on top of the curtain rod, calmly licking her paw. Then one day I heard a crash in the bedroom. I ran into the room to find the curtains in a pile on the floor and my precocious kitty across the room, sporting that "I-don't-know-what-caused-that-loud-noise-but-it-wasn't-me" look with which every cat owner is well acquainted.

But the absolute worst thing she would do was run up my back when I was cooking. I'd be standing at the stove, cooking away at some new recipe, when she'd take a running start and scamper up my back. Ouch.

The months went by, and Dink showed no sign of calming down. If anything, her energy increased as she grew. Finding the curtains on the floor of the bedroom became a daily occurrence. Christmas was just around the corner, and Randy and I debated whether or not to put up a tree. We knew we couldn't do a live tree because the temptation would be too great for our little climber. I couldn't imagine celebrating Christmas without a tree, so eventually we settled for an artificial tree with no tinsel and no ornaments or lights on the bottom branches. And there would be absolutely no ribbons on the presents to exacerbate her string fetish.

Once the tree was up, Dink surprised us by not trying to climb it. While she batted a little at the bottom branches, she became quickly bored with that occupation and settled for sitting under the tree and watching the lights twinkle on and off. She was content—and surprisingly—calm.

Christmas got closer, and as newlywed luck would have it, I came down with the nastiest stomach virus I'd ever had in my life. I dragged myself home from work, running a fever of 103 degrees and wishing the ground would just swallow me. The only thing I wanted to do was sleep, but unfortunately, it's hard to do that when your stomach feels like it's turning itself inside out. So I opted for pulling out the sleeper sofa in the living room and watching television while I waited for my husband to come home.

Dink had never seen the sofa bed opened up, so she jumped up to investigate. As it happened, the sofa bed opened up right next to the tree with all of its shiny ornaments and pretty baubles, and, in Dink's mind—cat toys—which were now at her eye level and in reach. She took one look at me, and determining that I was in no shape to do anything about it, proceeded to knock the ornaments off the tree—one by one.

I'm not exaggerating at all, that I was never before, nor have I ever been, as sick as I was that week I had the stomach flu—including the week I spent throwing up in the hospital because my doctor didn't realize I had an intolerance to morphine. I knew that the tree would be in shambles if I didn't stop the cat, but I didn't have the energy.

Finally, I decided to reason with her—a sure sign I had passed into some phase of fever-induced delirium, because no one in their right mind would try to reason with a cat.

"Dink," I began, "Mama's very sick. I know the ornaments look like a lot of fun to play with, but I just don't have the energy to deal with you playing with them right now."

Then my door-frame-climbing, curtain-destroying, back-shredding kitten did something that completely blew my fever-ridden mind. She took one look at me, then walked across the bed to the pillow next to mine, curled up, and went to sleep.

It was a Christmas miracle.

~Fran Veal

# Twinkie to the Rescue

*It is difficult to obtain the friendship of a cat. It is a philosophical animal… one that does not place its affections thoughtlessly.*
*~Theophile Gautier*

Although I was born in Oregon, my family spent five of my formative years in New York City where my father attended university. And every summer my folks, my older brother, John, and I packed up the car to return to Medford so that Dad could lumberjack with his brother, Sharkey.

During one of those summers, at Uncle Sharkey's Quarter Horse ranch, a half-grown barn kitten wound her way into our hearts and our easterly-traveling station wagon.

Twinkie was an aptly labeled tuxedo cat, sporting a brilliant black coat with white whiskers and markings under her chin and chest, punctuated with four white feet. Her personality and love of life matched her beauty.

She quickly took to the car, collar and leash and, long before the advent of seatbelts, lay between John and me as we slept in the back of the vehicle. My parents took turns driving, often through the night, and to this day I have warm memories of watching the stars out the window as Twinkie snuggled alongside and the aroma of thermos coffee filled the air.

Twinkie evolved into an apartment cat, and we shook our heads while she sat on the slightly ajar window, perusing the goings-on twenty-one stories below. And she was a daily source of laughter with her newly assumed role as a proficient clotheshorse gymnast.

Eventually my dad finished his education during a year in Berkeley, California, where my younger brother, David, was born. Then Dad was offered a position at the University of British Columbia in Vancouver and we once again packed up, but this time we were permanently Canada-bound. We lived in a series of different homes before we bought and settled in one within the beautiful Dunbar area. A large backyard served the young family, which included Twinkie.

I'd always been an animal lover and I assumed that each animal I encountered must reciprocate my feelings. So when I discovered that our neighbors regularly fed a feral cat, I was hurt that he wouldn't let me anywhere near him. The raggedy tom had all the hallmarks of a fighter with cauliflower ears and visible scars on his face and tail. But to a young girl, the marks simply made him more endearing. It meant he needed me.

One warm summer's day, the perfect opportunity presented itself. The tom was in our yard, pointing towards the neighbor's house, relieving himself. I knew that if I could just touch him, he'd realize that I was a friend and the bond would be instantaneous.

I tiptoed up behind, reached out, and stroked his back. If I'd not already understood the term, "All hell broke loose," I soon did! In one motion, the tom whirled and leapt onto my shorts-clad legs, digging in each claw, piercing and excavating shards of skin as he raked his back paws up and down, over and over. My small voice emitted a true primal scream.

And then, seemingly from out of the blue, charged my black and white knight in shining armour. Twinkie hit that tom with her own claws outstretched. Amidst the dreadful caterwauling that only two felines in battle can wail, the tom released his hold and made a beeline for the fence, with Twinkie an inch from his tail.

She stopped at the property line and trotted back to me, knowing that I was somewhat in shock. She waited until Mom, having heard the commotion, shepherded me into the house to address my wounds.

A couple of years later, Twinkie developed a tumour in her jaw.

There was no treatment and she was in pain with every movement. It's always difficult to have an animal euthanized. But when that animal is not only a family member and friend but a personal hero as well, the pain is multilayered.

As for the tom, he and I agreed to disagree and allow each other distance. Having since worked with feral cats, I completely understand his actions and reactions. No doubt, Twinkie was empathetic with his position, but she was not going to tolerate him hurting her girl.

More than forty-five years have passed, as have other much-cherished cats. Each has brought his or her own brand of love and joy. But no other has surmounted a challenge that put her life at risk, to protect me. In that, Twinkie, our endearing superstar cat, stands alone.

~Diane C. Nicholson

# Introducing a Second Cat

*One cat just leads to another.*
*~Ernest Hemingway*

I'm not sure what possessed me to get another cat. With three boys, a bouncy Golden Retriever, and the resident cat, Reuben, the house was full. But I decided Reuben needed a feline companion.

He'd become a completely indoor cat after the deaths of two neighbors' cats; one from poisoning and another from an unleashed dog. I didn't want Reuben's life to end like that. So I kept him inside and he sat at the patio door, staring out at freedom, telling me how unfair it was.

"Reuben wants a friend," I announced.

"I don't think he'll like another cat in the house," warned my brother-in-law, a veterinarian. "He's a dominant cat, and he won't want to share his territory. Besides, you can't afford another animal."

He was right. As a single mom, I was always stretching my paycheck to make ends meet. But somehow it worked, and I figured one more cat wouldn't cost that much.

And our household was evolving. My sons had entered the skulls and zombies era. Bizarre music came from their rooms. Black became the color of choice. I helped make the house creepier by leaving the summer plants in their pots long after frost arrived. I felt like Morticia

Addams as I passed the stiff, dead flower stalks and entered my somewhat Goth home. But it was missing something.

"Our house needs a black cat," I told my boys.

"Reuben won't like it," said my eldest.

"Sure he will," I insisted. "Reuben likes everybody."

"He used to hiss at the cats outside."

Actually, he used to get into scrapes with the neighbor's cat, but I ignored that and kept searching the SPCA adoption pages. There was one cat whose picture stayed up long after other black ones appeared and were adopted. For months she was on the page every time I checked. Finally I decided to go to the shelter—just to look, of course.

As soon as I said I was interested in a black cat, the staff person led me to an oversized cage in the cat section. A huge mass of black huddled in the back. Two yellow-green eyes stared at me from the darkness. "She's very sweet," said the young man, "and she has a wonderful purr."

I followed him to the shelter's visiting room and he set her down. She looked like an overstuffed sausage with four short sticks supporting her. She staggered slowly around the room, rolling from side to side on stiff legs. I'd never seen a cat move like that.

"Why is she so fat?"

"She's been in a cage for five months. She'll shape up as soon as she's out of here."

The cat lumbered over to me and pushed her face against my hand. Then she started purring. A long, loud trill. I was instantly captivated.

They had to give me a dog carrier to take her home because the cat crate was too small.

My sons were less than pleased when I arrived home. "She's gonna make Reuben spray again."

"No, she won't. He'll like her."

But I wasn't so sure when I saw our orange tabby stalk toward the dog carrier with huge, staring pupils and a bottle-brush tail. A loud hiss came from inside the crate.

"I'll just take her up to my room," I said. "We're supposed to keep them separated for a little while anyway."

A little while turned into over a month. Reuben camped outside my bedroom door, waiting for a chance to slip in and deal with the intruder. The new cat spent most of her time on my bed, not losing any weight. Occasionally she lowered herself down, landed on the floor with a loud thud, and watched with interest Reuben's paw, which appeared from underneath the bedroom door, swiping at her.

This was not the sleek, panther-like animal I had envisioned.

But she would lie by my shoulder at night, trilling me to sleep, and it was heavenly. When I woke up she was still there, waiting to greet me. The man at the shelter had been right; she was a very sweet cat.

I named her Belladonna after the deadly nightshade plant, an apt name for a black feline. And I was sure she and Reuben would eventually become friends.

After six weeks I put a child gate up in the doorway so they could see each other but still be separated. Reuben puffed up like an orange marshmallow and hissed. Bella retreated under my bed. A week later I decided they had to work it out. I removed the gate and she ventured downstairs.

The idea of Bella appearing on his turf had obviously never occurred to Reuben. As soon as he saw her, his eyes got huge, his fur fluffed out, and he chased her back upstairs under my bed.

I figured the exercise would help her with weight loss.

And it did eventually, but not until one corner of my mattress was in shreds from Reuben's claws.

To my amazement, Bella kept coming downstairs. Then one day I saw them sitting next to each other, looking out the window. Did Reuben realize she was there? I tiptoed past, afraid to disturb the miracle.

Reuben's tolerance grew. He allowed the usurper downstairs more often. And if she wasn't around, he'd search for her—acting as if he didn't care once he found her.

Now Bella comes down every day. Reuben still chases her when he's feeling cranky, and the corner of my mattress is still in shreds. But they eat side by side, sleep next to each other on the sofa, and stare out the patio door together.

And she still jumps on my bed at night, not panther-like, but a bit more gracefully than when she first arrived, and trills me to sleep. And it's heavenly.

~Joan Friday McKechnie

# Mondo's Miracle

*The power of love to change bodies is legendary, built into folklore, common sense, and everyday experience.... Throughout history, "tender loving care" has uniformly been recognized as a valuable element in healing.*

*~Larry Dossey*

Mondo had been severely beaten and abused. His face was covered with blistered, red skin instead of fur. His paw pads were thin and scarred with burns. Mondo was unrecognizable as the shorthaired, black cat he had once been. After being delivered to a local animal shelter by a concerned citizen, Mondo was out of luck again. The shelter could not provide the medical care he urgently needed. Instead, Mondo sat alone, shaking, facing the back corner of his cage with his head buried deep in his front legs. He jumped every time he heard footsteps approaching.

A shelter volunteer knew that Mondo needed help quickly. She used the power of social media to connect with hundreds of rescue organizations, hoping that one might have space and funding to help Mondo before it was too late. Her last e-mail plea was sent directly to me. Our rescue had helped special needs animals from their shelter in the past.

Although we did not have the funding, I had an open space in my home for a new foster feline. Working as an all-volunteer group with no paid staff, we hoped that the community would pull together once again to help with Mondo's mounting medical bills. And miraculously, they did. Mondo was out of the shelter, away from his abusers and living in his own private bedroom in my home while he recovered physically and emotionally.

Mondo's recovery didn't happen overnight. It took weeks for him to begin to trust me. I was thrilled the first time he purred. He was learning that the touch of a human could be gentle, the food and water in the bowls could be depended on, and the people who surrounded him were there to protect, not harm him. What a vastly different universe Mondo experienced as he eased into life in my home.

As Mondo purred and began to confidently raise his tail high, I opened the door to his private room and allowed him to meet my two dogs. He loved them instantly. I had feared that he would run and hide, but he trotted towards them and rubbed their muzzles with his wounded head, followed by flopping on the floor, paws in the air. He had certainly made an emotional recovery!

The veterinarian warned us that Mondo's physical wounds might never heal. Although we are never concerned about aesthetics, we worried about what chance he would have for adoption. Being a shorthaired black cat already gave Mondo the worst chance of being adopted due to the superstition about black cats. Add to that his scarred, red, furless face and he was facing tough odds. But at least he was safe. And after four months, Mondo began to grow hair again on his face. Soon he looked like a typical black cat and a family agreed to adopt him.

On adoption day, I shared Mondo's journey of rescue and rehabilitation with his adopter, Rita, and her family. They were shocked. Rita's eyes welled up as she looked at the photos of Mondo before he healed. She promised to love Mondo and provide him with a safe and caring home for the duration of his life. I had no doubt that Mondo was in good hands. As I turned to leave Rita's house that afternoon, I watched cheerfully as Mondo bounced from couch to couch like a small child on Christmas morning.

Mondo's journey is one of courage, trust and love. His story shows the impact that human kindness and compassion can have. We do indeed have the power to make miracles happen for these trusting, loving companions.

~Stacey Ritz

# Dreams Come True

*Some people come into our lives and quickly go. Some stay for a while, leave footprints on our hearts, and we are never, ever the same.*
~*Flavia Weedn*, Forever

Surprise was not the word for it when a beautiful longhaired black cat fixed her gimlet-green eyes on me, ran across the lawn, and demanded to be petted. Little did I know that she had even bigger plans in mind.

My husband, Prospero, and I had settled into our new home three months before. He had seen this pretty black cat and assumed she belonged to a neighbor because she was so perfectly groomed. Since that first encounter she hung out in our yard every day, even clinging to our bedroom window screen and meowing us awake each morning. We were careful not to feed her in fear that she wouldn't return home to her rightful owner.

This turned out to be a bit of a problem. You see, the weather was balmy and we had taken to eating our dinner on the terrace. When her meowing didn't get her a nibble, the cat simply caught a chipmunk and joined us.

"This is grossing me out," said Prospero.

"I know." The sight upset me too. "I can't handle it."

We agreed to discourage the cat from coming into our yard by shooing her away. Realizing that she was no longer welcome—most likely with her feelings hurt—the cat moved on to another location.

We felt bad, but were secure in the knowledge that it was for the best.

Weeks passed and we woke up one morning.

"I had a dream about the cat," said Prospero. "She was ours."

I simply stared at him and said, "You won't believe this, but I was just dreaming the exact same thing. It woke me up." Talk about synchronicity.

We walked into the kitchen and there was the black cat sitting right outside our glass door! After weeks of not seeing her, we both had the same dream and the cat showed up. There seemed to be a higher power at work.

Not being pet people, we agreed to feed the cat but declared she would continue to live outdoors. Toonsie—yes, we named her—seemed to like this arrangement and continued to leave us an assortment of chipmunks, squirrels, bunnies and birds as a thank-you present.

Summer came to a close and the chilly autumn nights made us realize that we had to come up with another game plan. Leaving Toonsie out in the cold was too cruel.

"She's coming inside, but she'll live in the basement!" said Prospero.

Ha! Toonsie came in the house and took over. Even the vet said that she had us very well trained. Before we knew it our lives revolved around the cat. We ran out to her favorite Japanese restaurant to get sashimi for her, because she refused to eat the supermarket variety. We stopped taking vacations, because we returned from a three-day trip only to find that she had stopped speaking to us. And as her fame grew—a Chicken Soup for the Soul story caught the attention of our local newspaper and they did a feature article on her—Toonsie became even more of a diva.

For two people who didn't want to take a cat into their home we never slept better than in those wee hours of the morning when Toonsie snuggled up between us.

Then one summer morning, as Prospero and I prepared to leave for a day at the Jersey Shore, Toonsie began wailing and crying. She stuck her nose in an electrical socket, which I took to be a shameless faux-suicide attempt in anticipation of being left alone indoors on a sunny day.

Prospero got down on his knees and stuck his nose in the outlet. "I need a screwdriver."

He unscrewed the switch plate and an arc of electricity sprung out. It was the beginning of an electrical fire. Toonsie not only saved our lives but inspired yet another Chicken Soup for the Soul story. Who knew we had adopted a literary lion?

With the passing of years, Toonsie gradually slowed down. Gone were the critter gifts and the mad escapes to prowl the neighborhood. We settled into a comfortable pattern of family life. Toonsie basked in being the pampered little princess of the house.

Toonsie had been with us thirteen years but since she was already a fully-grown cat when she arrived, we figured she was at least seventeen. We knew the end was near when her weight dwindled to a mere five pounds. But then one day we were sitting in the back yard when suddenly she dashed across the lawn, snagged a chipmunk and offered it to me. When I didn't take it, she devoured it in one sitting. Rather than being grossed out, I was thrilled that she ate.

For the next two weeks, Toonsie astounded us with several chipmunks a day but no longer ate them. The chipmunk gifts were—and always had been—her way of showing us how much she loved and appreciated us.

One afternoon an enormous black bird landed on the patio and snatched up the chipmunk that Toonsie had brought for me. A raven. Not good. Even I knew about that omen.

One Saturday morning Prospero woke up at five. "I just had a dream that Toonsie passed away." A quick check on her proved he was right.

Knowing it was her time still didn't ease our pain. A fluffy black kitty cat entered and exited our lives through dreams that came true, and we will never be the same.

Toonsie came into our lives to teach us how to love. Not the kind of love that Prospero and I already shared, but the nurturing and selfless kind of love that comes from caring for one of God's creatures. Even in our pain we realized that it was a magical experience for which we will be forever grateful.

~Lynn Maddalena Menna

# The Cat Did What?

## There's No Place Like Home

# I Came Home for This?

*The cat has nine lives: three for playing, three for straying, three for staying.*
*~English Proverb*

We had done it a million times before—leaving the front door open for just a second. But she usually didn't care. We would run in to grab "one more thing," and then scoot out the door, firmly locking it behind us. And she really didn't care. Sure, she might come and investigate, but she had food, water, a comfy blankie—she had it made on the "inside." What was so much better for her outside?

But then, one day, the unthinkable happened.

She got out.

Sam, our indoor-only, seven-year-old, collarless kitty, was gone—like GONE GONE. That kind of gone. She must have seen something really good out there, like another cat, a raccoon or a deer, and when the timing was right, and the door was open—if only for a second—she bolted.

Sam had only ever been outside once before, and at that time she barely got past our front yard, so fearful was she of the great outdoors. But this time, fear meant nothing to her. There was no finding her. We searched high and low—under neighbours' decks, in bushes, in garages—everywhere. Not a fuzzy kitty in sight.

With heavy hearts, my three men slouched around the house. Every sound outside had them running to the windows, scanning the grounds. Every time we drove through the parking area of our townhomes, we scanned the bushes for a fuzzy little kitty.

I know everyone was thinking the worst, not daring to speak dreadful thoughts. I tried to keep their hopes up, but it was hard.

Sam came to us from a local pet store, Pets West, who in turn got her through the local animal control/rescue. As she was a rescue cat, one of my sons wondered—did she have a chip or tattoo that we didn't know about?

So as requested, and only on faint-hope whim, I hustled to the pet store. Maybe they did, by chance, have a record of her being chipped or tattooed. It wouldn't find her, but if someone took her to the animal shelter, it might be easy to identify her. I secretly hoped they had implanted a microscopic GPS somewhere on our feline friend.

The store's sales clerk, Meghan, looked up our kitty's file. She said they didn't have a record of any chips or tattoos, but advised me to call animal control to see what they knew. I later did check, but with no luck.

But… Meghan gave us something more.

A bit of hope.

After handing me Sam's file number and the phone number for animal control, she gave me a few pointers. Meghan suggested I send her a photo and details of our lost kitty, and not only would she set up a "lost kitty" notification on Facebook—lots of "shares" of lost pets had helped in the past—but she said she would also post an ad on the store's website. And she would post a "lost kitty" poster in their store.

Wow!

I raced home and shared the news with my heartbroken men. I recapped the "Find Lost Kitty" plan, but sprinkled it with "no promises." But it gave them hope. The thought that someone was doing something lifted their spirits. They were most surprised that someone would go out of their way to do all that.

So with details sent to the store, and "lost kitty" posters posted around our neighborhood, all we could do was wait. And hope. And keep our paws crossed.

Two days later, I had two e-mails. One was from Meghan confirming her Facebook/website work, and the other from a concerned animal lover—a total stranger—who saw the advertisements. Not only did she express her concern for our family, but she also gave us a few tips to enhance our "Find Lost Kitty" plan. Pets West's Facebook page was full of "shares" and comments from other concerned folks—folks we didn't know. Two other folks took the time to phone with sympathy and words of encouragement—"Don't worry, she'll come back soon."

When I shared these e-mails and phone calls with my family they, too, were overwhelmed. It amazed us that so much was being done for us, and by people we didn't know. It was a lesson in community, in folks looking out for other folks. It gave us all a bit of hope, that maybe someone would see our furry Sam. We weren't paying anyone to do this; we didn't know any of these people. Everyone's kindness and concern overwhelmed us.

Days went by. On the recommendation of many, I left her favorite blankie outside, in the hope that her smell/homing beacon would kick in. Nothing.

And then, a week and seventeen hours later, there she was. When one of my sons and husband came back from an outing, there she was, sitting in our parking stall, as if waiting for them to come home. With barely any coaxing, Sam willingly came to my husband, and silently, and without excitement for fear of scaring her, we carried her into the house. And locked the door—double-checking it five times.

To this day, Sam is happy and healthy and is wearing her first collar ever, complete with engraved tag and a bell—just in case.

By the way she sulked around those first few days home, the unfamiliar "noose" around her neck tinkling and jingling with every step, I suspected she was thinking, "I came home for THIS?"

~Lisa McManus Lange

# The Miracle

*What greater gift than the love of a cat?*
*~Charles Dickens*

"Alex! Don't move," I whisper to our gray and silver Manx. She sits still on the deck railing, her ears lying back against her head, hair standing on end, a most violent sound emanating from her throat. Ten feet past Alex is a black bear. The bear looks merely curious, but Alex, in her usual feisty mood, is certain she is going to attack anything that comes into the yard. She has already been known to break up a three-way dogfight and teach the neighbor's dog a lesson. And here I am standing in the line of fire between a black bear and her.

I know I should probably go inside, but I'm terrified to leave Alex. I continue to soothe her. "Shhh, it's okay he's just curious. He means no harm. And if he did I'm pretty sure you wouldn't win." I pet the top of her head. The bear cocks his head and slowly saunters back into the woods. My legs turn to jelly with relief. "Goodness cat, I don't know where you get your attitude from but it sure is something."

"Are you talking to the cat again?" My husband ventures outside.

"Yep. Just talking her down from scrapping it out with a black bear. You know— everyday conversation." I grin. "Speaking of animals, when is Gunnar bringing Walker over?"

"He said he would bring him over tomorrow and they will pick him up again in December."

"I sure hope he and Alex get along. Even though he's a Doberman and looks intimidating, I'm still worried she is going to beat him up. I would hate to let your brother down."

"No kidding. Let's just see how it goes tomorrow."

The day is upon us and Walker has been left in our care for a few months. "Hey Walker, buddy, how are you?" I scratch our temporary resident's ears. Alex is sitting close by. She eyes him but surprisingly hasn't made her usual fuss. Walker doesn't seem to mind her either. He hasn't barked, growled or even tried to chase her. He is such a good dog. I'm at ease the rest of the day. Yes, this will work out well.

"Todd, have you seen Alex? I've been calling for her since I got up this morning." I peer into the woods, wondering where she could be. The early morning fall frost is still fresh on the step. "It's so unlike her. She is usually right at my heels looking for her ears to be scratched."

"No, I haven't seen her. Did Walker chase her off?" He looks puzzled.

"I don't think so. He hasn't even gone near her. I'm going to go ask the neighbors if anyone has seen her." I head off to ask around.

Hours later I'm home with no good news. I plunk down on the deck steps next to my husband. "Nothing. No one has seen her." I lay my head on his shoulder, weary with worry about my cat. "I guess we'll just keep looking. I won't give up on her."

"I know you won't. Maybe Walker told her where to go," he jokes, trying to lighten the mood. "Or maybe she thinks we replaced her," he wonders seriously.

I jump up. "Here kitty kitty." I walk off into the woods looking for her.

The snow is gently falling. It's been three months since we have seen Alex. I put her food out. It doesn't seem like it ever disappears but I refresh it daily. Hoping beyond hope that she is out there somewhere. I pause at Walker's dish. I don't need to fill his dish today; he went home with Gunnar. It sure is lonely without the furry babies around. I look up at the snowflakes gently falling. I wonder if God would hear my prayer.

God, wherever Alex is, please take care of her. I know she might be with you, or maybe just living with someone a few roads over, but wherever she is, please keep her safe. Especially tonight on Christmas Eve. I wish I could see her again. Amen.

I head indoors for the typical Christmas Eve festivities. The cookies are laid out for Santa with his milk. I write a quick note.

*Dear Santa,*
*All I want for Christmas is my cat.*
*xoxoxo*

Todd and I hit the bed exhausted. It's a restless, dreamless sleep. I clamber out of bed during the wee morning hours. The bathroom window is illuminated with bright moonlight. Beautiful sparkling snow shining in the moonlight. It's magical. I notice right where the moonbeams come down onto the yard sits a little animal, quiet, not moving. It's very small, like a cat. It doesn't move a muscle. I squint. Oh my goodness, it looks just like Alex. But no, it can't be. She's been gone for over three months. I blink and the yard is empty. I rub my eyes. I must have been dreaming or hallucinating. I hurry and go back to bed. Again I fall into a restless sleep but I dream of a gray and silver Manx curled up next to me.

"Mom! Mom! Mom and Dad get up! Santa came!" The kids are hopping up and down on the bed.

We stumble out to our recliners and watch the gift opening through squinty, sleepy eyes, inserting oooh's and ahhh's in the right places. All the gifts have been opened. The kids are playing quietly with their new toys. I am enjoying the quiet when I hear a knocking at the door. Who in the world could that be at this hour? I hop up from my chair and answer the door. When I open it I see no one looking at me, but I hear the sound again coming from the lower part of the screen door. I glance down and there sits my beautiful baby. Gray and silver, fluffy and fit. I stand awestruck for several seconds, sure that she must be an illusion.

"Meow." And she paws the door again.

"Honey, who is it?" Todd is asking.

"It's Alex… It's ALEX!" I gently open the door and scoop her into my arms. I squeeze her, hug her, kiss her, tears stream down my face.

Todd comes to inspect the miracle.

The kids come running. "Alex! Alex! Alex!"

I'm crying as I hold my beautiful gray and silver cat, my husband's arms around me. Our kids are jumping up and down around us, cheering. Hugs and kisses, and "oh we missed you" all around. It's the most beautiful sight. It's the most beautiful moment.

The moment is ours. Our family's most special moment. A miracle witnessed and the best Christmas ever.

~Denise Taylor

# Missing Inaction

*It is impossible to find a place in which a cat can't hide.*
*~Bill Carraro*

Frantic, my boyfriend Jeff called me at work one afternoon to say he was home early and could not find our cat. I asked him whether he had checked all the usual places—under the bed, under the sink, or under any clothes piles. He had, and Mr. Big was nowhere to be found.

I left work and raced home to join the search. Mr. Big was an indoor cat so our manhunt was confined to a 900-square-foot apartment. We checked and double-checked the clothes hamper, the cabinets, the closets, in and under the bed, and his favorite spot, the windowsills.

I gave the dry cat food bag a noisy shake and loudly opened a can of wet food, hoping the sounds and smells of dinner would lure him out of hiding. No luck.

After combing every square inch of the apartment, we turned our focus to the indoor corridors of our three-story building. Mr. Big enjoyed taunting the dogs in the building with drawn claws and a hiss. To get out, he often grabbed the bottom of the door and if it wasn't shut tightly, he could pull it open. On more than one occasion he actually stood on his back legs and tried to turn the doorknob.

Unfortunately, Mr. Big was not on any of the floors in the building so we had to face the possibility that he could be outside. We could not figure out how he would have gotten outside, but it was the only logical conclusion.

I hoped he had not traveled outside the general vicinity of our apartment. There was a very busy street two blocks away and the back of our building abutted a wooded area.

Jeff and I rounded up as many neighborhood kids as we could find. We gave each of them a handful of cat food and the promise of a cash reward to the one who found our cat. The kids scattered out, all calling, "Here kitty kitty."

We looked under cars, up trees, behind bushes, and called him until our throats were sore. We could not bear the thought of him being lost in the woods or the victim of a fox.

Later, as darkness approached, our search party dwindled as the kids were called one by one into their homes for the evening.

Jeff reluctantly suggested we go back inside. I followed him back to our apartment, lagging a few steps behind and unwilling to accept a new life without Mr. Big. Baffled, I kept thinking aloud, "How did he get out of a locked apartment?"

Mr. Big was twenty-three pounds when we brought him home from the animal shelter. With a thick coat of long, black and white fur, and big green eyes, he was the most handsome Maine Coon you would ever meet.

Nearly everyone who met Mr. Big for the first time said one of two things: "That's the biggest cat I've ever seen" or "That's the most beautiful cat I've ever seen." I'd seen enough detective shows on television to form somewhat of an educated guess as to how Mr. Big got out. My theory? Someone stole him!

I shared my theory with Jeff. I believed Mr. Big was relaxing in a window when he was spotted and admired by someone below. Somehow, maybe with a ladder and a screwdriver, they loosened the screen and took him. They properly replaced the screen from the outside leaving no trace of a crime. That is the only logical explanation for an indoor cat to be missing from a locked apartment.

Jeff listened but did not enthusiastically agree with my hypothesis. No matter what happened while we were at work, we both agreed that we could not give up.

We decided to create missing cat posters using Mr. Big's most recent photograph and offer a $1,000 reward. We printed copies at the local Kinko's, and in complete darkness, we attached them to poles and trees near our apartment. There was nothing left to do but wait for our phones to ring.

What a terrible night it had been for us. I couldn't imagine going to bed without knowing whether Mr. Big was safe. Jeff was collapsed on the couch, silent and distraught.

I decided to make phone calls to let family and friends know what had happened. While I was on the phone with my sister, I heard Jeff yell from the other room. I dropped the phone and ran into the living room.

Jeff said he felt something from inside the couch. We removed all the couch cushions to find our cat sitting inside the wooden frame. He had torn a hole in the lining and crawled inside! He sat there staring up at us looking precious and innocent.

This vocal cat, who was not afraid to meow when it was mealtime, or when the tub faucet was not dripping, or when he wanted what we had on our plates, never made a peep throughout the entire evening. He was probably silently laughing at us the whole night from his secret hiding place.

Mr. Big gave us twelve years of enjoyment after the infamous couch night. He's in heaven now, but I'll never forget the night he brought us frustration, fatigue, and tears of joy.

~Donna M. Reed

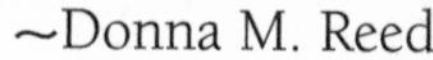

# Cat-astrophe Avoided

*A cat is the only domestic animal I know who toilet trains itself and does a damned impressive job of it.*
*~Joseph Epstein*

Even though my house was very full, with three cats and two large Retrievers, I had just adopted a little kitten. She spent her days exploring her new house and getting into all sorts of trouble. I named her Mouse, because she squeaked instead of meowed, and she would run around in short bursts of energy, just like a mouse.

One day, as I was relaxing after a long day at work, I sat down to watch television and it wouldn't turn on. After trying various light switches around the house, I realized that half of my house was without electricity. I went outside to flip the breakers, and the moment I did, there was a loud pop sound in the house. I ran back in and smelled smoke, but I couldn't see any sign of smoke or fire. I couldn't figure out where the smell was coming from.

Since I couldn't detect any overt signs of fire, I called the non-emergency number of the fire station to ask what I should do. The dispatcher asked me several questions. I told her all I knew, and she told me the fire engine was already on the way. That's not what I had expected to happen, and hurried to tell her I didn't think it was an emergency. She said that's the normal response on all calls. Then I started panicking.

I grabbed all four cats and stashed them in the back seat of the car, thinking that I'd move my car across the street and away from the house in case it did in fact go up in flames. I figured I'd be able to run to the back yard to get my dogs, but as soon as I parked the car in the street, not one but two big fire engines came roaring down my street followed by the fire marshal's truck. They had all their lights flashing and sirens blasting, and came to a stop right in front of my house.

As the firemen poured out of the fire engines, I tried to tell them that I hadn't called for an emergency but had just smelled smoke. They assured me that they'd take care of it. We all crowded into the house, and they scattered all over to find the source of the smoke. The fire marshal called me over and had me walk him through exactly what had happened, so I went over the story again.

As we were talking, one of the firemen walked up to me.

"Do you have a cat?"

I was puzzled but replied, "Yes, I have four cats."

He told me that they had found the source of the problem and asked me to follow them down into the crawl space under the stairs.

"Can you smell urine?" he asked.

What an odd question, I thought, but I sniffed, and sure enough there was the scent of cat urine. I was very confused, as I knew there was no way the cats could have gotten into the crawl space, since it involved lifting a heavy trap door in a closed closet.

"I do smell it, but I don't understand where it's coming from," I replied.

He grinned and pointed at the ceiling.

"Your cat peed in the outlet."

My mind boggled.

"Excuse me? My cat did what?"

He laughed, and by this time, some of the other firemen were laughing too.

"Your cat peed in the outlet and shorted out half your house."

Thoroughly confused and rather mortified, I followed them back upstairs into the living room, where he pointed out the one outlet built into the floor. My coffee table was above it, and he had me kneel down and look underneath the table. He pointed out the large scorch mark on the underside of the coffee table.

"You were really lucky, and I'm not sure how your cat didn't fry herself, but when she peed in the outlet, a flame would have shot upward and could have destroyed your whole house."

By this time, the firemen were standing around grinning at me, all of us so relieved that there was no real emergency. They filed outside to their fire engines, and the fire marshal tipped his hat and said goodbye, suggesting that I have an electrician come fix the problem.

I walked outside with them to pull the car back into my garage and realized that every one of my neighbors was standing around watching. I was so embarrassed and couldn't even get the words out that my cat had peed in the outlet, so I just smiled weakly at them and moved my car.

After I brought the cats back into the house, I checked them all over carefully, but found no marks on any of them. But I knew exactly which cat was the culprit. Silly little Mouse, but she must have learned her lesson, because she never did that again.

~NL Shank

# Kitty Kidnapping

*One must love a cat on its own terms.*
*~Paul Gray*

It had been in all the local newspapers. There was even a story about it on the evening news. People all over the county were discussing it—everyone seemed to know someone who was a victim.

The crime was petnapping.

Crooks stealing family pets, keeping them until the owners advertised a reward; then the crooks would return the "missing" pet and collect the reward money.

Paulette the Pomeranian fetched someone a $200 reward. Sylvester the Border Collie garnered a $500 reward. Even Thor, the elderly Dachshund, was returned for a $50 reward.

Now, living on a rural country road I wasn't too worried about petnappers striking my household. Besides, I didn't have any Pomeranians or Border Collies. The closest thing I had to a pet was the woodchuck that ate most of the tomatoes in my vegetable patch and the robin who built her nest near my bedroom window where she loved to start singing her arias at 5:15 every morning. And, of course, there was Clancy.

Clancy was the big black and white cat who had adopted me years ago.

Clancy was overweight, cranky, committed to taking long naps and almost always hungry. I could see a lot of myself in Clancy, so, even though most people thought he was miserable, we got along just fine.

Friends and family learned when they came to visit, if Clancy is sleeping in a chair, don't try to move him; it's best to just find another spot to sit. If Clancy is eating, that's not a good time to interrupt him. And when Clancy wakes from a nap, the last thing he wants is anyone petting him or cuddling him or telling him he's a "pretty kitty."

A few years ago, at the veterinarian's suggestion, I put a collar and ID tag on Clancy, although it seemed doubtful the cat would ever get lost—he rarely traveled farther than the front porch.

Every evening, after dinner, I open the door and call Clancy. He slowly saunters into the house and sits by his food dish waiting to be served, before he heads off to his corner of the couch for a good night's sleep.

But, one evening when I called, Clancy didn't show up. It wasn't like him to miss dinner, or food at any time for that matter.

I went outside to search for him, checking all his usual hangouts: the lounge chair on the patio and the shady spot under the willow tree. He was nowhere.

The next morning Clancy was still missing. It seemed unlikely that he would run away, especially since I had never seen the cat run at all.

Two full days went by with no sign of Clancy.

Early the next morning there was a knock at the front door. It was a young man carrying a cardboard box, the top secured with duct tape.

"Can I help you?" I asked.

"Yeah," the kid replied. "Is there a reward for your cat, Clancy?"

"What?" I couldn't believe my ears.

"Your lost cat," he repeated. "Is there a reward?"

It didn't take a genius to figure out what was in that box. I was the victim of a petnapping. But I had everything under control. I lived with Clancy. I had read O. Henry's "The Ransom of Red Chief." And this young man had a desperate look in his eyes. I knew just how to handle the situation.

"No," I replied. "No reward."

"Well, I got your cat here," he said, holding up the box. "You can have him back for a reward."

"No, that's okay," I answered, smiling. "Your reward is you can keep Clancy."

"Well, um, no," said the kid, somewhat confused. "I don't want this cat. He's mean."

"Yeah, he's miserable," I agreed. "And that's when he's in a good mood."

"I just need a reward…"

"No," I said. "You keep the cat."

"But he scratched me a bunch of times," the kid complained. "And he eats everything. He ate my potato chips—I didn't even know cats ate potato chips."

I nodded. "Clancy is very expensive to feed."

"That's not the worst part," explained the kid. "He made a mess all over my couch."

"Clancy was probably just happily marking the territory of his new home," I said. I turned to go back in the house.

"Wait," said the kid. "No reward at all?"

"Nope. Good luck with Clancy."

"Okay, okay." The kid set the box on the porch. "I don't need a reward. Just take your cat."

"He's your cat now." I reached down and handed him back the box.

"I don't want that cat!" He quickly set the box back down.

"Let's see if he comes to you when you call him," I said as I began pulling the duct tape off the box. "That will prove he belongs to you."

"Do not open that box," the kid said. "He'll scratch me again. He hates me."

"Don't take it personally, Clancy hates everybody. So what are you going to do?" I asked, impatiently. "You can't leave your cat here."

"It's not my cat!" the kid insisted. "You keep it!"

"This isn't an animal shelter," I replied. I slowly began pulling more tape off the box.

"Wait, I have an idea!" The kid held up his cat-scratched hands in surrender. "How about if I give you five bucks and you keep the cat?"

"Five bucks?" I laughed. "I'm not taking your cat for five bucks!"

The kid frantically dug in his pockets. "Look! Here's eight bucks—that's all I've got. Please, just take the money and the cat!" He handed me the cash and jumped off the porch.

"Don't you want to say goodbye to Clancy?" I called after him.

The kid didn't reply—he hopped in his car and began backing out of the driveway, quickly.

I pulled the lid off the box and found Clancy safe inside, curled up with an empty bag of potato chips, purring peacefully.

All was well. Clancy was back home. I had an extra eight dollars in my pocket and Clancy and I had taught a young petnapper the error of his ways. It was a very good day.

~David Hull

# Left Behind

*Cats are absolute individuals, with their own ideas about everything, including the people they own.*
*~John Dingman*

Our cats were always outside cats. When we moved, which was often, we usually kept our cats in the house a few days until they got used to living in the new place. One cat, however, decided he preferred the old neighborhood. No matter how many times we moved him, as soon as we let him outside he returned to the old home. Finally the neighbors at the former residence said, "Let him stay. We'll feed him with our cats."

Lily, a calico cat, always sensed when a move was starting. She would dash into the house and curl up in a moving box to make sure she went with our family. One time we moved a mere block away. At that time Lily was busy with a litter of five newborn kittens so she did not leave them to jump into a moving box. We finished moving late in the evening and decided that Lily and her family would be fine until the next morning. We would then move her and the kittens and keep them in the house until they adjusted to the new place.

That night, as we scrambled through boxes in the kitchen trying to fix dinner, we heard scratching and meowing at the back door. We opened the door to find Lily with a kitten in her mouth. She was making sure that she and her family were not left behind.

~Martha Hawn VanCise

# My Boyfriend Bob

*Cats know how to obtain food without labor, shelter without confinement, and love without penalties.*
*~W. L. George*

"So, Lenka, do you have a new boyfriend? Who's this Bob you've been raving about?" My coworker leaned against the side of my cubicle with a curious smile on her face. She must have overhead me talking to our receptionist.

"Bob came over last night, so we were just hanging out. We had dinner together and then we just snuggled on the sofa. I watched *Grey's Anatomy* while he dozed off. I might see him again tonight."

I winked at my coworker as I reached to answer my phone. She was so eager to learn about my mysterious admirer. Where did you meet him? What does he look like? Does he have a head full of dark hair? Her inquisitiveness put me into a mischievous state of mind. Why not keep Bob's identity a secret for now? It certainly sounded like I got myself a loyal companion—and I did.

Bob was a neighborhood cat who started hanging around our apartment building one day. My neighbor Alex and I thought that he might be a lost cat and she even called a local SPCA to see if they could take him. It's a good thing that she didn't succeed in her attempt. As she later found out, his owner lived across the street. Ever since she moved to her apartment, Bob turned into a wandering star—and our street was his playground. He'd stay at home during the day, resting after a busy night. When the evening rolled around, he'd get up and set out to make rounds. It was time to check on his neighborhood friends, including Alex and me.

Overtime we established a routine, with Bob waiting devotedly for me at the doorstep every evening. He'd come in, have a snack, tuna being his favorite, and he'd fall asleep on the sofa next to me while I was catching up on my favorite TV shows. After a couple of hours he'd wake up, stretch his long paws—and take off, walking down the shared balcony. His next stop was Alex's apartment, just two doors down from me. Sometimes he'd take a long nap, and that's when Alex would come knocking on the door, making sure he hadn't forgotten about her. "It's my turn, now," she'd chirp softly, trying to lure Bob into her arms. We found ourselves in this love triangle, with Bob being the center of our attention—and we were getting a kick out of it. Both Alex and I wanted to make sure Bob divided his time equally between the two of us. His name, so unusual for a pet, confused quite a few people, including my coworkers and even one of my dates.

One Friday evening I was meeting a new guy for drinks. Bob was still snoozing on the couch while I was getting ready for the date. I decided to wake him up, hoping he could walk out with me so he wouldn't be stuck in my apartment. I gently stroked his back and scratched his belly but he was sound asleep. Bob suddenly took a swipe with his paw, sinking his claws into my skin. As I quickly backed off, his claws ran down my hand, leaving ribbons of scratches behind. I tried to pick him up and carry him to the door but he skillfully escaped my embrace and curled up on the couch again. We wrestled a little longer before Bob finally got up and left. I wasn't necessarily happy about my victory. But I didn't want him to be stranded in my place when he woke up and I was not there.

Now I was running late, and by the time I got to the bar the marks on my hand were puffy and burning a bit. "I'm so sorry I'm late," I apologized. "Bob was hanging out at my place and when I tried to get him to leave, he scratched me." I waved my scratched hand in front of his eyes. I was sure he'd understand. After all, this was Bob we were talking about.

So why was the guy still staring at me blankly?

"So… there's a guy at your place? And he doesn't want you to go out? So when you do, he scratches you?" My date hesitantly put down the cocktail menu. Who is this woman who has a man at home, goes on a date with another one and brags about the wounds he inflicts on her? I burst out laughing. I forgot that my date had no idea who Bob was. It was our first meeting after all. I told him about my part-time cat over a couple of raspberry mojitos and we shared a good laugh. Bob's escapades eventually became a favorite topic to discuss during most of my first dates, especially when there was no connection or no common things to talk about. It turns out Bob was a good judge of character, too. I ended up dating one of the guys but Bob would not come near him. He must have sensed that I was not in good company—and he was right.

There were days when Alex would get home late, and by then Bob had already left my place. I'd occasionally hear Alex roaming around the neighborhood and whistling into the dark. "Bob! Where are you?" Bob sometimes stayed at her place overnight. One night I was woken by a noisy banging at my front door. I quietly tiptoed to the door but couldn't see anyone through the peephole. So who was making this loud ruckus at two in the morning? I groggily looked out the window. Two eyes glowed in the dark of the night, staring in my direction. Bob sat at the doorstep and was using his paw with all his might to hit the screen door that wasn't closed all the way. He figured that if he did that, it would slam against the main door and make enough noise to wake me up. I kept the screen door slightly opened all the time so that Bob could come in and out when the main door was open. I later found out that Alex was not home that night and, since I was just steps away from her apartment, Bob decided to stay at my place.

I was adopted by a cat—but I didn't mind at all. I enjoyed his company without having to worry about keeping a litter box in my small apartment or finding someone to take care of him when I traveled. He wasn't the snuggly type that jumps into your lap, but he enjoyed being in close proximity to me and often followed me curiously around my place. And one thing was for sure—I knew that I'd always see him again the following day.

Unfortunately our property manager wasn't taking good care of the building and it got to the point that I decided to look for a new place. I wanted to stay in the same neighborhood—and after a couple of weeks, I found an apartment just one street down. I was finishing cleaning the apartment when Bob sneaked in through the open door. He quickly scanned the place that was empty except for a few things lying around. He shot me a bemused look—and that's when his inner feline came alive, wildly roaring around the hardwood floors, chasing a couple of plastic bags, jumping all over the clean counters and into the bathtub. Was this the same cat? Was this Bob? As I taped up the last box, I realized this was his way of letting me know he was upset. I wished I could explain to him that I was tired of sketchy neighbors and the building crumbling away in front of my eyes. Could I just smuggle him into my new apartment in one of the moving boxes? I knew he'd be safe frequenting Alex's place but I still felt saddened as I closed the door of the empty apartment.

"Bob is waiting for you at the doorstep," Alex texted me a few weeks later. My heart sank. By then a new tenant had moved into my old apartment but my furry friend still kept coming back to the same doorstep. Who says cats aren't loyal? Although I only lived one block down, it was a long walk for a cat. I decided it was my turn to pay Bob a visit. So whenever I had the chance, I'd stop by Alex's place to hang out with Bob, the busiest cat on the block.

~Lenka Leon

# Stowaway

*I travel not to go anywhere, but to go. I travel for travel's sake.*
*The great affair is to move.*
*~Robert Louis Stevenson*

Whenever Bubba saw my suitcase on the bed, he'd wiggle in among my socks and underwear and make himself right at home.

"You're not going with me," I explained time after time. "I'll only be gone two nights. You've got food and water and everything you need right here."

But Bubba would always give me "the look."

"I'll be back Sunday night. I promise!" I'd say, as I lifted him gently from the suitcase to continue packing. Unconvinced, he'd follow me from room to room, clinging like Velcro, supervising my every move.

He was always under my feet, right up until it was time to depart. And then, just as I was about to go out the door, Bubba often "disappeared," off pouting somewhere as if to punish me for not giving in and taking him along.

I traveled on weekends once or twice a month, so I was used to his little routine and didn't worry too much about not finding him to say goodbye. He was always waiting at the door for me when I returned, and then I'd "love him up" to make amends for my weekend absence.

On one such excursion, I had driven for about an hour when I decided to stop at a gas station for a cup of coffee and a leg stretch.

When I turned off the ignition, the radio, which I'd been singing along with as I drove, also became silent.

And that's when I heard it—the unmistakable sound of a cat meowing—and it was coming from my trunk!

Somehow, the little rascal had wriggled in behind my suitcase, spare tire, tennis shoes, and the usual assortment of miscellaneous trunk gear, and had stowed away with me.

The friends with whom I planned to stay did not have a cat. There was no welcoming cat box, litter, or any other cat essentials at their house.

There was nothing to do but head back home, this time with Bubba curled up in the front seat of the car, purring softly to the music on the radio.

~Jan Bono

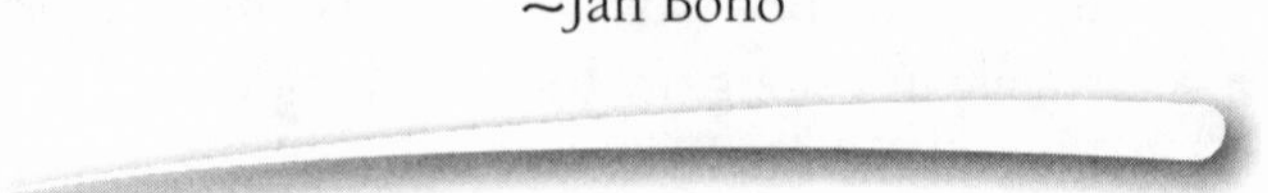

# Welcome to the Navy

*A meow massages the heart.*
*~Stuart McMillan*

I walked in laps through my new home. My fingers glided along the glossy walls. My home! Under my brand new last name! Jason had had enough time to get the residence key from the naval base housing office and walk through the apartment with me before he had to report for duty. Our luggage sat in the corner of our bedroom. Outside, a moving truck held all my worldly belongings and several pieces of second- and third-hand furniture.

The carpet smelled new, though it scratched at my soles like sandpaper. I had grown up near a United States Navy base, so I knew all the stories about how base housing wasn't always a pleasant place to live. That didn't dim my excitement, though. This was my house! I imagined where everything would go as we unpacked—where the mattresses would sit until we could afford a proper bed, where the tiny TV would rest.

That's when I heard the yelling.

The next-door neighbors were engaged in a full-on fight. He yelled. She screamed and cried. Doors slammed. The walls filtered the noise like cardboard. Wherever I stood in my new house—even thirty feet away, through closed doors—I could hear them. It didn't sound violent, but it did sound awful, profane, and unlike anything I had heard before.

My new home didn't feel so welcoming now. It felt scary. I was keenly aware that we didn't have a phone yet. I couldn't call for help if things turned worse. Other than Jason, I didn't have any loved ones within three thousand miles.

I burst out crying. I wanted my mom. I wanted my familiar house, the place I'd lived from age seven to twenty. I wanted my cat, Adventure, who always sensed when I was upset and knew to curl up on my lap and purr.

That thought made the tears worse. Adventure was slowly dying of cancer back at my parents' house. I had moved away, knowing I'd likely never see him again.

The horrible argument continued next door. I couldn't stay and listen to them and wallow in my own self-pity. I dried off my face and then I headed outside and began to ferry boxes from the truck.

Over the next days and weeks, I busied myself by unpacking everything. The possessions that had completely filled a moving truck looked very spare inside our small two-bedroom apartment. We were so poor we couldn't afford a car. I walked a mile in the sticky South Carolina mornings to buy packs of ramen and cake mix at the commissary. As hot as it was, we wore clothing more than once to avoid trips to the Laundromat.

I had known it would be a hard transition, financially and emotionally, but logic didn't prepare me for reality.

Jason did what he could, but he was away most of the day in training. I looked for a job, but no place nearby was hiring. Therefore, I wandered the house all day long. The apartment felt so empty. I called my mom every few days and tried not to cry as I asked how things were going, how Adventure was doing.

I loved Jason so much. I didn't want to end up like the couple next door. I desperately wanted to be a good wife, but the simple fact was that I was miserable and full of doubt. I had married a sailor. If I couldn't cope with being a newlywed, how would I deal with deployments? How could I survive on my own?

A few more wedding gifts trickled in. One came in the form of a check. As we shopped for a much-needed microwave, we realized we would have a bit of money left over.

"Maybe we can stock up on cheese. There's a good sale at the commissary this week," I said. "Macaroni is cheap."

"I was thinking of something else," Jason said.

"What?"

"I know where the SPCA is," he said. "I think this would be enough to get a cat. It wouldn't be a replacement for Adventure, but..."

"A cat. Really?" My eyes filled with tears—this time, tears of joy.

We headed to the SPCA as soon as we could. Puppies whined and birds cawed for attention, but I went straight for a cage holding four kittens. A black and gray one pressed against the bars and mewed at me.

"I want to hold this one, please," I said to the attendant.

As soon as I held the kitten, she began to purr. My terrible loneliness began to melt away.

"There's another one," said Jason. Sure enough, there was another tabby at the rear of the cage. A minute later, I cradled both kittens against my chest. I looked at Jason, biting my lip.

"We can't split them up. They're brother and sister. Spaying and neutering will be really expensive and I don't know if..."

Jason held up a hand. "Stop. I know you're already trying to figure out the budget in your head. You need these cats, Beth. I can eat less if it means we'll save some money, if it will make you happy."

We returned home poorer and richer at the same time. I dubbed the kittens Palom and Porom, named for twins in one of our favorite video games. The two rambunctious tabbies immediately made themselves at home. Within an hour, they managed to explore every nook and cranny, break a candleholder, and damage the kitchen cabinets.

That night, we sat on our itchy secondhand couch. We each had a kitten; Palom, the boy, had claimed me, while Porom latched onto Jason. The kittens were exhausted from their rampage, their striped bellies rounded with dinner.

I looked around the room. My house. My couch. My husband. My kittens. Sure, the place still looked empty, but something major had changed. No matter where the Navy sent us in the coming years, no matter how much Jason worked, I wasn't going to be alone.

Palom purred and nuzzled against me, perfectly cozy. With my kittens close by, I realized I was finally cozy, too.

~Beth Cato

# The Blankie

*There is no such thing as "just a cat."*
*~Robert A. Heinlein*

"Do you know there's a small black cat hanging by his teeth from the yellow blanket you've hung on your clothesline?" asked a neighbor. "The wind is blowing, but he's still hanging on."

"That's George the Cat," I said. "He will not leave his yellow blanket. He sleeps on it, runs to it when he's frightened, claws and kneads his paws into it. The blanket was so dirty that I had to wash it, but he's found it on the clothesline."

"George the Cat?"

"Yes, George. He's part of our family, now."

Our son John, then in third grade, had come home from school with something clasped in his hands. Pleading, knowing we'd rejected the idea of a pet, he said, "The mother cat at a neighbor's house had kittens. She had too many. They're going to take some to the animal shelter. This one has to go, they say. I think he's the smartest. Just look. I've named him 'George.'"

The tiny black kitten, with a spot of white fur on his throat, was sucking on our son's finger. He was really too young to leave his mother.

There was no way to say "No" to George. John warmed milk for him and put a yellow blanket in a box beside his bed. That night, the cat and the yellow blanket ended up on the bed, tangled with boy.

Because George had come into our family when he was so young, he didn't always act like a normal cat. He played flag football with the boys. Reluctantly, he played dress-up with the girls. He pounced on my husband John for roughhouse games when son and daughter did. He helped me unload grocery sacks and claimed every cantaloupe for himself. He waited outside at exactly the time our kids would be returning from school. Eventually, he ventured to the edge of the nearby schoolyard, sat and waited for them.

When my son or daughter had mumps, colds or just felt down, George climbed into their beds and curled up, after he demanded I bring his yellow blanket. I thought he was a better restorer of health than any doctor or soup.

Our kids passed through grade-school years, and George learned along with them. He'd had no fear of dogs; in fact, he played with a Chihuahua. Then, a large dog chased and nearly killed George. He made it home to his yellow blanket, got underneath it, meowed out the story. The next day, George jumped onto a high wooden partition between our garage and house. He twitched his tail. The large dog saw that. The large dog ran toward the partition, ready to attack.

George jumped down and grabbed the dog's nose. The dog ran, yelping. George did not let go. A while later he came home, strutting, a winner.

After that he didn't fear any dogs, and when we moved to a new town where the neighborhood dogs ran free, George asserted his territorial rights. He leapt from some hidden place onto a lead dog's nose, and the whole pack ran away, baying. George trained them to stay away and we didn't have to worry about their messing up our lawn.

One spring day, George went out serenading some female cats as usual, but when he came home, he stretched out in front of the fireplace, limp. He lay there on his back, trying to run, and we knew it was time. We called our daughter and we all held George. Then we wrapped him in his yellow blanket and buried him in a sunny place. I still think about that special cat, with his own blankie, and the way he protected and cared for our children and our property.

~Shirley P. Gumert

# The Cat Did What?

## Bad Cat!

# The Cat Who Came to Dinner

*We do not quite forgive a giver. The hand that feeds us is in some danger of being bitten.*
*~Ralph Waldo Emerson*

We were a young family with three children under eight years old, two Collies and two cats. We also had an adopted family member—actually one who adopted us. I think many families experience this. This person is always the husband's good old buddy, who is either single or recently divorced. Our addition was still single.

Even though all the subjects in this little tale have long since passed away, I will change our guest's name. And "Charlie" was a constant guest. He would invite himself to every meal he could possibly attend and then include himself in our evenings watching TV, going to a movie or even bowling. It was as if he had no life away from our family.

When the kids started calling him "uncle" I told my husband that he simply had to have a word with Charlie. It wasn't that he was rude or obnoxious in any way. He was very nice. It was just that he was always there. We had no private time and in reality, he ate as if each meal was his last. It was breaking our already tight budget. My husband agreed, but found it very difficult to bring up the subject with his pal. How do you tell someone you really do like that enough is enough? It was quite a quandary.

The dogs liked him. The kids liked him. Even the cats liked him. If fact, it was how much one of our cats liked him that solved our problem. Johnny was a small, black and white cat that was basically a homebody. Even though I kept a window open for the cats to come and go, he preferred the indoors to the world outside. On the other hand, Ringo, our huge, gray tabby tomcat, loved the outdoors. He was a proficient hunter and was well known in the neighborhood for his skill. I was even offered quite a bit of money to sell him to a neighbor when he saw how good Ringo was at catching the gophers that plagued his vegetable garden.

One Sunday afternoon in the fall, I was making a pot roast dinner complete with homemade apple pie for dessert. Naturally, good old Charlie was already seated in our living room watching TV, waiting for the feast. I'd pulled my husband aside and told him that there would definitely be no leftover roast for his lunches the coming week, and that he really must talk to Charlie about being at every dinner, every day—without an invitation.

"I can't hurt his feelings." It was the normal reply I got from my dear husband.

"I'm not going to be the bad guy in this. Charlie is your friend," I always replied. He said he promised to talk to Charlie—maybe tomorrow. I sighed and started setting the kitchen table for dinner.

There was a sports show that both my husband and Charlie wanted to watch on television, so they opted to eat in the living room. They sat on the couch, using the coffee table for their plates and drinks. The girls and I ate our dinner at the kitchen table that evening.

Halfway through the meal, a commotion broke out in the living room. I assumed that some great event had happened in the game they were watching. Then the hollering became louder and turned into a male version of screams of terror. It was Charlie.

At the same time, my husband was laughing so hard, I was afraid he'd choke. I rushed to the doorway between the kitchen and living room. The girls scrambled from the table and huddled behind me, stretching to look out at their father and Uncle Charlie.

A giant, dead, bloody rat was lying in the middle of Charlie's pot roast. Gravy was spattered all over the table, Charlie's trousers and shirt. Some even made its way onto my husband, who was now so red in the face from trying to choke back his laughter he looked like he was ready to have a stroke.

Ringo was sitting on the back of the couch, purring loudly and rubbing back and forth against Charlie's head, proudly viewing the "gift" he had given to his friend to eat. To the cat, nothing on earth could possibly be better than a nice, fat, fresh rat. He had killed it, brought it in through the open window and hopped onto the back of the couch carrying his gift.

Charlie was hunched over his plate, his eyes on the TV screen. Ringo simply crawled onto his back and dropped the rat over Charlie's shoulder, directly onto his plate of pot roast. Then the cat retreated to the back of the couch to watch his friend devour the feast he had provided.

"Look, Mommy," my oldest girl said. "Ringo really loves Uncle Charlie. He brought him a present." I couldn't help it; I burst out laughing too.

Charlie was now on his feet and waving his arms frantically. He gulped a few times then took off running for the bathroom. Sounds of him heaving up his dinner almost drowned out the television.

"I'm sorry, hon. I couldn't help laughing," I said to my husband. "But, you were laughing first. You're not innocent. You'd better go help him."

My husband got up and went to see what he could do for Charlie. I got a paper lunch bag, a bottle of spray cleaner, and a massive wad of paper towels and went into the living room to wipe up the mess and deposit Charlie's dinner and extra condiment, into the bag for the trash bin outside.

Ringo watched me with puzzlement. How could anyone trash a delicacy like that? He jumped from the couch to follow me. My oldest grabbed him, put him in the bedroom and closed the door.

Charlie and my husband came back into the living room. Charlie was cleaned up as much as possible. I explained to him how Ringo really thought he was doing something great. It was an honor, actually.

Charlie didn't see it that way, but he accepted it. "Yes, we're all used to Ringo's little gifts," my husband added.

"He does this all the time?" Charlie stammered.

"Sure," my eldest daughter said. "But, this is the first time he ever thought anyone but us was good enough to get a present. He must really love you, Uncle Charlie."

I offered to heat up a new plate of food for Charlie, but he seemed to have lost his appetite. He suddenly remembered someplace he needed to go and even refused a slice of apple pie to take with him.

Needless to say, my husband never had to have "that uncomfortable talk" with his best friend. And Charlie never showed up for dinner uninvited. When he was invited, we always assured him that Ringo would be kept in the service porch to avoid any future gift-giving during dinner.

~Joyce Laird

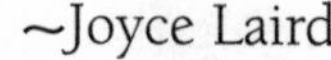

# Tattle Tail

*If animals could speak, the dog would be a blundering outspoken fellow; but the cat would have the rare grace of never saying a word too much.*
*~Mark Twain*

"Okay, what is it now, Patches?" Patches, my fat little calico, was once again trying to tell me something—something of utmost importance, mind you. A usually quiet cat (other than her incessant "I'm so happy" purr), Patches would only get vocal when she needed something. The food bowl is empty? "Meow, meow, meow" would resonate through the home until I would finally obey Princess Patches' commands and follow her to the kitchen to replenish. Time to go outside? Again, meows would echo off the walls until I made my way to the front door, where she would be sitting with her paw on the door waiting for someone with thumbs to come along and release her.

Granted, I was aware—and appreciative—of my cat's intelligence. When she wanted something, she would make it happen. (I'd like to think she got that from me.) But honestly, the needy meows were sometimes annoying. And this particular morning was no exception.

Patches and I had just made a move. The sweet man in my life and I had just decided to combine our homes and take the next step in our future together. And although he and I both knew we were ready, one little question remained hanging in the air.

How were our cats going to take the news?

He, too, had a ruler of the roost. A muscular, sleek, gray cat named Mittens. At first glance, you would think Mittens was not a very nice little fella. The first time I ever saw him, I almost laughed at the irony of such a sweet, cuddly name as Mittens paired with such a fierce looking tiger-like cat. But I soon learned not to judge a book by its cover. Under that fierce exterior lay the sweetest, most cuddly fur ball I'd ever met. Falling in love with Mittens didn't take long at all.

Would it be that easy for Patches?

Well, we were about to find out.

The inevitable came. After moving everything else I could think of, it was finally time to pack up Patches and move her as well. She wasn't too thrilled with the forty-five-minute drive (no more little quiet kitty, that's for sure). But, much to my surprise, once we arrived at the home and I put her down to wander through the house, she seemed to be immediately at ease. She sniffed around, circled the perimeter of every single room, and eventually made her way to the living room where she found her favorite resting spot on the radiator, and promptly went to sleep. Wow. That was easy.

Now, on to the hard part.

Patches, meet Mittens.

We let Mittens inside, and he immediately knew something was "off." He made his way through the home sniffing around until he finally found the culprit—a massive pile of sleeping multicolored fluff resting on "his" radiator. Patches woke up—and thus, the fighting began. The hisses, the growls, the shrieks.

Sigh. So much for love at first sight, huh?

Over the next few weeks, the cats seemed to come to a truce. There was definitely no love lost between them, but at least they were learning to coexist—even managing to share from the same food bowl (just not at the same time, mind you!). As long as no blood was shed, we considered the status quo a success.

Which brings me to this particular morning. The incessant "meow, meow, meow" could be heard throughout the whole house. I was getting ready for work so I didn't immediately go to find out what was going on. I figured whatever it was would pass. But the meows started getting closer, and soon Patches stood in the doorway of the bathroom staring up at me with that "Hello? Didn't you hear me calling for you?" face. "What, Patches? What is so important?" I knew her food and water bowls were filled—those were the first things I had taken care of when I woke up that morning. I knew she didn't want to go outside (Miss Lucy, the sweet, playful outside doggy took care of making sure Patches would now, and forevermore, be considered an "inside cat.") So, what on earth had my little fat cat in such a tizzy?

I let curiosity get the best of me (I guess I learned that one from her), and decided to stop what I was doing and follow her. We made our way down the hall, with her looking back every second to be sure I was coming, and ended up in the kitchen. Patches made it there first, and calmly and methodically sat down on the floor and looked up at the counter. And there, up on the counter, chomping down on last night's leftovers that were mistakenly left out and not put up in the refrigerator, was Mittens.

Patches had just told on Mittens.

I immediately burst out laughing. I mean, yes, Mittens was doing a bad thing and was eventually shooed off the counter and scolded—but seriously? He got told on? By a cat? Once my giggle fits finally subsided, I realized that there was a deeper meaning to be taken from this whole thing. Yes, our kitties were learning to coexist; yes, the fighting had stopped; and no, there was no cuddling or playing between the two, much to my dismay. But, finally, there was this. This incident told me all I needed to know.

Mittens and Patches had now become brother and sister. Tattle "tails" and all.

Mission accomplished. Our happy little family was complete.

~Melissa Halsey Caudill

# Why Cats Paint

*An artist is someone who produces things that people don't need to have but that he—for some reason—thinks it would be a good idea to give them.*
*~Andy Warhol*

To my cat, doors are the enemy. That includes the hall door where the evil vacuum lives, and the dreaded bathroom door, which she has learned to push open—self-taught—to the surprise of guests who mutter, "Wait, wait. There's someone in here."

Any door she can't open herself must immediately be opened by the nearest owner of an opposable thumb. Any delay results in cringe-inducing door scratching, her claws like ten keys dragged down the side of a new car.

Knowing this when my husband and I started some home projects—me painting the hall, and him setting black accent tiles for the bathroom floor—I said, "I'm not locking Alley away. She hates it. And besides, she's asleep."

"I don't think that's a good idea," my husband said.

"She'll be fine," I said. And she was fine—until she woke up.

My cat has a fine mousing instinct, but unfortunately no mousing ability. A Mr. Magoo with fur, she's been known to stalk balls of yarn and wool socks, but I never expected her to stalk the paint roller.

Quicker than I could yell, "Alley! Don't!" she did a classic four-legged pounce into a tray full of yellow paint. Then the race was on. She shot straight up, executed a bank-turn off the wall, and, performing a high-speed talk-to-the-tail, raced down the hall leaving a trail of yellow paw prints. In hot pursuit, I followed in the number-two position, shouting useless commands such as, "No! Stop! Don't jump on the sofa!"

With paint flying from her long-haired tail, she darted into the living room, onto an end table, down the sofa, across the oriental carpet, then into the dining room and onto the buffet, skidding its length before making an Olympian leap over the table and landing on the kitchen counter, where she finally ran out of gas. There she sauntered over to her food dish and sat nonchalantly, like she was asking, "So… what's for dinner?"

All through her bath she yowled, and for the rest of the day she wouldn't come near me.

It took hours to remove my feline Picasso's yellow period. That night I fell into bed exhausted, but still angry at the indignity of public bathing, my cat refused to join me.

Early the next morning though, she woke me, pawing at my neck. Then something hit my pillow with a dull thud. Oh, yuck! A revenge offering.

But to my surprise her "gift" wasn't a dead mouse or worse, a half-dead mouse; she'd brought me a small black tile. Though not particularly mouse-like, she obviously disagreed.

Then from the bathroom my husband yelled, "Cripes! She's ruined the floor! Every tile is crooked. And one's missing."

Purring, my cat nudged her gift closer to me, her way of saying, "I forgive you for the bath."

I picked a little paint off her whiskers, then scratched her chin and said, "What a good kitty."

~Pam Tallman

# The Standoff

*Dogs have owners, cats have staff.*
*~Author Unknown*

It was a rare, blissfully quiet day with no one home but the cat and me. I was coming out of the laundry room with a huge basket of clean clothes when I saw our small, sleek gray tabby, Pussywillow, glide up the stairs and turn the corner toward my toddler's bedroom. I went on my way, delivering clean, folded laundry to each bedroom, until I reached the nursery.

And then I saw it. "Eeeek!" I yelled, dropping the laundry basket. "There is a chipmunk in the baby's room and it is alive!" There on the hardwood floor a fat chipmunk was backed up against the wall. No cat in sight.

As quickly as I could, I threw the clean laundry back in the basket, set it inside the crib, and ran out, closing the bedroom door.

Pussywillow, looking imperious as only a cat can, sat calmly washing her paws at the other end of the hall. "This is YOUR doing!" I said as I scooped her up. "You brought that chipmunk into our house! You take care of it." With that I unceremoniously dumped our recalcitrant cat in our youngest son's bedroom. She must have stunned the chipmunk before carrying it inside through our tiny cat door, and when it came back to life she dropped it.

Half an hour later I peered in, hoping the deed would be done and I could dispose of it. But no. The cat was sitting on her haunches at one end of the room, tail jerking like a metronome. The chipmunk was shrunk into a corner at the other. Seven-pound cat. Three-ounce chipmunk. A standoff.

"Oh thanks," I said to Pussywillow. "You want ME to do this? I cannot kill anything bigger than a mosquito! Aarrghhh!"

I removed the cat, closed the door. Now what? I wasn't sure who was more scared, the chipmunk or me. I love nature. But I love it outside, not in my one-year-old's bedroom!

Dumping out a gallon-sized plastic jar of blocks and gathering up my nerve, I crept up to the tiny thing, which cowered in a corner of an empty closet. With a flourish I dumped the plastic jar over the chipmunk, reached for a cardboard book to slide underneath, and turned it over, chipmunk scrabbling and squeaking inside the plastic jar. One hand under the jar, one hand on the cardboard "lid," I stared at the still closed bedroom door. How do I get into these messes? And why is it always when no one else is home? Holding the cardboard book precariously on top with my chin, hoping little rodent teeth would not find a way to chew through the plastic, and feeling like the upstairs maid with a full chamber pot, I quickly made my way outside and down the hill to the meadow, where I set the poor creature free.

The cat stayed out of sight for several hours. A really good decision.

~DJ Kinsinger

# The Vet Visit

*My cat does not talk as respectfully to me as I do to her.*
*~Colette*

I don't know why I get elected to do all the "fun" stuff at our house, but that seems to be the case. For instance, I am always the one who has to take the animals to the vet for their checkups and shots. When it was time for our cat to make that trip, I spent several days dreading the task. But finally, I decided to square my shoulders and get it done.

"Cat" is what we call the black and white shorthaired feline who adopted us some seven years ago after turning up on our front porch one October night. She actually does have a "real name"—it's Mary Catherine—but no one ever calls her that.

Since Cat is very seldom sick or in need of medical attention, trips to the veterinarian have been few over the years. That's a good thing because Cat is not one to be trifled with when it comes to things she doesn't like to do. And going to the vet is definitely one of those things.

Knowing I would have to resort to trickery to even get Cat in the carrier for the car ride, I first placed her favorite rug and a couple of cat treats inside, then set it on the floor with the door open. I nonchalantly walked away, but hid behind the door to watch. Since Cat is curious, as most cats are, she soon began sniffing around the little cage. In only a few minutes, she had walked into the carrier, whereupon I quickly shut the door.

That's when she let me know what she thought of my deception by emitting the first howl from hell. I am not kidding, she actually sounded like a demon cat in some Stephen King horror movie. I was almost afraid to even pick up the carrier in case she somehow managed to charge the door and escape. But she stayed safely inside, although she continued to screech and hiss all the way to the veterinarian's office. To say she was unhappy is definitely an understatement.

When it was her turn to be seen, I warned the vet that Cat was not your typical kitty.

"She's not one to cuddle and purr," I said. "And when I get her out, she is going to be one angry cat."

Sure enough, when I opened the cage, she exploded onto the exam table like a big furry bomb with claws and teeth bared. The vet's assistant managed to grab her before she hit the floor, but she bucked and jumped, hissed and hollered like some possessed creature. The assistant held on, however, although I'm not sure just how, and the doctor was able to do an exam. Two injections were called for, and if we thought Cat had gone wild BEFORE the shots, we had seen nothing. When she felt the first needle, in her shoulder, she became even more enraged. She puffed up so big, she actually seemed to double in size. However, the assistant aptly kept her in place without being clawed to pieces. After the second shot, we managed to stuff her back in the cage, where she continued to loudly let us know just how unhappy she really was.

The whole thing was over and done with in only a matter of minutes, and soon Cat and I were on our way back home—with her hollering loudly all the way.

When we reached the house, I set the cage on the living room floor and opened the door. I was prepared for a mad dash from the carrier, but she surprised me. Instead of being a crazed and frantic feline, she just quietly walked out, looked around, then went to her favorite spot beneath the dining room table.

When I checked on her later, she was leisurely attending to her personal hygiene duties. After all, an ordeal like that takes its toll on a gal's appearance.

~Anna B. Ashley

# Murphy's New Law

*Curiosity killed the cat, and satisfaction brought it back.*
*~Eugene O'Neil*

Who ate all the cat food and left none for the others? Murphy.

Who waited till I washed the car, then pussyfooted all over the windshield? Murphy.

Who gifted me with half a dead mouse on the doorstep? You get the idea. It was… Murphy.

Whatever the question, whatever the mischief, the answer was always the same. Murphy. Soon after Murphy joined our household, I began to refer to this phenomenon as Murphy's New Law.

This gray fur ball came to me with his sister and mama after someone abandoned them in the dead of winter. I was a volunteer foster mom for a local pet rescue, and they asked me to keep the feline trio till we found homes for them. Murphy was a solid dark gray with long, very soft hair, and a big personality. His sister Maddie was adopted right away, but Murphy and his mama became part of my posse.

In just a few months, Murphy grew into an extra big, beefy boy. But the funny thing about Murphy was, in spite of his unusually large body, he had the tiniest meow. It never got louder than an adolescent squeak. What he lacked in voice, he made up for in mischief.

He loved to sit and watch me, tilting his head as far to the side as possible, as he did. Then, I believe, he'd file away the information he got by observation, and use it to his advantage. Like how he would watch me from the sidelines as I spent an hour washing the car. I'd pull the car in the garage and go in the house. Within minutes I'd see a path of dusty kitty feet across my windshield. I always wondered how long he'd walked in the dust to heighten the impact of those paw prints.

It didn't take long for me to realize that all the whodunnits in our house could pretty much be attributed to the mischievous Murphy. But when I was asked to take in a new foster cat named Zoey, Murphy took his mischief to a new level.

Zoey was a gorgeous, though timid, white Siamese. She was also an escape artist, and one evening, escape she did. She was somewhere in the neighborhood, and I needed to get her back as soon as possible. So I borrowed a humane trap from the rescue. They told me to lock up my other pets, then bait the trap with smelly sardines. Leave the trap door open, they said, and cover the rest with a blanket. They explained the blanket would allow Zoey to feel more secure going in.

This is exactly what I did. Then I tried not to think about it, though I kept peeking into the garage, hoping to find the trap door was triggered. Hours passed, but no luck. Finally I looked out and saw the trap door had sprung. I was so excited. I crept up on the trap eager to see my Zoey. Gently, I lifted the blanket and there was… you guessed it, Murphy. He didn't bother to apologize. In fact, he didn't even look at me. He was too busy licking the sardine oil off his thieving paws.

We went through this time after time, through several cans of smelly sardines. I couldn't figure out how Murphy was getting out of the room I confined him in. I guess the sardines were enough of a draw that he somehow found his way to them.

Thanks to Murphy's thievery, the humane trap didn't work. But I did manage to get Zoey back without it. She simply walked into the house one day. Murphy, on the other hand, decided there was too much competition here. He liked visiting my neighbor's house and she liked him. So eventually he packed his bag and moved in with the neighbor.

Murphy has been known to visit us, just to keep us on our toes. I seldom actually see him. I've just come to accept that when odd things happen—food disappears, items are knocked off the table, the ever faithful dusty cat prints appear—Murphy has paid us a neighborly visit during the night. He may not live here now, but Murphy's New Law is in effect. Whatever the question, whatever the mystery, the answer remains… Murphy.

~Teresa Ambord

# Puffed-Up Pussycat

*Never wear anything that panics the cat.*
*~P. J. O'Rourke*

As I am known as the "animal whisperer" of my family, I was surprised when my sister Sharyn cautioned me to be careful around our parents' cat.

"Why, what's the problem?" I asked.

"He's mean," my sister replied, describing a few unusual encounters she had had with the animal. My sister, who is a nurse practitioner, had a theory. "You know, he used to be nice. I think something happened to his brain when he had that surgery. He's never been the same."

"Really, Sharyn," I replied. "How bad can he be? Maybe you're the one who should be cautious. He likes me." My sister gave me a look as if to say, "You'll see."

Mom had waited a while before getting this cat, having lost two cats within a few months of each other. But one day, a mouse scampered across the kitchen floor of our timeworn home and Dad announced, "We're getting a cat!" So off to the shelter we went. Mom picked out an orange and white tabby called "Orange Juice."

"Not very original," I said to my mother when she informed me of the name.

"Well, what else are we going to call him?" she asked, as I stared into the four-month-old cat's amber eyes and sweet expression.

"I guess it'll do," I replied. You have to understand that my mom, Jan, has a way with words and especially pet names. I recalled her last cats' names: Mozzy, named for Mozart [Mom's a musician], and Biddy, for his spinster sister, short for "itty bitty kitty," a play on words. Somehow, O.J. seemed all too common. Eventually, his name morphed into Oj.

Like his predecessors, we felt sure Orange Juice would live in tranquility in the quiet Horn household. Mom played fetch with Oj, even bathed him. He was active but gentle. He had the most handsome face with large soulful eyes. He drew you in with a mesmerizing half-smile. Dad was not a cat person at heart but his fear of mice or anything rodent was strong, so he bonded with Oj. Dad would curl up with one of his mystery novels and before long, Oj would be lying on the top of the sofa, relaxing. Then, crisis! Oj stopped eating.

He was about six months old at the time, and a few hundred dollars later, the vet said he would need surgery for an obstruction. Though a hardship for the retirees, Mom and Dad scheduled the surgery.

"This is what was blocking Orange Juice's intestines," the veterinarian explained, handing an object to Mom. "He'll be fine now."

The object was a small metal religious statue. How had an indoor cat swallowed an object that didn't come from his home environment? That mystery would never be solved. Oj came home with a cone on his head and stitches in his belly. All seemed well. At his follow-up appointment, the trouble began: Oj hissed at the veterinarian.

"Understandable," Mom said to me, "after all he's been through." Another time, Oj swiped a paw at Dad's leg, causing a scratch. My dad, now loyal to the feline, brushed off the incident. "I must have startled him," was all he would say. Little attacks were common and the mystique grew. The whole family became cautious around Oj but no one had the heart to get rid of him.

That summer, my parents decided to take a vacation. My sister Sharyn and I, the designated cat sitters, staggered our schedules. My day came and I entered the house. Oj was in the hall, no smile, his fur puffed up all over his body, like a dog raises his hackles. But this was a cat, an average-sized cat, looking large, his neck hair like a lion's mane. He stared me down and growled.

"Here to feed you, buddy," I said, moving toward him, dismissing his reputation. He disappeared behind the sofa and I have to admit I was relieved. I made my way to the kitchen. I cleaned the litter box, put out fresh food, and washed and refilled his water bowl. He trotted over to me purring, no more puffed-up pussycat. I patted his head. See, my sister was wrong. He is a good cat, I told myself.

My next encounter was one to remember. I arrived and didn't see the cat. "Here Oj, here kitty kitty," I called. No sign of him. Exiting the powder room, I turned. In a nanosecond, an enraged puffed-up Oj attacked. I was wearing a cat on my jeans! I tried to pull him off me but he clung tightly, biting my hand in the process.

"Ouch, Oj. Stop. Let go. You're hurting me." He let go and dropped at my feet, looking angelic. My leg stinging and my hand red, I didn't blame the cat. I had startled him. Sharyn did the next few feedings and gave me a tip. "Go in with an open umbrella; keeps him at bay."

"That's a little extreme," I commented, with visions of a lion tamer and a chair.

"Your choice," she said knowingly.

My next visit was on a Sunday morning. I picked up the paper from the doorstep and a sample bottle of hairspray fell out of a plastic sack attached to the paper. I opened it and smelled—nice. I unlocked the front door and entered. My heart flipped as I saw the puffed-up "catzilla" staring me down. I should have taken the umbrella from the porch. Oj stalked. I backed away. He came closer. I shimmied to the side. In that moment when you are in total fear and not thinking clearly or not thinking at all, you act. I lifted the hairspray and gave a squirt. The cat froze then fled up the staircase. Oj was afraid of hairspray. I quickly did my duties and emerged unscathed, that day, onto the front porch.

My folks returned home and though Oj was an occasional aggressor with them, he generally was okay. Years later, when my father was ill, I came to spend some time with him and help out my mother and sister. I slept in the bedroom at the top of the stairs. In the middle of the night, flashlight in hand, I emerged in my thigh-length nightshirt, bare legs exposed, to use the powder room. As I padded to the bathroom, unaware in my sleepy state that I might encounter Oj, I remembered!

Panic. I'd forgotten my trusty hairspray. My nemesis was running up the stairs toward me, tail high, determined, puffed-up. I prayed. Dear God, help him calm down. I sucked in a terrified breath. Should I go back in the bedroom? Should I make a run for the bathroom? Oj was going to tear me apart. My sister had been right! With the cat advancing and my lack of protective clothing, I ran barelegged into the bedroom, barricading myself behind the closed door, breathing hard. Then, I turned in horror to find the puffed-up Oj in the room with me. "Ouch!"

~Ellyn Horn Zarek

# The Bad Influence

*The mathematical probability of a common cat doing exactly as it pleases is the one scientific absolute in the world.*
*~Lynn M. Osband*

The first cat was so mild-mannered and easy to train that I thought nothing of bringing a second cat into the household a year later. And besides, they looked enough alike that they could have been brothers.

But in direct opposition to Cat Number One's calm and serene disposition, Cat Number Two quickly raised enough havoc in the household for me to wonder if he wasn't actually an evil twin.

No amount of squirting him with the squirt gun, sharply clapping my hands, or hollering "Get down!" could convince him to stay off the kitchen counters, dining room table, or the upper window ledge. Even the "Cat Off" spray had no effect on his penchant for walking on all forbidden surfaces.

And the worst part was that instead of Cat Number One teaching him good manners, Cat Number Two taught the first cat to follow his misbehaving lead!

Right away, the pint-sized Peeping Tom streaked for the bathroom every time he heard the shower come on, stationing himself on the laundry hamper behind the door to "watch me" take a shower.

Now the first cat races to the bathroom right along with him, and takes up residence on the opposite side of the room, which happens to be the toilet seat, and sits on the closed fuzzy lid while I bathe.

Cat Number Two preferred sitting on a chair at the dining room table while I ate, so Cat Number One now takes a seat at the other end of the table. I never, ever, feed them at the table, of course, but it looks to all the world like they certainly expect a place setting in front of them. After all, we're all dining companions, right?

Someone must have fed Cat Number Two people food, because he climbs on the drain board and attempts to lick the plates in the sink before I can get them into the dishwasher.

And whereas Cat Number One never before responded to the sound of a can opener, now they both start caterwauling at any electronic sound coming from the kitchen, whether it be the garbage disposal or coffee grinder!

I used to have floor-length sheer drapes in my living room. Cat Number One always politely nosed underneath the hem to come up and sit peacefully on the windowsill to sun himself.

It took Cat Number Two only a week or so to tear a hole in the curtain to put his head through to look out the window. Now they both lie on the back of the couch, side by side, and peer out any one of a myriad of torn peepholes.

The other day I scolded the second cat for gnawing on one of my potted plants. He must have thought I was calling to him, as he came over to the couch and plopped down in my lap. He playfully head-butted my hand to get me to pet him. Naturally, I complied, but aloud I said, "Is this an apology? Are you honeying up to me now cause you know you're not supposed to eat my plants?"

I absentmindedly scratched his ears and looked to see what Cat Number One was up to.

And there he was—gnawing away on the very same potted plant! Number Two wasn't apologizing, he was running interference for Number One!

These two little buddies of mine were polar opposites at first. Number One was an angel until Number Two came along. Now I affectionately refer to Number Two as "My Little Terrorist." But despite his terrible behavior and his bad influence on Number One, I can't imagine a better pair of almost brothers.

~Jan Bono

# Bad, Bad Kitty

*A cat pent up becomes a lion.*
*~Italian Proverb*

Maybe it was her name, Art, that caused my little female cat so much confusion. Whatever the reason, she was simply not interested in chasing birds or catching mice. Weighing in at only three pounds, Art was most happy on someone's lap or sitting on the porch watching all the activities in the back yard.

Skinny, Art's mother, was an expert hunter. Even with warning bells on her collar, she had no trouble catching the birds and mice unlucky enough to venture into our yard. Skinny took her job as a mother seriously as she tried to teach Art to hunt. But Art would just stretch slowly and walk away.

Shortly after my husband Paul and I were married, my two cats moved in with us. I hoped Skinny and Art would adjust to their new home.

We had a sliding glass door in our dining room. It opened onto a deck and the back yard. But while Art loved to just look out the window, Skinny paced and meowed by the deck door. She also perched herself on the back of a chair. It became her favorite lookout spot. After a week Skinny seemed to be settling in and I relaxed. But when the deck door was left open accidentally, she raced outside, never to be seen again.

Art moped around the house for a couple of weeks.

"Do you think Art has grown?" I asked Paul.

"I think so," he said.

Without her domineering mother, Art doubled in size. It was amazing. She walked with a little more swagger. She puffed out her fur and swished her tail. She perched herself in Skinny's lookout spot.

"I swear Art looks like Skinny now," I said.

"She really does. Especially when she swishes her tail. I wonder what she'll do next," Paul said.

Three months had passed since Skinny disappeared. I thought it was safe to let Art outside. I started leaving the deck door open so Art could go in and out whenever she wanted.

"M-e-o-w."

I looked up to see Art saunter into the house. "Paul, what's that in Art's mouth?"

We both watched Art let a live mouse go in the dining room. The mouse scampered into the kitchen cupboards.

"No, Art. Bad kitty."

Paul and I spent the next three days trying to entice the mouse from its hiding place. Art paid no attention. Paul finally set a trap with peanut butter and we got the mouse out of our house.

For the next month, the deck door was shut tight each time Art was let outside. Art tried to bring a chipmunk into the house but the door was firmly shut. She let the chipmunk go. It scurried away.

"No, no," I said to Art. "Bad kitty."

The deck door was accidentally left open one day and Paul and I heard a loud "M-E-O-W."

"Oh no," Paul said. Art had dragged in a full-sized rabbit and dropped her on the dining room floor. The rabbit looked stunned for a second and then hopped and jumped all around the living room and kitchen.

Paul grabbed a laundry basket, turned it upside down, and the chase was on. I tried to corner the rabbit that was leaping frenetically about the kitchen. We blocked the kitchen exit and zeroed in. The laundry basket went over the rabbit and we eased the basket through the dining room and out the deck door. The rabbit hurried away.

Art had watched the whole pursuit while sitting on a chair.

"No, no," I said to Art loudly. "Bad, bad kitty." I looked at Paul in disbelief. What had gotten into Art?

The door was shut tightly for another month. I knew we couldn't keep the cat inside forever, so one day I let Art outside. I thought I had closed the door behind her. It was open enough for her to push it the rest of the way and come back into the house.

"M-E-O-W."

"Oh, my God. I don't believe it," I said.

Art swaggered into the house with an adult mourning dove in her mouth. She let it go. It flew through the house wildly.

I seized a broom and ran after the now frantic dove. Paul had a bathroom towel handy in case I actually hit the bird with the broom. After circling the living room several times, the bird twisted quickly and flew right into the window. It fell to the floor dazed. Paul put the towel around the bird and brought it outside. Since it was still bewildered from hitting the window, Paul laid it on the deck. It flew away after a couple of minutes.

"Okay, Art. That's it. BAD, BAD KITTY," I yelled. I had never raised my voice to Art because she was so timid. She started shaking until even her whiskers were moving in all different directions. I didn't have the heart to shout at her anymore.

"Why do you think Art is bringing all these animals into the house?" I asked Paul that night.

"I think she just wanted to show us that she could catch them. Actually, Skinny would be proud."

Art never hunted again after the incident with the dove. When she went outside, she stayed on the deck. Inside, she lived out her days sitting on the floor with our new baby Anne and watched the back yard from her perch on the chair.

~Mary Clare Lockman

# The Housewarming Gift

*Let nature be in your yard.*
*~Greg Peterson*

A yard! After four years of marriage, my husband Jack and I were finally going to have a yard. I had long dreamed about working on a house of our own. Mowing the lawn, designing the garden and playing in the dirt. It had finally happened. I finally got my own personal playground.

We bought a small farmhouse that needed quite a bit of work. When I say work, I mean a complete overhaul. We knew going into it that we would be tearing down and putting up walls, installing floors, painting over the pink kitchen cabinets… creating our dream home.

One of our most frightening challenges was introducing our two cats to their new home. Scooter and Yaicha had always been indoor cats, as our previous places were apartments in high-rise buildings. Except for the actual moves from building to building, the two never set foot outside. I was sure they would continue to show no interest in the outside world. The fact that they were skittish about new noises and people convinced me that they would stay indoor cats.

Scooter and Yaicha's eyes were as wide as saucers as they entered their new home. Once inside, they dropped to the ground and took off running, searching for a place to hide. Scurrying through the kitchen and down the hall they quickly found a familiar couch in the living room and crawled behind it. We didn't see them until later that evening when their stomachs told them, fear or not, they wanted dinner.

The next few days we saw little of our Scooter, but Yaicha was feeling bold. New noises and new smells seemed to invigorate her. She was curious about where she was and what all these new scents were. Where were they coming from? She wanted to know. So one day she sneaked by me and ran outside.

I was horrified. Where would she go? Would she know how to get home? Would a car hit her? Would someone take her? I ran after her calling her name but she ran through the shrubs that bordered our property. I looked for her for over an hour and returned home feeling certain that I had lost her forever.

Yaicha returned home soon. She held her tail high and had a skip in her step. Just by looking at her I knew. She, too, had found paradise. Yaicha would be a lover of nature.

As the days passed, Jack and I spent all our free time working on the interior of the house. Every room needed attention.

Once I completed some of my more grueling interior chores, I allowed myself to go outside and work on my lawn and garden. My special treat.

Yaicha would often spend time with me in the yard. She'd softly brush my leg as I tackled some stubborn weed or planted a perennial. I'd watch her jump as she chased a butterfly. Sometimes she would just lie in the sun as I worked nearby. She was my garden companion.

Granted our property was small, a quarter acre, but to me it was paradise. I pruned and pulled and planted. I would work until I could no longer stand. And then I would stop, feeling almost paralyzed.

This was also when I first learned how euphoric naptime could be.

After spending hours outside I would sneak inside, plop on the couch, and fall asleep. One afternoon I lay there, in and out of a deep sleep, when I felt Yaicha jump on the end of the couch. She slowly walked alongside me, stopping at my head. It was time for me to get up so I welcomed the chance to be awakened by my little girl. But something was off. I felt her soft paws on my arm, but there was another movement I couldn't identify. Something was wiggling in harmony with Yaicha's purrs. I opened my eyes just in time for Yaicha to drop a snake on my chest.

She seemed surprised and hurt that I let out such an alarming scream.

After realizing that the snake was now loose in the house, I started the search. It wasn't in the couch. I searched the room, which was not an easy feat, as there were paint cans and tools scattered all over the floor. Lifting cans and newspapers, I finally saw its tail extending out from under a drop cloth. I picked up a tool from the fireplace and grabbed it by the tail. I was actually a bit embarrassed after I saw how small it was in comparison to the sizeable scream I had let out. Yaicha looked at me, trying to figure out what the fuss was all about and why I did not seem happy with her fabulous gift.

I took the wiggling snake outside and threw it as far back on the property as I could. When I returned to the living room Yaicha was still sitting there, looking quite dejected. I picked her up and told her that I appreciated the thought, but slithery reptiles weren't my idea of a housewarming gift.

I would like to say that that was the first and last time my darling brought me a gift, but it wasn't. For the first summer we were in that house, Yaicha brought me a total of five snakes. They were always presented to me when I was on the couch in deep slumber.

I guess she felt that I would warm to the idea of having another living creature in the house. Or maybe she thought it would make a fine dinner. Either way, I appreciated the gesture but was even more grateful when she decided to just join me on the couch herself.

~Jeanne Blandford

# Meet Our Contributors

**Teresa Ambord** is a senior editor and writer for a major publisher. She works from her home in rural far Northern California. For fun she writes stories about her family, her faith, and her posse of small, rescued dogs. Her dogs inspire her writing and decorate her life.

**Monica A. Andermann** lives and writes on Long Island where she shares a home with her husband Bill and their latest addition, a cat named Samson. Her work has been included in such publications as *Sasee*, *Woman's World*, *Guideposts*, and several other Chicken Soup for the Soul collections.

**Anna B. Ashley** worked at a small town newspaper for over forty years. She began writing while in elementary school and was the editor of the high school newspaper. Joyce writes short stories, commentaries, articles, profiles and features for the newspaper and other publications. She is married with three children and four grandchildren.

**Jill Barville** is a freelance writer in Spokane, WA. Her first cat, Tyler, was one of seventeen feral cats in her uncle's orchard. After she tamed and claimed him, Tyler rewarded her love by paw kneading, purring and protection from any mouse within a quarter mile. Contact her at www.jillbarville.com.

**Gretchen Bassier** holds a B.A. degree in Psychology from the University of Michigan-Dearborn. She lives in Michigan with four cats, eleven doves, and four horses—all sources of inspiration for her writing. She has written numerous short stories, one and a half novels, and hopes to start a nonprofit to benefit feral cats.

**Valerie D. Benko** writes from Pennsylvania when she's not busy rescuing and re-homing stray kittens and cats with her Dr. Dolittle husband. She is a frequent contributor to Chicken Soup for the Soul and has more than two dozen essays and short stories published in the U.S. and Canada. Visit her online at http://valeriebenko.weebly.com.

**Kathleen Birmingham** writes from Phoenix, AZ, where she lives with her husband, three children, dog, cats, and fish. Kathleen and her family have always chosen their pets from animals who needed rescuing, giving them their "forever homes," a solution that works well for both their rescued pets and Kathleen's family.

**Jeanne Blandford** is a writer/editor who, along with her husband Jack, is currently producing documentaries and creating children's books. When not in their Airstream looking for new material, they can be found running SafePet, a partnership between Outreach for Pets in Need (OPIN) and Domestic Violence Crisis Center (DVCC).

**Jan Bono's** specialty is humorous personal experience. She has published five collections, two poetry chapbooks, nine one-act plays, a dinner theater play, and written for magazines including *Guideposts* to *Woman's World*. Jan is writing a mystery series set on the Southwest Washington coast. Learn more at www.JanBonoBooks.com.

**Robert J. Brake, Ph.D.**, is a retired college teacher, freelance writer, jazz aficionado, friend of animals, friend of nonprofit organizations, and resident of Ocean Park, WA. He loves a good story and being the center of attention. E-mail him at oobear@centurytel.net.

**Karla Brown** is married and lives on the outskirts of Philadelphia, PA. She loves swimming, British movies, chocolate and gardening. She also writes paranormal romantic suspense, YA and middle grade, and hopes one day to be a novelist.

**Cathy Bryant** is a former childminder, life model and civil servant. She has blogged for The Huffington Post, won nine literary awards, and co-edited the poetry anthologies *Best of Manchester Poets Volume 1*, 2 and 3. Her latest book is *Look At All the Women*, available at www.themothersmilkbookshop.com.

**Lori Bryant** is a public speaker, author and inspirational storyteller. Lori is a four-time contributor to Chicken Soup for the Soul. She also writes for *Zoe Life* devotionals. Her passion is helping people live life to the fullest! Contact Lori at www.LoriBryantsstories.com or on Facebook at Lori Bryant's Stories.

**Jill Burns** lives in the mountains of West Virginia with her wonderful family. She's a retired piano teacher and performer. She enjoys writing, music, gardening, nature, and spending time with her grandchildren.

**Liane Kupferberg Carter** is a journalist whose articles and essays have appeared in many publications, including *The New York Times*, the *Chicago Tribune* and The Huffington Post. She writes a monthly column for *Autism After 16*. She wrangles cats with her husband and two adult sons.

**Beth Cato's** the author of *The Clockwork Dagger*, a steampunk fantasy novel from Harper Voyager. She's had stories in over a dozen Chicken Soup for the Soul books. She's a Hanford, CA native transplanted to the Arizona desert, where she lives with her husband, son, and requisite cat. Learn more at www.BethCato.com.

**Melissa Halsey Caudill** is thrilled to have her second story published with Chicken Soup for the Soul. She is a paralegal and shares her life in North Carolina with her supportive boyfriend Richard and their four combined children. She is currently working on her first novel. Visit her blog at www.missyspublicjunk.wordpress.com.

**Linda Cheshire** is mom to four grown children, a grandmother, and loves her faith, family, animals, writing, singing, crafting jewelry, and traveling with her husband. Her writing interests are inspirational, humorous, children's and music. She resides in South Texas with her husband and collection of beloved rescued dogs and cats.

**Margrita Colabuno** is a single mom and full-time marketing-communications professional. She graduated *cum laude* from Hiram College with a bachelor's degree in Business Management. She enjoys designing and crafting jewelry, to wear and to share, and lives with her teenage son and sassy feline in Northeast Ohio.

**Harriet Cooper** writes personal essays, humor and creative nonfiction for newspapers, newsletters, anthologies and magazines and is a frequent contributor to the Chicken Soup for the Soul series. She writes about family, relationships, health, food, cats, writing and daily life. E-mail her at shewrites@live.ca.

**J.J. Crowley** is a freelance direct response advertising copywriter/creative director. A graduate of New York University, he now lives in Connecticut with his wife, two daughters, two cats, two dogs, two parrots, and a varying number of goldfish. He enjoys fast cars, fast motorcycles, slow dancing and long naps.

**Jo Yuill Darlington** is a writer of short stories and poetry. This is her second story published by Chicken Soup for the Soul.

**Mary Dempsey**, a former teacher and bookstore owner, resides in Bluffton, SC. Her writing has appeared in newspapers, magazines and four Chicken Soup for the Soul anthologies. She is a freelance writer for a local newspaper. Mary enjoys traveling and is an avid cycler.

**Peggy Dover** is a freelance writer/columnist living in the Rogue Valley of Southern Oregon. Her bi-weekly column, "Southern Oregon Journal," publishes in the *Mail Tribune* newspaper. Peggy is working with an agent regarding her debut novel. She enjoys nature, reading, the arts, and traveling (without cats).

**Laurie Carnright Edwards** has been involved in Christian ministry for over thirty years with her pastor husband, Dale. She enjoys working with children and teens, and seeks to honor God with her gift of writing. Laurie received a B.A. degree from Berkshire Christian College and a MATS from Gordon-Conwell Theological Seminary.

**Manley Fisher** has a Bachelor of Education degree and has taught English classes to adults for nearly twenty years. He lives in Spruce Grove, Alberta, and enjoys cross-country skiing, fishing, and, of course, writing. His other work includes pieces for professional publications and hopes one day to be an inspirational speaker.

**John Forrest** is a retired educator who writes about the exceptional events and wonderful people in life. He lives in Orillia, Ontario, with his wife Carol, where they enjoy golf, travel and following the life adventures of their children Rob and Dana. E-mail him at johnforrest@rogers.com.

**Claire Fullerton** is the author of the novel *A Portal in Time*. Her second novel, *Dancing to an Irish Reel*, will be published in early 2015. She is a three-time award-winning essayist, and a newspaper columnist.

**Heidi Gaul** lives in Oregon with her husband and four-legged family. She loves travel, be it around the block or the globe, and reading is her passion. Active in American Christian Fiction Writers and Oregon Christian Writers, she is currently finishing her third novel. E-mail her at dhgaul@aol.com.

**Shirley P. Gumert** is a writer who lives with her husband, John, in the

Texas Hill Country. Her story "My Parents' Pears" appears in *Chicken Soup for the Soul: Home Sweet Home*. Her family knows that George, the smartest cat in the world, still visits them, to tell of new adventures. Meanwhile, he drops off stray kittens.

**Bonnie Compton Hanson**, artist and speaker, is author of thirty-seven books for adults and children, plus hundreds of articles, stories, and poems (including thirty-four for Chicken Soup for the Soul). A former editor, she has taught at several universities and writing conferences—plus loves cats! Learn more at www.bonniecomptonhanson.com.

**Susan Harris** is the author of *Remarkably Ordinary: 20 Reflections on Living Intentionally Right Where You Are*, *Golden Apples in Silver Settings*, *Little Copper Pennies* and *Little Copper Pennies for Kids*. Born in Trinidad, she lives on the Canadian prairies with her family and their gregarious cats. E-mail her at susan@susanharris.ca.

After earning a B.A. degree with honors in both Psychology and French, **Janet Hartman** worked as an IT professional for many years before returning to her love of writing. Her work has appeared in national magazines, online, and various anthologies including several for Chicken Soup for the Soul. To learn more, visit JanetHartmanwrites.com.

**Jill Haymaker** is a family law attorney in Fort Collins, CO. This is her third story published by Chicken Soup for the Soul. She enjoys outdoor activities with her three children, three grandkids and her Shetland Sheepdog. E-mail her at jillhaymaker@aol.com, blog at jillhaymaker.wordpress.com or twitter @JillLHaymaker.

**Emily Ruth Hazel** is a New York City-based poet and writer who aims to capture the beauty, hope, and humor in everyday experiences. Her first poetry book is titled *Body & Soul*. Emily's poems are also featured at www.sparkandecho.org and have appeared in magazines, journals, anthologies, music albums, and science museums.

**Cheryl Heide** currently lives with her husband Dick, four cats and two horses on their farm in northeastern Kansas. She has written a collection of stories about her experiences and the animals that shared her life at Leap of Faith Farm in southern Minnesota. She is also a singer and a writer of prose as well as poetry.

**Marijo Herndon's** stories appear in several books, including the Chicken Soup for the Soul series. She has also developed stress management strategies that benefit the coaching programs for a leading health plan company. She lives in New York with her husband, Dave, and two rescue cats, Lucy and Ethel.

**Georgia A. Hubley** retired after twenty years in financial management to write full-time. Vignettes of her life appear in various anthologies, magazines and newspapers. Once the nest was empty, Georgia and her husband of thirty-six years left Silicon Valley in the rearview mirror and now hang their hats in Henderson, NV. E-mail her at geohub@aol.com.

**Carol Huff**, co-owner of Sudie Belle Animal Sanctuary in Northeast Georgia, enjoys writing about the rescued animals on the farm. She is a frequent contributor to Chicken Soup for the Soul and has also been published in several other national magazines. E-mail her at herbiemakow@gmail.com.

**David Hull** received his Bachelor of Arts degree from SUNY Brockport in 1986. He has published numerous short stories in magazines and Chicken Soup for the Soul books. Retired from teaching in 2013, David enjoys, reading, writing, gardening and spoiling his great-nephew. E-mail him at davidhull@aol.com.

**DJ Kinsinger** knows the value of stories: in teaching life lessons, in helping people in the healing process, and in knitting hearts together in laughter and in love. She has been a writer forever, finding magic in words. DJ is delighted to share life's tender, funny, and poignant moments with others through her stories.

**Mimi Greenwood Knight** is a freelance writer living in south Louisiana with her husband, David, and four spectacular kids. She enjoys gardening, baking, karate, knitting, Bible study, and has recently jumped on the backyard chicken wagon. Mimi is blessed to have essays in thirty Chicken Soup for the Soul books.

**Kathleen Kohler** writes stories about the ups and downs of family life for numerous magazines and anthologies. She and her husband live in the Pacific Northwest, and have three children and seven grandchildren. Visit www.kathleenkohler.com to read more of her articles or enter her latest drawing.

**Melisa Kraft** resides in Benton, KY, with her husband and two boys ages five and nineteen. She also has two stepsons, one grandson and one granddaughter on the way.

**Joyce Laird** is a freelance writer living in Southern California. Her features have been published in many magazines including, *American Fitness*, *Cat Fancy*, *Grit*, *Mature Living*, *I Love Cats* and *Vibrant Life*. She is a regular contributor to *Woman's World* and Chicken Soup for the Soul.

**Lisa McManus Lange** is a frequent contributor to Chicken Soup for the Soul, this being her fourth book. She likes cats, writing, her kids, and peace and tranquility—but not in that order. Visit her at www.lisamcmanuslange.blogspot.com or e-mail her at lisamc2010@yahoo.ca.

**Jody Lebel's** short stories have sold to *Woman's World* magazine, *Pages of Stories* and dozens of others. Her romantic/suspense novel, *Playing Dead*, was released by The Wild Rose Press in 2012 to excellent reviews.

Jody resides in southern Florida with her two cats. The three of them enjoy beachcombing.

**Mark Leiren-Young** is the author of two comic memoirs, *Free Magic Secrets Revealed* and *Never Shoot a Stampede Queen* (winner of the Leacock Medal for Humour). He is also a screenwriter, playwright, performer, journalist, filmmaker and cat lover.

**Gretchen Lendrum** is a retired English teacher from Middletown, RI who enjoys reading, writing, music, all animals, and long walks with her husband and dog. She has had essays published in *Chicken Soup for the Soul: Grandmothers*, the *Providence Journal*, *The Newport Daily News*, *Newport Life Magazine* and *The Sun* magazine.

**Lenka Leon** is working on a collection of personal essays. She was born and raised in the Czech Republic and came to the San Francisco Bay area via London where she caught the travel bug that keeps her wandering shoes polished and ready for new adventures. She's a diehard Bon Jovi fan who loves to volunteer and swim with dolphins.

**Lisa Leshaw** has now officially retired as a therapist and is busily exploring new careers for the second stage of life. She is still at her happiest (and best) side by side with her grandkids, Mush and Gab, and her husband Stu. Secretly she dreams of the day that a magazine editor calls and says, "Yes, Lisa Leshaw, you're hired!"

**Mary Clare Lockman** is a retired Oncology/Hospice RN. She also has a B.A. degree in Writing and has written three books. The most recent is *They're Always With You*. Her stories have appeared in Chicken Soup for the Soul books and magazines. Mary has four daughters and four grandchildren and has been married to Paul for thirty-six years.

**Laird Long** writes in various genres. Big guy, sense of humor. His writing credits include: *Sherlock Holmes Mystery Magazine*, *Woman's World*, *The Weekly News*, *that's life!* and stories in the anthologies *Amazing Heroes*,

*The Mammoth Book of New Comic Fantasy*, and *The Mammoth Book of Perfect Crimes and Impossible Mysteries*.

Newspaper columnist, retired teacher, counselor and psychologist, **Janet E. Lord** is the mother of one child and is from Illinois. The majority of Janet's professional life has been in the education arena. She currently focuses on writing children's books and a weekly newspaper column for families.

**Morna Murphy Martell** has written numerous articles, plays, TV and film reviews, and was Broadway Critic for *The Hollywood Reporter*. Morna enjoys hiking, reading, live theater and coffee with friends. Her books, *Classics 4 Kids* and *Shakespeare in an Hour*, are published by Shakespeare, Inc.

**John McInnes** was a teacher. He received his diploma of teaching in Melbourne, Australia in 1960 and his B.A. at Flinders University in Adelaide, Australia in 1970. Since retiring he has written short stories, memoirs, etc. Some of which have been published. He taught seniors at colleges and coached Australian Rules Football at League level for thirty-plus years.

**Joan Friday McKechnie** has a B.S. degree in Bible from Cairn University. She works in a local elementary school as an instructional aide. Joan enjoys reading, writing, swimming, walking, and kayaking. She has three grown sons, two cats, and a very happy Golden Retriever who loves going for walks with her.

**Lynn Maddalena Menna's** young adult novel, *Piece of My Heart*, was listed on *Seventeen* magazine's list of must-read books for the summer of 2013. A song from that book, "(You have) No Soul" is available on YouTube. Lynn and her husband, Prospero, live in Hawthorne, NJ. E-mail her at prolynn@aol.com or on Facebook.

**Nanci Merczel** lives in Poplar Grove, IL with her husband, daughter, and two cats who do not consider her their favorite—but she loves them anyway. She enjoys art and photography and is currently working on a picture book for children.

**Marya Morin** is a freelance writer. Her stories and poems have appeared in publications such as *Woman's World* and Hallmark. Marya also penned a weekly humorous column for an online newsletter, and writes custom poetry on request. She lives in the country with her husband. E-mail her at Akushla514@hotmail.com.

**Linda Newton** is an Empowerment Educator, and the author of *12 Ways to Turn Your Pain into Praise*. She speaks all over the country, and currently hosts a popular blog with her husband, "Answers from Mom and Dad" on YouTube https:/www.youtube.com/user/answersfrommomanddad and https://www.facebook.com/answersfrommomanddad.

**Diane C. Nicholson** is a writer and professional photographer/photo-artist, specializing in companion animals and special needs children. A longtime vegan, her affinity and respect for animals and her patient understanding of children with special needs are reflected in her art. Diane has eight stories published by Chicken Soup for the Soul.

**Alicia Penrod** received her Bachelor of Science degree in Sociology from Brigham Young University-Idaho in 2004. She currently does accounting for an insurance company in Utah. Alicia enjoys running in competitive races with her husband as well as hiking with him and her four big dogs.

**Saralee Perel** is an award-winning nationally syndicated columnist who is honored to be a multiple contributor to the Chicken Soup for the Soul series. E-mail her at sperel@saraleeperel.com or visit www.saraleeperel.com to learn more.

**Felice Prager** is a freelance writer and educational therapist from Mesa, AZ. She is the author of five books: *Waiting in the Wrong Line*,

*Negotiable and Non-Negotiable Negotiations*, *TurboCharge Your Brain*, *SuperTurboCharge Your Brain*, and *Quiz It: ARIZONA*. She has five cats and vacuums a lot.

**Diane Quinn** is a freelance writer living in Las Vegas, NV. Diane and her husband are allowed to live with their two spoiled cats. She enjoys reading, playing tennis and is fascinated by wildlife and nature every day.

**Tim Ramsey** is an educator in the public school system and an instructor at his local community college. Many of his past adventures from campus are chronicled in his book, *The Hugs on My Shirt*. Tim lives in Arizona with his wife, daughter and seven cats.

**Julie Reece-DeMarco** is an attorney, educator and author. She is married with four daughters and enjoys being a mom, spending time outdoors in the great Northwest and playing sports. Approximately one million copies of her books are in print.

**Donna Reed** received a Bachelor of Arts degree from the University of Massachusetts and a Juris Doctor from the University of New Hampshire Law School.

**Stacey Ritz** is an award-winning freelance writer and the Executive Director of Advocates 4 Animals, Inc. Learn more at www.Advocates4Animals.com.

**Janet Ramsdell Rockey** is a freelance writer living in Tampa, FL, with her Realtor husband and their two cats. Her dedication to writing survives the demands of a full-time job, her husband's constant home improvements, and her furry feline "children." See her Amazon Author page at www.amazon.com/author/janetrockey.

**Heather Rodin** is mother to six grown children and serves as Executive Director for Hope Grows Haiti. She and her husband Gord live with their Great Dane, Bogart, near Peterborough, Ontario. Family needs, charity demands, speaking and writing keep her schedule full.

**Gail Sellers** enjoys writing animal, children's and inspirational stories. She loves cats and enjoys relaxing at her cottage. E-mail her at gailsellers2011@gmail.com.

**NL Shank** has been creating stories throughout her life and now chooses to share them with others. Her travels around the world and exposure to many cultures, combined with a vivid imagination, give her rich fodder to draw from. She currently lives in Southern California and is happily owned by a rather fierce feline.

**Charlotte Blood Smith** has been a freelance writer for fifty years. She has written for over 115 publications. Charlotte has had cats since she was four and spent a lot of time watching them, especially their interaction with other animals.

**Deborah Sosin** is a writer and clinical social worker whose essays have appeared in the *Boston Globe Magazine*, on Salon, and elsewhere. Her picture book, *Charlotte and the Quiet Place*, will be published by Parallax Press in 2015. A longtime meditator, Debbie lives outside Boston with her skittish cats, Sophia and Sascha.

**Alvena Stanfield** is fairly new to writing, She is delighted, energized and amazed when a reader says her writing is interesting. Publishing success sent her back to NKU. She now studies writing and electronic media. Her suspense novel and screenplay are looking for agents. E-mail her at stanfieldwrites@gmail.com.

**Nicole Starbuck** started scribbling as an infant and hasn't stopped since. After receiving her BFA degree in Studio Art from the University of Arizona, she gathered her snow gear and settled in the foothills of the Colorado Rockies to write novels and short stories. E-mail her at nicolita@email.arizona.edu.

**Pam Tallman** holds a master's degree in theater arts, but is constantly fumbling and dropping her degree in life skills. This gives her plenty of fodder for her humorous essays. The mother of three felines, Pam enjoys baking, quilting and cat herding. She hopes to soon sell her novel. Please… anyone.

**Austin Tamillo** is an elementary school teacher in Northlake, IL. He resides with his beautiful wife Joy, his two amazing children, one pampered pooch, and four fabulous felines in Elgin, IL. His hobbies include writing, running, and cheering for his beloved Kansas City Royals.

**Tsgoyna Tanzman**, life coach, writer, speech pathologist and memoir teacher, considers writing her ultimate "therapy." Her published works appear in numerous Chicken Soup for the Soul anthologies, More.com, the *Orange County Register* and *Soul Matters*. Her humorous, wise and scientific-ish blog can be read at tsgoyna.tumblr.com.

**Denise Taylor** is the busy mom of eleven children, eight of whom are still living at home. Thankfully she has her husband Todd to help out around the house. She also keeps company with one cat named Flower P. Cat. Denise loves to write, camp, hunt and fish in the quiet forests of Michigan's Upper Peninsula where she resides.

**Stephen Taylor** is a writer and graphic artist. He lives in the San Francisco Bay area. He remains a devoted cat lover; he lives with his cat, Maxi; performs catsitting duties for various feline friends; and continues to volunteer as a cat care partner at a local animal shelter.

**Martha VanCise** grew up in Indiana, but lived in Bolivia, Guatemala, and Haiti. She also worked in the English as a Second Language program at Indian River State College in Florida. Along with writing, she enjoys nature photography and visiting her two granddaughters. E-mail her at 43martha43@gmail.com.

**Fran Veal**, author of the Finding My Escape book series, currently resides in the beautiful city of Murfreesboro, TN, with her husband of twenty-eight years, sixteen-year-old daughter, and one extremely snarky cat. She enjoys reading, hiking, and playing video games with her daughter.

**David Warren** has been writing part-time for three years. This is his second story to appear in the Chicken Soup for the Soul series. David has also appeared in *Grand* magazine and is the author of *Mealtime Guests*, a nationally released children's book. David resides in Kettering, OH with his wife Angela and daughter Marissa.

**Susan Graham Winslow** lives in Gloucester, MA. She has a B.A. degree in English from the University of Massachusetts and writes for a number of magazines in the equine industry. She is also a Therapeutic Riding Instructor, mom to Lexie, Sam and Keelie, owner of three cats, Manchego, DeDe and Finn, and a Shire named Dancing Bear.

**Susan Yanguas** is a four-time contributor to the Chicken Soup for the Soul series; this is her second cat book. She is a nonfiction writer/editor for a government agency and author of the Po-po Poker Mystery series. Susan also blogs about health and wellness at http://susanyanguas.wordpress.com.

**Ellyn Horn Zarek** is a freelance writer from Jupiter, FL. She is a member of the Writers' Circle at the Kravis Center for the Performing Arts. An alumnus of the University of Massachusetts Boston, Ellyn enjoys local beaches, her job at The Weiss School, and time with friends and family. E-mail her at ezarek@bellsouth.net.

# Meet Our Author

**Amy Newmark** has been Chicken Soup for the Soul's publisher, coauthor, and editor-in-chief for the last six years, after a thirty-year career as a writer, speaker, financial analyst, and business executive in the worlds of finance and telecommunications. Amy is a Chartered Financial Analyst and a *magna cum laude* graduate of Harvard College, where she majored in Portuguese, minored in French, and traveled extensively. She and her husband have four grown children.

After a long career writing books on telecommunications, voluminous financial reports, business plans, and corporate press releases, Chicken Soup for the Soul is a breath of fresh air for Amy. She loves creating these life-changing books for Chicken Soup for the Soul's wonderful readers. She has coauthored and/or edited more than 100 Chicken Soup for the Soul books.

You can reach Amy with any questions or comments through webmaster@chickensoupforthesoul.com and you can follow her on Twitter @amynewmark or @chickensoupsoul.

# About Miranda Lambert

Grammy Award-winning singer-songwriter Miranda Lambert is the reigning four-time CMA and reigning five-time ACM Female Vocalist of the Year. Her last album, *Four The Record*, made history when it debuted atop Billboard's Top Country Albums chart, making Miranda the first country artist in the forty-seven-year history of the chart to have each of her first four albums debut at # 1. All four of those albums have also been certified Platinum.

Miranda's highly-anticipated fifth album *Platinum* was released June 3rd. Her lead single "Automatic," written by Miranda, Nicolle Galyon and Natalie Hemby, is an autobiographical song that reflects on the days of pay phones, learning to drive a stick shift, driving to Dallas to buy an Easter dress, recording the country countdown on her cassette recorder and more.

In addition to her award-winning music, Miranda has designed a shoe line that is available at DSW, and other retailers across the country. She also dedicates much of her time to her MuttNation Foundation. The foundation has raised more than $1,500,000 to aid organizations and entities whose purpose is to build animal shelters for better care; increase pet adoption and encourage responsible pet guardianship; rehabilitate sick or unsocialized animals; fund spay/neuter programs; reduce/eliminate euthanasia of healthy animals. She also owns two lifestyle boutiques, general stores she named The Pink Pistol. The stores are located in her hometown of Lindale, TX and Tishomingo, OK.

American Humane Association™

# About American Humane Association

For over 100 years, one organization has been standing guard over America's children and America's animals, keeping them safe and working tirelessly to improve their futures. Born in the years after the Civil War, American Humane Association has been behind virtually every major advance in the protection of our most vulnerable, from creating the nation's first child labor laws to saving the Bald Eagle, rescuing animals from war, hurricanes, tornadoes and floods, and pioneering programs to prevent abuse, cruelty, and neglect.

Today, American Humane Association helps ensure the welfare of one billion farm animals, works to keep pets and children safe from harm, protects 100,000 animal actors each year on film and television production sets, brings life-saving and life-altering emergency services to children, animals and communities struck by disasters, uses animal therapy to provide healing and hope to military families and children with cancer, and researches ways to keep more of the eight million pets abandoned each year in loving, forever homes.

The country's first humane organization, and the only one dedicated to protecting both children and animals, American Humane Association has been uniquely effective in working with others for the common good: parents, teachers, scientists, farmers, ranchers, animal advocates, and anyone interested in speaking for the voiceless and effecting lasting change.

A moderate and mainstream voice in a sometimes contentious world, American Humane Association bases its programs on both science and sentiment, "heart" as well as "smart," as it strives to bring commonsense solutions to some of our most complex challenges so that together we may build more humane communities and a more humane world.

To learn more or join them in their important work, please go to www.americanhumane.org or call 866-242-1877.

# Thank You

Thank you cat lovers! I owe huge thanks to every one of you who shared your stories about your beloved, intuitive, supportive... and mischievous cats. You make a strong case for running right down to the animal shelter to adopt a new friend. Your stories made us laugh a lot, nod our heads in recognition, and cry a few times.

I know that you poured your hearts and souls into the thousands of stories and poems that you submitted. Thank you. All of us at Chicken Soup for the Soul appreciate your willingness to share your lives with us. We could only publish a small percentage of the stories that were submitted, but our editorial team read every single submission—and there were thousands! Even the stories that do not appear in the book influenced us and affected the final manuscript.

First of all, I want to thank Miranda Lambert for taking the time out from her busy schedule to write her foreword for us. I loved her story about the cat throwing up on her very first performing contract! And I want to thank our editor Jeanne Blandford, who is also the director of marketing for our pet food business, for educating all of us about shelter cats and the important issues that we needed to cover through our story selection.

Our regular editorial team did its normal fabulous job. Our VP & Assistant Publisher D'ette Corona worked with all the contributors as we edited and perfected their stories, and she and Senior Editor Barbara LoMonaco proofread the manuscript, while Managing Editor and Production Coordinator Kristiana Pastir oversaw the long journey from Word document to finished manuscript to proofs to cartons of finished books.

Lastly, I owe a very special thanks to our creative director and book producer, Brian Taylor at Pneuma Books, for his brilliant vision for our covers and interiors.

~Amy Newmark

# Sharing Happiness, Inspiration, and Wellness

Real people sharing real stories, every day, all over the world. In 2007, *USA Today* named *Chicken Soup for the Soul* one of the five most memorable books in the last quarter-century. With over 100 million books sold to date in the U.S. and Canada alone, more than 200 titles in print, and translations into more than 40 languages, "chicken soup for the soul" is one of the world's best-known phrases.

Today, 21 years after we first began sharing happiness, inspiration and wellness through our books, we continue to delight our readers with new titles, but have also evolved beyond the bookstore, with wholesome and balanced pet food, delicious nutritious comfort food, and a major motion picture in development. Whatever you're doing, wherever you are, Chicken Soup for the Soul is "always there for you™." Thanks for reading!

# Share with Us

We all have had Chicken Soup for the Soul moments in our lives. If you would like to share your story or poem with millions of people around the world, go to chickensoup.com and click on "Submit Your Story." You may be able to help another reader, and become a published author at the same time. Some of our past contributors have launched writing and speaking careers from the publication of their stories in our books!

We only accept story submissions via our website. They are no longer accepted via mail or fax.

To contact us regarding other matters, please send us an e-mail through webmaster@chickensoupforthesoul.com, or fax or write us at:


Chicken Soup for the Soul
P.O. Box 700
Cos Cob, CT 06807-0700
Fax: 203-861-7194


One more note from your friends at Chicken Soup for the Soul: Occasionally, we receive an unsolicited book manuscript from one of our readers, and we would like to respectfully inform you that we do not accept unsolicited manuscripts and we must discard the ones that appear.

We all rejoice in the simple absurdities, funny habits, and crazy antics of our cats. They make us smile every day, but sometimes they really outdo themselves. You will love reading all the heartwarming, inspirational, and hysterical stories in this book. We know after reading the stories you'll say, "I can't believe a cat did that!"

978-1-935096-92-4

More Fun

From kittenhood through the twilight years, our feline companions continually bring joy, love, and laughter to the lives of their "staff." This collection of 101 new stories captures the experience of living through the natural life cycle with our cats. Stories cover each age and stage with all the fun, frustrations, special bonds and routines involved. The book also holds a special chapter about grieving and recovery when our feline friends leave us.

978-1-935096-66-5

for Cat Lovers

Cats are wonderful companions and playmates that brighten and enrich the lives of their "staff," but they're also amazing teachers, often leading by example! Cat lovers, both lifelong and reluctant, share their feline-inspired lessons about determination and perseverance, self-confidence and self-acceptance, and unconditional love and loyalty. Any cat lover will nod, laugh, and tear up as they read this new collection of 101 amazing stories.

978-1-935096-37-5

More Lessons

We are all crazy about our mysterious cats. Sometimes they are our best friends; sometimes they are aloof. They are fun to watch and often surprise us. These true stories, the best from Chicken Soup for the Soul's library, will make readers appreciate their own cats and see them with a new eye. Readers will revel in the heartwarming, amusing, inspirational, and occasionally tearful stories about our best friends and faithful companions—our cats.

978-1-935096-08-5

and Love